THE ARTISANS AND ENTREPRENEURS OF DONGYANG COUNTY

Studies on Contemporary China

THE POLITICAL ECONOMY OF CHINA'S SPECIAL ECONOMIC ZONES
George T. Crane

WORLDS APART
RECENT CHINESE WRITING AND ITS AUDIENCES
Howard Goldblatt, editor

CHINESE URBAN REFORM
WHAT MODEL NOW?
R. Yin-Wang Kwok, William L. Parish, and Anthony Gar-on Yeh with Xu Xuequang, editors

REBELLION AND FACTIONALISM IN A CHINESE PROVINCE
ZHEJIANG, 1966–1976
Keith Forster

POLITICS AT MAO'S COURT
GAO GANG AND PARTY FACTIONALISM IN THE EARLY 1950s
Frederick C. Teiwes

MOLDING THE MEDIUM
THE CHINESE COMMUNIST PARTY AND THE *LIBERATION DAILY*
Patricia Stranahan

THE MAKING OF A SINO-MARXIST WORLD VIEW
PERCEPTIONS AND INTERPRETATIONS OF WORLD HISTORY IN THE PEOPLE'S REPUBLIC OF CHINA
Dorothea A.L. Martin

POLITICS OF DISILLUSIONMENT
THE CHINESE COMMUNIST PARTY UNDER DENG XIAOPING, 1978–1989
Hsi-sheng Ch'i

CONQUERING RESOURCES
THE GROWTH AND DECLINE OF THE PLA'S SCIENCE AND TECHNOLOGY COMMISSION FOR NATIONAL DEFENSE
Benjamin C. Ostrov

THE PARADOX OF POWER IN A PEOPLE'S REPUBLIC OF CHINA MIDDLE SCHOOL
Martin Schoenhals

CHINA'S ECONOMIC DILEMMAS IN THE 1990s
THE PROBLEMS OF REFORMS, MODERNIZATION, AND INDEPENDENCE
Edited by the Joint Economic Committee, Congress of the United States

CHINA IN THE ERA OF DENG XIAOPING
A DECADE OF REFORM
Michael Ying-mao Kau and Susan H. Marsh, editors

DOMESTIC LAW REFORMS IN POST-MAO CHINA
Pitman B. Potter, editor

POLITICS AND PURGES IN CHINA
RECTIFICATION AND THE DECLINE OF PARTY NORMS, 1950–1965
Frederick C. Teiwes

MORNING SUN
INTERVIEWS WITH POST-MAO CHINESE WRITERS
Laifong Leung

CHINESE FIRMS AND THE STATE IN TRANSITION
PROPERTY RIGHTS AND AGENCY PROBLEMS IN THE REFORM ERA
Keun Lee

THE MARKET MECHANISM AND ECONOMIC REFORMS IN CHINA
William A. Byrd

CHINA, THE UNITED STATES, AND THE SOVIET UNION
TRIPOLARITY AND POLICY-MAKING IN THE COLD WAR
Robert S. Ross, editor

AMERICAN STUDIES OF CONTEMPORARY CHINA
David Shambaugh, editor

CHINA'S AUTOMOBILE INDUSTRY
POLICIES, PROBLEMS, AND PROSPECTS
Eric Harwit

DECISION-MAKING IN DENG'S CHINA
PERSPECTIVES FROM INSIDERS
Carol Lee Hamrin and Suisheng Zhao, editors

PRIVATE BUSINESS AND ECONOMIC REFORM IN CHINA
Susan Young

MAKING URBAN REVOLUTION IN CHINA
THE CCP-GMD STRUGGLE FOR BEIPING–TIANJIN, 1945–1949
Joseph K. S. Yick

CHINA'S ECONOMIC FUTURE
CHALLENGES TO U.S. POLICY
Joint Economic Committee, Congress of the United States

THE POLITICAL ECONOMY OF CORRUPTION IN CHINA
Julia Kwong

FAREWELL TO PEASANT CHINA
RURAL URBANIZATION AND SOCIAL CHANGES IN THE LATE TWENTIETH CENTURY
Gregory Eliyu Guldin, editor

PROVINCIAL STRATEGIES FOR ECONOMIC REFORM IN POST-MAO CHINA
Peter T.Y. Cheung, Jae Ho Chung, and Zhimin Lin, editors

THE ARTISANS AND ENTREPRENEURS OF DONGYANG COUNTY
ECONOMIC REFORM AND FLEXIBLE PRODUCTION IN CHINA
Eugene Cooper with Jiang Yinhuo

AFTER THE COLD WAR
DOMESTIC FACTORS AND U.S.–CHINA RELATIONS
Robert S. Ross, editor

Studies on Contemporary China

THE ARTISANS AND ENTREPRENEURS OF DONGYANG COUNTY

Economic Reform and Flexible Production in China

EUGENE COOPER
with Jiang Yinhuo

An East Gate Book

M.E. Sharpe
Armonk, New York
London, England

An East Gate Book

Copyright © 1998 by M. E. Sharpe, Inc.

All rights reserved. No part of this book may be reproduced in any form without written permission from the publisher, M. E. Sharpe, Inc., 80 Business Park Drive, Armonk, New York 10504.

Photographs in this book were taken by Eugene Cooper.

Library of Congress Cataloging-in-Publication Data

Cooper, Eugene, 1947–.
The artisans and entrepreneurs of Dongyang county : economic reform and flexible production in China / Eugene Cooper with Jiang Yinhuo.
p. cm.
"An East Gate book."
Includes bibliographical references and index.
ISBN 0-7656-0321-7 (cloth : alk. paper)
1. Wood-carvers—China—Tung-yang hsien (Chekiang Province)
2. Cabinetmakers—China—Tung-yan hsien (Chekiang Province)
3. Furniture industry and trade—China—Tung-yang hsien (Chekiang Province)
4. Marxian economics. I. Jiang, Yinho, 1928–. II. Title
HD8039.W52C63 1998
338.4′76841′00951242—dc21
98-11092
CIP

Printed in the United States of America

The paper used in this publication meets the minimum requirements of American National Standard for Information Sciences— Permanence of Paper for Printed Library Materials, ANSI Z 39.48-1984.

BM (c) 10 9 8 7 6 5 4 3 2 1

Contents

Tables and Illustrations	vii
Introduction	ix
Abbreviations	xix

1.	Dongyang County	3
2.	Traditional Woodcarving and Its Revolutionary Transformation—The First Transition of Tradition	41
3.	Xia Qi Tan Village	70
4.	Li Tang Village	88
5.	Guo Zhai Town	109
6.	Heng Dian Town	124
7.	The Dongyang Woodcarving Factory and Economic Reform—The Second Transition of Tradition	138
8.	Conclusion—Flexible Production in Dongyang?	168

Appendices

Appendix 1:	Ham Production	183
Appendix 2:	Camphor Tree Mothers	191
Appendix 3:	The *Huichang* (Country Fair) Cycle	194
Appendix 4:	Specimen *Cheng bao* Contract	209
Appendix 5:	The Thirteen Room House	216
Appendix 6:	Eight Immortals Cross the Sea (One Version of the Myth in Translation)	220

Glossary	227
Bibliography	253
Index	263

Tables and Illustrations

Tables

1.1	Production Figures for Rural Industrial Enterprises in Zhejiang Province	19
1.2	Dongyang Rural Industrial Enterprise Performance in 1988	27
1.3	Dongyang Rural Industrial Enterprise Performance for Selected Years	28
6.1	Production Figures for Heng Dian Woodcarving Arts and Crafts Factory	126
7.1	Production Figures for the Dongyang Woodcarving Factory	165
1A	Ham and Bacon Production Figures	186

Figures

1.1	Surname Distribution in Wu Ning	36
3.1	Founders of the Wu Lineage of Xia Qi Tan	71
3.2	Mantang's Segment of Xia Qi Tan #2 Fang	75
4.1	Founders of the Zhang Lineage of Li Tang	89
4.2	Li Tang Genealogical Poem	89
4.3	Mingyao's Segment of Li Tang #2 Fang	94
4.4	Agricultural Cycle of Li Tang Village	95
5.1	Guo Genealogy	110
5A	Thirteen Room Head	216

Maps

1.	China, showing provinces	x
2.	Zhejiang province, showing location of Dongyang County	4

3. Dongyang County, showing the county seat, Wu Ning, and assorted market towns.   6
4. Dongyang County map from the Qing dynasty gazetteer, Kang Xi reign period (1662–1722)   7
5. Wu Ning Town, showing principal roads and notable sites   32
6. Wu Ning Town, from the Qing dynasty gazetteer, Kang Xi reign period (1662–1722)   33
7. Xia Qi Tan Village   73
8. Li Tang Village   91

Photographs

Hardware stall on West Street in Wu Ning, the county town	34
Looking west on West Street in Wu Ning	35
"Cow shanks" in the eaves of a traditional structure in Huai Lu village depicting immortal Lü Dongbin	44
"Cow shanks" on a structure in Fang Jun town depicting a *qilin*	45
Master carver Zhou Fangchun at his carving bench at home in Fan Jun township	56
Worker inking motifs onto wood panel in preparation for carving	60
Restored Leishan Ancestral Hall in Xia Qi Tan village	72
Ploughing with a power tiller in Xia Qi Tan village	79
A "two headed crow" pig valued for the production of Dongyang hams	184
Crowds attending the rural market fair in Hu Qi town	203
Carved wood furniture for sale at the market fair in Hu Qi	204
A maker of wooden tubs displays his proceeds of the day at the market fair in Hu Qi	205
A blind singer performs at the market fair in Huang Tian Fan	207

Introduction

This book represents a continuation of research begun in Hong Kong in the early 1970s among expatriate artisan furniture makers and woodcarvers from Dongyang county, Zhejiang province (Cooper 1980a). That work traced the evolution of the mode of production of Chinese carved wood furniture from its origins in an architecturally based part-time rural sideline craft, through a transitional regime of urban-based factory "hand manufacture," to full-scale industrial production, based first in Republican Shanghai, and later in post–World War II Hong Kong. It explored in detail the development of the craft in the capitalist environs of Hong Kong, and analyzed the evolving division of labor of production, and changes in the relations between labor and capital as the industry expanded and the carpentry shop became mechanized. It also traced the ways in which received cultural categories that segmented the labor force gradually lost significance as production took on a more proletarian character. The differing woods in which members worked (rosewoods as opposed to teak), the differing native places from which members hailed (Guangdong as opposed to Zhejiang), and the differing craft traditions in which members were trained (carving, carpentry, and painting/varnishing), were clearly superseded by the overwhelming imperatives of the polarity between labor and capital (Cooper 1980a).

Rural Dongyang county has produced generations of artisans skilled in the techniques of woodworking since as early as the Song dynasty (A.D. 960–1127), and possibly even the Tang dynasty (A.D. 618–907), and continues to do so to this day. It was a core group of its expatriates in Shanghai and Hong Kong who were the principal agents of the twentieth-century evolutionary transformations described above in the guise of both labor and capital.

Having conducted in-depth field research among Dongyang

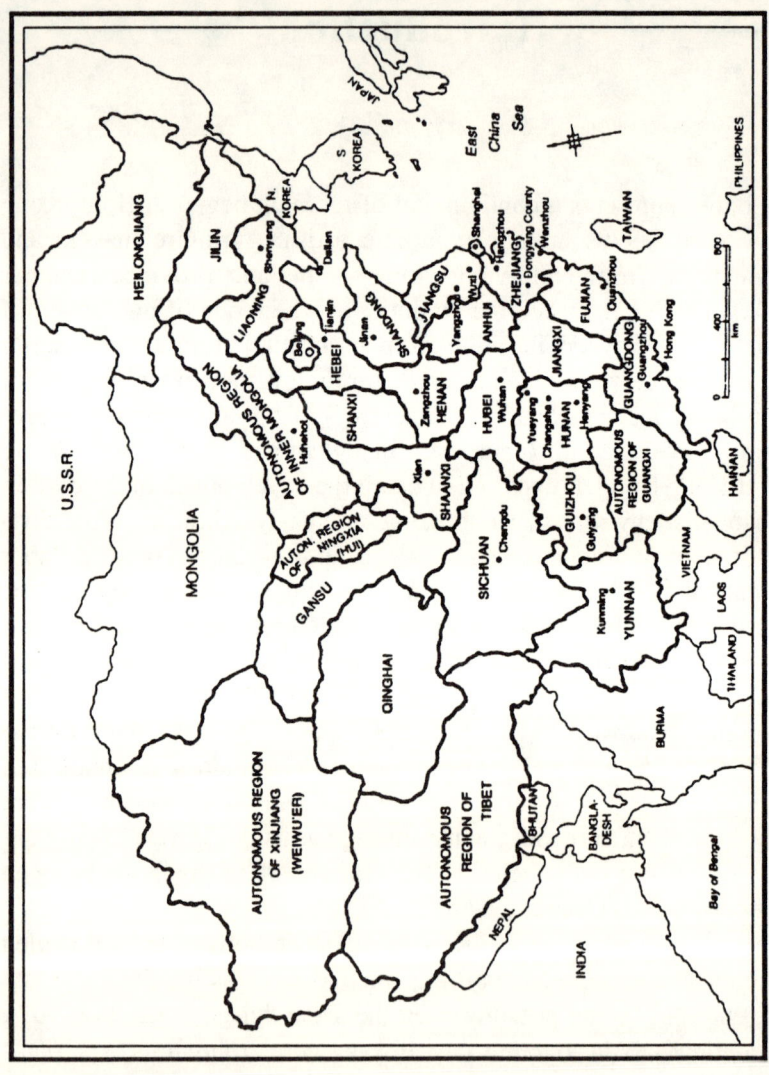

Map 1. China, Showing Provinces.

county's expatriates working in the carved wood furniture industry of modern capitalist Hong Kong in the 1970s, it seemed an intellectually and logically compelling course to investigate the fate of the same craft in the hands of the same folk under totally different socioeconomic conditions in their native county in the Communist People's Republic of China. Such a project would make possible the isolation of systemic features of the socioeconomic environment influencing the evolution of the mode of production, with the technical requirements of production and regional/ethnic variability held constant as it were.

However, access to Dongyang county proved elusive for several years, due in part to a moratorium on anthropological investigations instituted by the Chinese Academy of Social Sciences in 1983, just when the proposed project had succeeded in winning grant support from U.S. sponsors. But Dongyang county, for reasons I was never able to determine, remained closed to foreign visitors for several years after the Zhejiang coastal cities of Shaoxing, Ningbo, and Wenzhou had already "opened up." It was only in the summer of 1986 that I succeeded in visiting Dongyang for a couple of weeks informally, and only late in 1987 and early 1988, through the good offices of Zhejiang University, that I began the collaboration with Professor Jiang Yinhuo of the economics department that allowed the research in Dongyang to go forward, and of which this book is the result.

Field research by anthropologists in the modern world is a sensitive issue with most governments, but especially so with the People's Republic of China. We did not enjoy the luxury of the classic year-long stay in a single peasant village to observe the social life of the community unfold before us in the full round of its annual agricultural and ritual cycles. Indeed, although my original research proposal had called for just such a year-long stay, repeated failure over several years to win approval for the project from Zhejiang provincial public security authorities had led to numerous rewrites and compromises designed to minimize possible security concerns. When the proposal was finally approved, it called for a much reduced research agenda to be implemented over two separate three-month field seasons. There is no way to determine whether this arrangement indeed proved less threatening or was simply approved due to continuing relaxation in the Chinese political climate in 1987 and 1988.

My association with the expatriate Dongyang community of Hong Kong, and the fact that Professor Jiang was himself a native of the county, compensated in some respects for the relatively brief periods actually spent in the field. Our most intensive investigations centered on two villages, Xia Qi Tan and Li Tang, and two market towns, Guo Zhai and Heng Dian.

Mr. Wu Mantang, of Xia Qi Tan village, was the proprietor of the Hong Kong furniture factory in which I was apprenticed as a carver during fieldwork in 1972–73 (Cooper 1980a). Mr. Zhang Mingyao of Li Tang village was one of Hong Kong's premier carving practitioners of that era (Cooper 1980a: 125ff.). Mr. Guo Youxing of Guo Zhai town had lived and worked in Hong Kong during the 1930s and 1940s, but returned to China in the early 1950s. In 1978, I met Mr. Guo during a visit to the Shanghai No. 1 Carving Factory where he worked until his retirement the following year (Cooper 1980b: 447ff.; and Cooper 1994).

Heng Dian came to our attention during visits to one of its woodcarving enterprises (see Chapter 6), and by chance it figured prominently in the life experiences of the Guo family. This resulted in several subsequent visits, and made possible a somewhat more detailed documentation of its remarkably successful experience under the economic reforms.

It was hoped that long familiarity with the expatriate branches of these communities in Hong Kong and Shanghai would serve as a basis for relations of trust and informality in the collection of data. That hope was largely fulfilled. We were warmly welcomed by the villagers and entrepreneurs in each locale, who willingly and openly shared with us their life experiences, as well as the changes wrought in rural social life under recent economic reforms.

In addition, we were afforded the opportunity of conducting a near countywide survey of woodcarving enterprises, which gave us an excellent overview of social life throughout the broader region. We were able to observe the operation of state, local collective, and private enterprises in a period characterized by broad scope for experimentation with individual initiative, private investment, and accumulation in the promotion of rural industry.

Quite by chance our survey itinerary happened to coincide with the cycle of rural market fairs—*hui chang*—as it coursed through several of the towns we visited in succession (see Appendix 3). This happy coincidence gave us the occasion to observe what can only be described as the economic effervescence and vitality of a relatively backward county in a relatively advanced coastal province, under the economic reforms of the 1980s.

There is something of an irony in the fact that although our research was motivated by a desire to compare the development of artisan production under capitalist conditions in Hong Kong with that under socialist conditions in China, by the time we were able to begin our study, national policy in China was already emphasizing the adoption of capitalist rationality as a model for enterprise organization and management (see Chen 1995: 143). Indeed, many of the woodcarving enterprises we visited in Dongyang evoked in their organization and division of labor the small businesses of their expatriate cousins in free market Hong Kong of the 1960s and 1970s. There was, however, a great diversity in size and administrative arrangement under which the enterprises operated, and the investigation of that diversity became one of the principal focuses of our work.

Our presentation continues and elaborates an earlier tradition of scholarly inquiry into Chinese artisanry exemplified in the work of H.B. Morse (1909), C.C. Ch'u and T.C. Blaisdell (1924), J.S. Burgess (1928), J.B. Tayler (1930), H.D. Fong and Y.T. Ku (1934), R.P. Hommel (1937), T.C. Liao (1948), and others. In examining the effects of socialist revolution and recent economic reforms on the artisan sector, the present work updates that tradition, providing new perspectives on the changes wrought by contemporary development processes in the lives of Chinese rural craftsmen as their activities increasingly place them on the pathways of transnational capital (Dirlik 1994: 88).

Like its forebears, this work is firmly grounded in an analysis of the division of labor and organization of craft production, but also seeks to explore the role of the artisan sector in economic development more broadly, and as a window on new theoretical perspectives and approaches.

The enterprises of the artisan sector have figured prominently as organizational models, particularly suited to a new global industrial order in which flexible specialization (Piore and Sabel 1984), flexible production (Dirlik 1994), or flexible accumulation (Harvey 1990) is said to be outcompeting Fordist mass-production on many fronts. There is much in the landscape of China's rural industrial sector under current economic reforms that evokes the elements said to characterize such "flexible" industrial regimes (see, e.g., Gates 1996: 3). After presenting a historical and economic overview of Dongyang county's artisan and rural industrial sectors, we will return in the conclusion to consider the theoretical issues surrounding such flexible regimes, and explore their implications for understanding the contemporary Chinese economy.

Chapter 1 provides a historical and geographical background of Dongyang county, taking note of the dramatic changes that have marked the development of the county town, Wu Ning, under contemporary economic reforms. It situates Dongyang county in the context of national and provincial economic development strategy and policy, and explores the effects of the implementation of economic reforms in the rural industrial sector on Dongyang county as a whole.

Chapter 2 examines the development of the woodcarving profession up to the present period of economic reform. The chapter documents early efforts on the part of newly victorious Communist authorities to reestablish Chinese crafts by reviving earlier treaty port understandings about the organization of production and division of craft labor. It charts the suppression of the art crafts during the cultural revolution, and their second revival under contemporary economic reforms.

Chapters 3, 4, 5, and 6 introduce the two villages and two market towns in which our first season's fieldwork was concentrated—Xia Qi Tan, Li Tang, Guo Zhai, and Heng Dian. Each chapter traces the historical and expatriate experience of each community, and presents data on the local entrepreneurial activity that has proliferated in all four locales under the economic reforms. Not surprisingly, each locale is also represented by at least one woodcarving establishment.

Chapter 7 presents an account of the fortunes of the Dongyang Woodcarving Factory, the largest artisanal enterprise in the county, and formerly a local state-run *(difang guoying)* enterprise. It examines the transformations and innovations introduced in the organization, administration, and management of the enterprise during the reforms.

Chapter 8 concludes with an examination of theoretical issues concerning the role of the artisan sector in economic development. The development experience of Dongyang county is considered in the context of a discussion of "flexible" industrial regimes, and the implications of that experience for understanding the contemporary Chinese economy explored.

In recent years, considerable controversy has erupted in the field of anthropology over the writing of ethnography, and the old functionalist ethnographic paradigm, which persisted long after functionalism's theoretical limitations were recognized, has increasingly been called into question. That paradigm in which at least a little bit of information on economics, politics, religion, kinship, and social organization was presented, with some stress on the functional interrelationship between these various dimensions of social life, has fallen victim to a critique of the unwarranted objectivism it presents with the authority of a disempowering "imperial voice."

In a "post-orientalist" world, a flock of colleagues has rushed to give voice to their "informants" in a "new" ethnography liberated from the conventional literary shackles of "scientific" reportage of "facts." Increasingly, we as readers are invited to share the deeper emotional and expressive, symbolic worlds of informants, and in some quarters within the discipline the literary medium of delivery has become as important as the information conveyed. I am generally sympathetic to such trends insofar as their birth was enabled by the study of a political economy which recognized as relevant the categories "imperial" and "colonial," and was informed from the outset by an awareness of the specter of anthropology's association with imperialism. In addition, it is difficult to argue with the proposition that ethnography which is innovative and interesting in its mode of presentation is preferable to a stale and boring presentation of facts.

Thus, Michael Taussig's *Shamanism, Colonialism and the Wild Man*, employs the "wild man" as a thematic leitmotif throughout a work dealing with terror as a political instrument, presented as a series of montages derived from the author's field experiences in Colombia. Stephen Gudeman and Alberto Rivera's *Conversations in Colombia* describes the analytic discussions between the coauthor "alien and native" anthropologists concerning the household mode of production, most of which took place in Gudeman's run-down automobile as the two drove through the countryside in the course of their collaborative field work.

The present work, constrained by the nature of the field setting in China, is much less innovative in its methodology, and less ambitious in its literary devices and conventions. The investigation was to a large extent structured by local administrative and public security conceptions of how research was to be conducted, in which the formal recording of "facts" was deemed good enough, and in which even the scope of the facts to which we might be privy was a constant subject of dispute, debate, and negotiation.

While at the time of our investigation, the toleration of a diversity of industrial forms was an operative policy in the countryside, and the newly legitimized private sector was booming, field research by social scientists was something with which county public security operatives had little experience. Foreign "guests" were still an oddity in the county when our work commenced, and those who did visit the county rarely stayed longer than overnight. Our activities were closely supervised and monitored, and we were inevitably escorted in our perambulations in the county by a functionary from the county foreign affairs office (read public security) or, at minimum, by an operative from the rural industrial bureau (*xiangzhen qiye ju*). Despite the genuine official duties of our several successive "guides" from the rural industrial bureau with respect to administering local industry, as our escorts their primary responsibility was to report on our activities to the foreign affairs office.

There were frequent disagreements and arguments with the foreign affairs office about how broad the scope of our investigations was to be, about whom we might interview, about appropriate lines of questioning, about what documents we should be allowed to see, about lengths of time to be spent in various locales, about the necessity of supervision at all. Generally speaking, rather than my association with Professor Jiang opening doors that would otherwise have been closed to a foreign researcher, Jiang's association with me served to close doors that would otherwise have been open to a native Chinese researcher.

Although the county was officially "open" *(kaifang)* as of 1986, it was explained to us over and over that there were "degrees" of openness, and that at this particular stage in Dongyang's history, the relatively free and unsupervised movements of foreign researchers that was already common in larger urban centers was simply not to be expected in Dongyang.

There were no old cars available for purchase to drive at will through the countryside, and precious few opportunities to plumb the depths of informants' symbolic beliefs and intimate experiences of the world. Rather, there was an accumulation of impressions gained from observation in the course of supervised perambulations through the county, visiting with and interviewing villagers and factory managers. Professor Jiang's "native" perspective close at hand helped to make initial sense of those impressions, providing an important second opinion confirming or not my interpretation or construction of events.

The restraints and limits placed on us during our ever too brief periods in the field, prior to the Tiananmen massacre it should be noted, made the conduct of research an often frustrating and occasionally humiliating experience. Indeed, perusing the data of our two seasons of field research, I am reminded of Woody Allen's quip about the restaurant in which "The food was lousy... and such small portions!"

Notwithstanding our difficulties, I remain convinced that for the most part the data we were able to gather, and the observations we were able to make, offer a generally accurate portrayal of the rural industrial sector of Dongyang county as it was experiencing new opportunities for dynamic development under Communist Party policies of economic reform. If further evidence were needed, it was provided by follow-up data-gathering trips undertaken by Professor Jiang unencumbered by my presence during the summers of 1991 and 1993.

The policies promoting the development of the productive forces of society through a diversity in industrial form were indeed having an observable effect. The overall rural standard of living and the technical level of the rural work force were rising. The bureaucratic constraints on the ordinary citizen, although present, were considerably loosened, most notably with regard to the ability to save and invest, but also with respect to geographic and occupational mobility. Rural folk were enjoying the opportunity of seizing control of their own destinies, and making of them what they were able (see also Huang 1990: 246).

In light of the obvious economic dynamism of the county during the period of our research, the preoccupation of the public security apparatus with limiting the scope of our investigations and closely monitoring our movements and contacts seemed all the more surprising. And yet, given the inexperience of the local public security operatives with scholarly investigations of their "turf," and the subsequent "crackdown" that occurred in Tiananmen just two weeks after our departure from the county in 1989, perhaps their concern to treat us "according to the regulations" *(anzhao guiding)*, narrowly interpreted, "by the book" as it were, was understandable. While they might not have expected it to come quite so soon, undoubtedly they felt there might come a time when they would be called upon by their superiors to account for their treatment of this foreigner. Being able to respond that such treatment had been accorded "by the book," to the great and well-documented dismay of the foreigner himself, might provide some comfort. However, that did not make our investigations any easier or less frustrating, as such treatment was visited upon us by local public security authorities over two field seasons.

Still, the spirit of ethnography continues to lie in overcoming all obstacles in the effort to convey to one's readers something of one's informants' way of life. In this regard, I have done my best to stitch the materials at our disposal into as clear and understandable a characterization of the structure and process of Dongyang county's recent economic development as possible, given the observational limitations and my own theoretical predilections with respect to the continued importance of "thick" descriptive political economy.

In this post-modern age, I find myself most in sympathy with the Comaroffs' prescriptions for a "neomodern" anthropology, which recognizes that "the meaningful world is always fluid and ambiguous, a partially integrated mosaic of narratives, images, and signifying practices" (Comaroff and Comaroff 1992: 30), but which also assumes that "the human world . . . remains the product of discernible social and cultural processes; processes partially indeterminate yet, in some measure, systematically determined; ambiguous and polyvalent, yet never utterly incoherent or meaningless; open to multiple constructions and contest, yet never entirely free of order—or the reality of power and constraint" (1992: xi).

The fieldwork in Dongyang county on which this book is based would not have been possible without the good faith and cooperation of the Economics Department of Zhejiang University, in Hangzhou. Professor Zhou Wenqian was the architect of the cooperative agreement that made my collaboration with Professor Jiang possible. Without the patience and concern of both Zhou and Jiang, this project would never have got off the ground.

The project was funded by a grant from the United States National Academy of Sciences, Committee on Scholarly Communication with the People's Republic of China. The work of 1989 was also supported by a grant from the Faculty Research and Innovation Fund of the University of Southern California. Both sources are gratefully acknowledged.

Abbreviations

DDZGZJ. 1989. *Dang Dai Zhongguo de Zhejiang* (Contemporary China's Zhejiang Province). 2 volumes. Shang Jingcai, ed. Beijing: China

DYMDBAO (*Dongyang Mu Diao Bao* —Dongyang Woodcarving News)

DYSZ. 1993. *Dongyang Shi Zhi.* (Records of Dongyang City). Dongyang City Gazetteer Editorial Committee. Shanghai: Hanyu Da Zidian Publishers.

DYWZX. 1985. *Dongyang Wenshi Ziliao Xuanji* (Selections of Dongyang Historical Materials). Volume 1. Dongyang: Historical Materials Committee.

DYXXLJS. 1910. *Dongyang Xian Xiangtu Lishi Jiaoke Shu* (Textbook of Dongyang County Local History). 4 parts. Dongyang: County Government.

DYXZ. 1978 (1829). *Dongyang Xian Zhi* (Dongyang County Gazetteer). 2 volumes. Taibei: Taibei City Dongyang Same Native Place Association.

FSZ. 1985. *Dongyang Fengsu Zhi* (Habits and Customs of Dongyang). Dongyang: Dongyang Cultural Palace.

JHFSZ. 1984. *Jinhua Difang Fengsu Zhi* (The Local Habits and Customs of Jinhua). Jinhua: Arts Palace of the Masses.

JHWSZL. 1987. *Jinhua Wenshi Ziliao* (Historical Materials of Jinhua). Jinhua: Zhejiang People's Publishers.

NCNA. 1972. New China News Agency, Dispatch No. 5278: 19.

ZJNCDC. 1932. *Zhejiang Sheng Nongcun Diaocha* (Rural Investigation of Zhejiang Province) esp. pp. 66–97, "Dongyang County." Hangzhou: Provincial Government Press.

ZSQGY. 1986. *Zhejiang Sheng Qing Gai Yao* (Outline of the Condition of Zhejiang Province). Hangzhou: Zhejiang Province Economic Study Center.

THE ARTISANS AND ENTREPRENEURS OF DONGYANG COUNTY

Chapter 1

Dongyang County

Historical Background

Located in a mountainous region virtually equidistant (ca. 170 km) from Zhejiang province's coastal port cities of Hangzhou and Ningbo (see Map 2), Dongyang county was traditionally a land poor and grain deficient area. Indeed, with no more than 30 percent of its total land area arable, scarcity of land has been noted as acute since the Dao Guang reign period (1821–1851) of the Qing dynasty, when the county's population reached 500,000 people.

Dongyang county of the present day is somewhat smaller than in the past. In 1985, two of its eastern districts were divided off into a separate county, Pan An, leaving Dongyang with about one-third less territory. Its present area is about 1,740 square km, and its population in 1992 was 761,400. The county is divided into 7 districts *(qu)*, 48 subdistricts *(xiang)*, and 1,270 villages *(cun)*. There are two large towns *(zhen)*— Wu Ning (the county seat) and Wei Shan, each of which is administered by the county government. Arranged in descending order, county *(xian)*, district *(qu)*, town *(zhen)*, subdistrict *(xiang)*, village *(cun)* represent the levels of the present rural administrative hierarchy.

From very early on in the county's history, Dongyang residents had come to rely on extra-agricultural sideline occupations and outmigration to supplement their livelihood, and since the Ming dynasty (1368–1644), Dongyang has enjoyed a reputation as a "county of 100 skills" *(bai gong zhi xiang)*. Besides purveying their distinctive woodcarving skills, Dongyang expatriates also engaged in carpentry, masonry, and other construction trades, while back in the county itself residents engaged in ham curing, bamboo weaving and basketry, hosiery knitting, cord and thread production, pottery and soap manufacture, silk weaving, and the production of traditional medicinal preparations and fireworks.

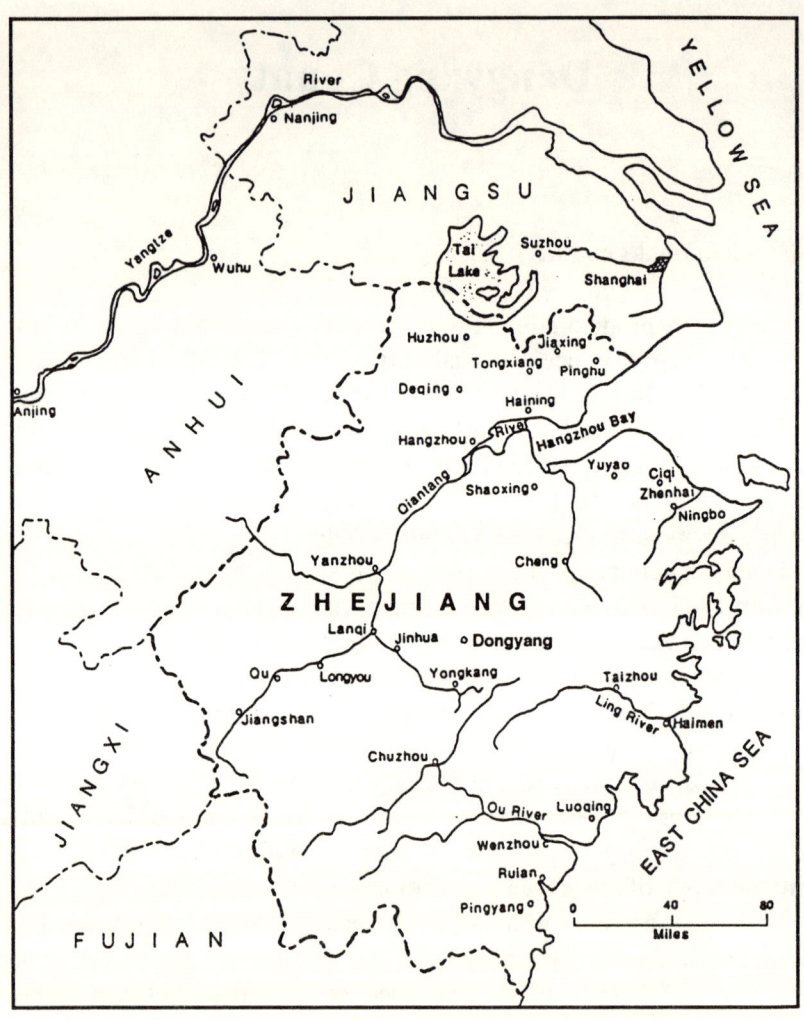

Map 2. Zhejiang province, showing location of Dongyang county.

During late imperial times, Dongyang was part of Zhejiang province's Jinhua prefecture, and remained under the prefectural jurisdiction of Jinhua until 1988, when its county town Wu Ning was upgraded in administrative status to "city" *(shi),* under the direct bureaucratic supervision of the provincial authorities.

Geographically, Dongyang is characterized by three distinct economic zones (ZJNCDC 1932: 70). The first is a level plain extending eastward from the county town of Wu Ning, which is itself located on the western edge of the county near to the border of Yi Wu county (see Map 3). The first zone is the county's most productive agricultural area, and livestock raising is most advanced; mainly pigs, but also goats, ducks, and chickens are raised. The pigs are processed into a variety of hams that differ according to the curing process employed, the season in which they are processed, and the kind of pig from which the meat derives. Roughly one-fourth of so-called Jinhua hams, which came to enjoy a national reputation during the latter part of the Qing dynasty (1644–1911), are actually produced in Dongyang (see Appendix 1 on ham production).

The second economic zone lies further to the east of the county town at a slightly higher elevation. Silk production is carried out in this zone centered on the town of Hu Qi, in the immediate suburbs of which the village of Li Tang is located, birthplace of Mr. Zhang Mingyao (see Chapter 4). In this zone also, the woodcarving centers of the county lie in an arc from southeast to northeast, including the market towns of Heng Dian (see Chapter 6), Nan Shang Hu, Hu Qi, Guo Zhai (the birthplace of Mr. Guo Youxing described in Chapter 5), Lou Xi Zhai, Wei Shan, Huailu, Zhang Cun, and Liu Shi Kou (near Xia Qi Tan, the native village of Mr. Wu Mantang described in Chapter 3) (see Map 3).

In the third zone, which lies in an arc still further east of the county town, the land becomes mountainous, and the temperatures cooler. Grain production is more difficult, and most of the land that is cultivated is planted in tea and medicinal herbs, which do well at higher elevations. This zone also produced the lumber for house construction and woodcarving in traditional times, marketed in the towns of Heng Dian and Ma Che Bu. Nowadays, indigenous supplies of lumber have for the most part been depleted, with many forests cut down for fuel for the ill-fated "backyard steel furnaces" of the Great Leap Forward in the late 1950s. Wood for the industry now comes mainly from north-

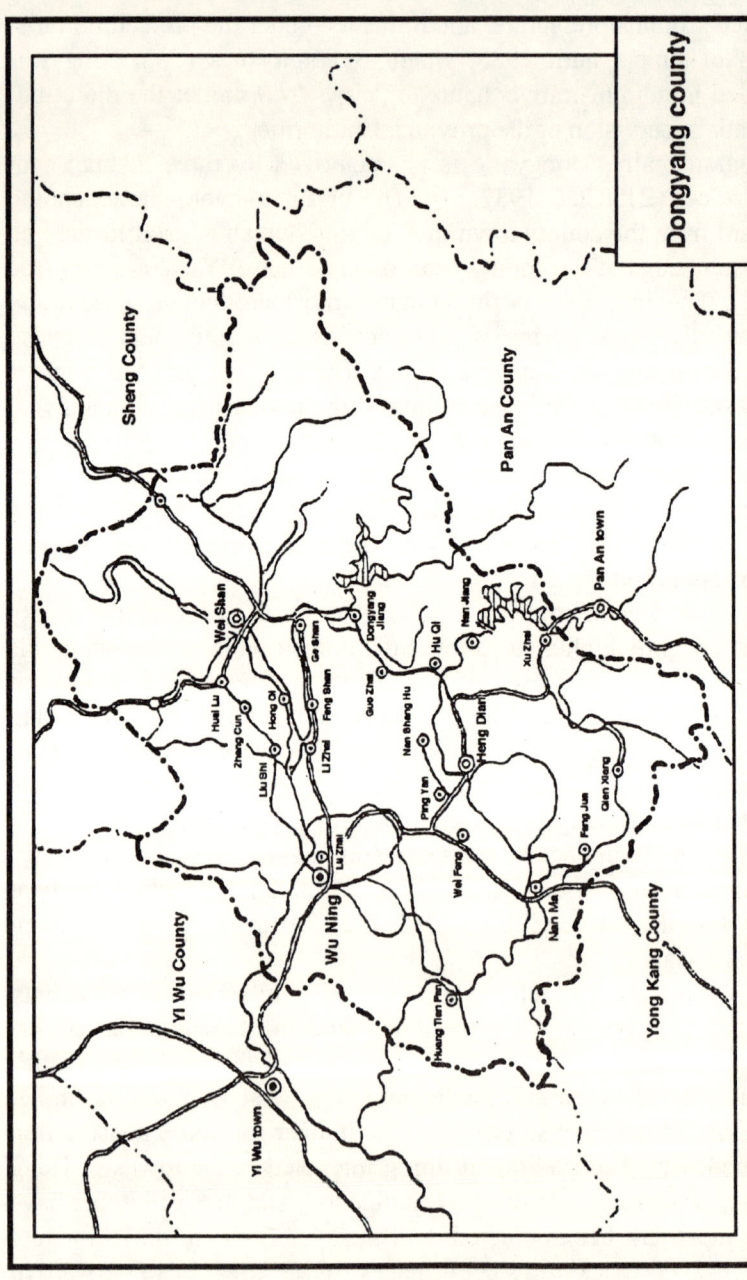

Map 3. Dongyang county, showing the county seat, Wu Ning, and assorted market towns. Li Tang village is near to the town of Hu Qi; Xia Qi Tan village is just south of Zhang Cun; Guo Zhai is a market town in its own right.

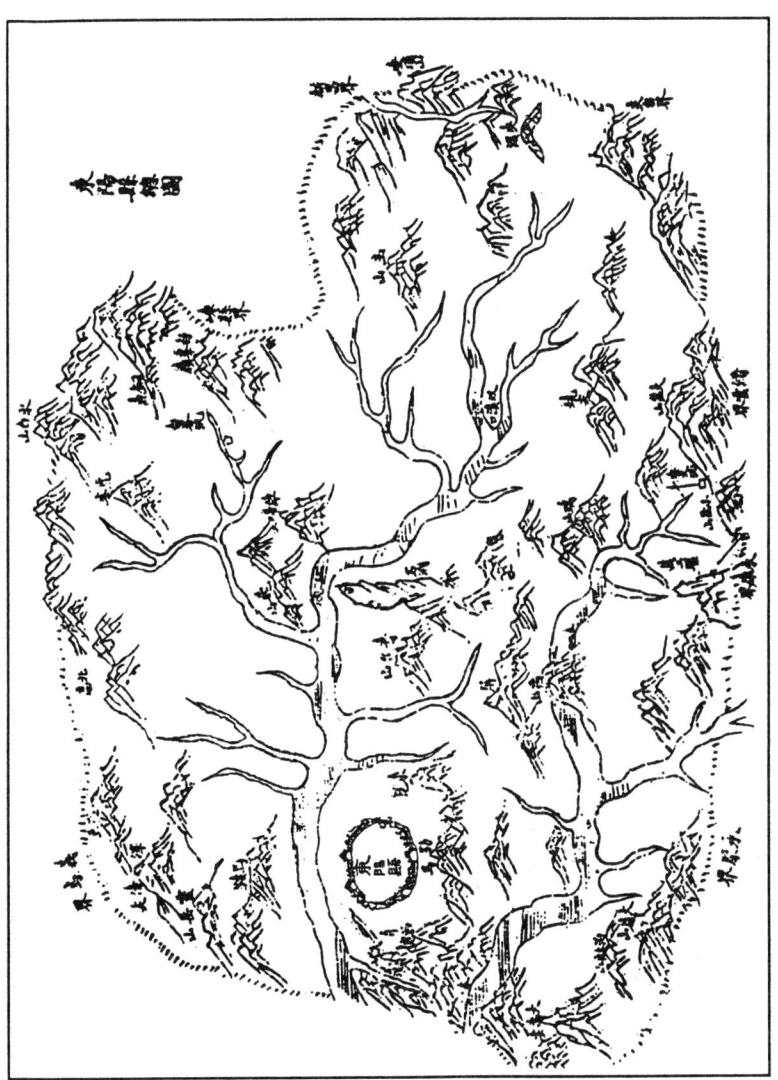

Map 4. Dongyang county map from the Qing dynasty gazetteer, Kang Xi reign period (1662–1722).

east China (Manchuria), and from the hills of Jiangxi province to the west and south.

Occasionally, one still sees a great spreading camphor tree near the entrance to a village, or adjacent to a square or courtyard. Such trees provided the raw material for the camphorwood chests produced by traditional workers in wood for bridal trousseaus, and later for export, but local supplies of camphorwood are now quite scarce, and camphorwood for the products of the contemporary industry comes from outside the county. Such camphor trees as remain in Dongyang have been spared by traditional beliefs in their efficacy as protective mother spirits (see Appendix 2 on camphor tree mothers).

In Southern Song dynasty times (1127–1278), the royal court in Beijing fled south, establishing itself in the Zhejiang provincial capital Hangzhou, bringing with it a variety of influences—in education, Confucian values, diet (wheat, bread, and noodles), and division of labor between the sexes. Several centers of learning were established in Dongyang at the time, including the famous Stone Cave Academy (Shi Dong Shu Yuan) where neo-Confucian philosopher Zhu Xi taught classes, wrote poetry, and left specimens of his calligraphy. Six other academies, and a variety of lineage-sponsored private primary schools, *shu guan,* flourished in Dongyang during the Qing dynasty, and a 1910 textbook on county history proudly proclaims that the county produced more than 500 *sheng yuan* degree holders during this era (DYXXLJS 1910: 74; Jiang n.d.d).

Since that time, Dongyang has maintained a tradition of scholarly excellence and there is a great sense of pride in the educational achievements of county citizens that continues down to the present. Dongyang achieved universal primary education in 1962, and near universal lower middle education in 1969. Since 1977, county middle schools have sent nearly 1,000 new students each year to colleges and universities, among the highest numbers sent from any single county in the country (Zhou 1987a: 6).

At present, there are 67,300 students in the county's 834 primary schools, 38,000 students in its lower middle schools, more than 8,000 students in its upper middle and specialized upper middle schools, and more than 10,000 students in 312 vocational middle schools in a variety of specialties including mechanics, accounting, health, construction, horticulture, farm machinery, household electronics, animal husbandry, and fruit cultivation (Jiang n.d.d).

Local annals assert that from the beginning of the Ming dynasty (late fourteenth century), the familiar Confucian values—*san gang wu chang*—the three duties of a man as prince, father, and husband, and the five constant virtues of benevolence, righteousness, ritual propriety, wisdom, and sincerity—*ren yi li zhi xin*—were firmly established, as were the various manifestations of the Confucian patriarchal social order (FSZ 1985: 2). A survey and investigation carried out in 1961 by county, province, and national cultural departments identified twelve extant buildings and structures associated with Ming dynasty estates in the county, of which the grandest in scale is Su Yong Tang—Hall of Solemn Harmony in Lu Zhai village (described in Chapter 2). These structures are noteworthy for the light they shed on the development of woodcarving skills and the association of such skills with household and temple architecture and construction.

From the late eighteenth to the mid-nineteenth centuries during the Qing dynasty, Dongyang experienced a period of peace and prosperity. From the end of the reign period of the Qian Long emperor (1736–1796) on through that of Jia Qing (1796–1821) and Dao Guang (1821–1851), a generally stable society with a flourishing and increasingly commercialized economy provided a setting in which local traditional folk arts underwent an expansive development.

The opening of the treaty ports of Shanghai, Hangzhou, and Ningbo in mid-century would accelerate the commercialization of agriculture and craft production in the hinterland counties of Zhejiang province, but much of the province was ravaged by the armies of the Taiping rebels in the 1860s. The Taipings took Dongyang on October 1, 1861, the eleventh year of the Xian Feng emperor, and held it until March 3, 1863, second year of the Tong Zhi emperor (fieldnotes, 5/8/89, Jinhua), when they were finally expelled. The population of Dongyang county, as well as that of Jinhua prefecture, was depleted by nearly 50 percent by the end of the rebellion, as many were killed and thousands more fled (DYXXLJS 1910: 44; Rankin 1986: 56).*

With the advent of the Republic, Dongyang was subject to the

---

*Elderly residents of Xia Qi Tan village still recount the story of Wu Xiankui, a *juren* (degree holder) of the Wu lineage who was executed by the Taiping rebels for refusing to cooperate with their administration. His grandson, Wu Shixiao, was awarded an honorary hereditary official post in acknowledgment of his grandfather's loyalty by the Guang Xu emperor after the Taipings were defeated.

influence of the larger political and cultural forces affecting the rest of the nation. Students at Dongyang Middle School participated in demonstrations on the streets of Wu Ning town during the May 4th movement of 1919, opposing concessions granted to the Japanese in China after the First World War. The students engaged in propaganda work and organized a boycott of Japanese goods, at one point going from shop to shop in the county town, confiscating the goods, and burning them in a great bonfire at the school gate. In 1925, students organized strikes in support of the May 30th movement. They demonstrated in support of the Shanghai workers, protesting the massacre, boycotting foreign goods, and extending their organizational network more broadly into other schools in the county (DYWZX 1985: 1: 85–86).

The 1920s and 1930s were hard times in rural Dongyang. Imported foreign goods—cigarettes, kerosene, and fertilizer—were perceived to be draining the wealth of the county (ZJNCDC 1932: 70), and social disorder was pervasive in this era of warlordism. Interlineage conflict and violence were widespread, and banditry, both spontaneous and organized, led to increased instability and insecurity (Schoppa 1982: 119).

A 1932 survey of eight Dongyang villages shows that distribution of landholdings was becoming increasingly polarized, with high rates of tenancy (ZJNCDC 1932: 89). Rents were generally due three days after the solar term *li qiu,* the beginning of autumn, and were paid in kind, averaging 40 percent to 50 percent of the crop (ZJNCDC 1932: 91; Jiang n.d.d), a figure consistent with village studies conducted in other parts of China during this period (see e.g., Fei's study of Jiangsu 1939).

A variety of surcharges and rent deposits often made tenancy even more onerous, and the elements also took their toll. Hail storms from March to May, excessive rain and flooding in May and June, heat and drought in early and mid-July, typhoons and more flooding from July to September, and early frost in the beginning of September, spelled ruination for many households, leaving others on the bare margins of subsistence. Hardship during the period of "green and yellow not connected," *qing huang bu jie,* when the new grain was ripening and the past year's grain was already consumed, was commonplace, and many households were forced to make up their grain deficits by selling what they could, even children, in years of severe flooding or drought (Jiang n.d.d).

In those years it was said,

San nian liang tou han, yi chang da yu bian wang yang; Dongyang liang tiao lan duchang, sha ren bu yong qiang—[Every three years there are two droughts and one great inundation; Dongyang has two rotten intestines, to kill a man, one does not have to shoot him.] (DYSZ 1993: 87)

The two rotten intestines refer to Dongyang's North and South rivers, whose irregular flows brought frequent hardship if not disaster for the local population.

One of the accomplishments of the Maoist regime in the 1950s was the establishment of an effective water control system, which not only ensured a measure of protection against the vagaries of the elements, but also made it possible for most areas in the first and second economic zones to rely more heavily on irrigated rice for their subsistence rather than millet and corn. Nowadays, corn is mainly pig food, although there are a variety of tasty local festival foods that are prepared with corn flour or cornmeal.

Not surprisingly, outmigration from the county was an attractive alternative to wrenching poverty and insecurity. One estimate of outmigration during the early 1930s suggests a figure of nearly 30 percent of the poor agricultural peasant population expatriated, with still larger percentages for nonagricultural households (ZJNCDC 1932: 72, 87–88). Outmigration remained a fact of life into the late 1930s and 1940s as the Japanese invasion of China, World War II, and civil war further undermined rural stability (Xu 1986: 10–11). One encounters outmigration repeatedly in elderly woodcarvers' accounts of their work lives and careers during this period.

With established traditions of work outside the county, Dongyang residents maintained extensive expatriate networks in Shanghai, Hangzhou, Hong Kong, and Guangzhou and worked in construction, carpentry, masonry, furniture manufacture, and silk weaving till Japanese occupation cut them off from their markets. But these networks were reestablished after the Communist victory in 1949, and have taken on renewed significance for county residents seeking opportunities under the market-oriented economic reforms of the 1980s.

A Communist Party special branch was first established in Dongyang in late 1927, and a county central committee was set up in 1933. By 1935 there were 3 district party committees, 53 branch offices, and more than 650 members in Dongyang. In that year, the party was preparing to seize the county town on lunar 8/13. The plan was to use the Hu Gong temple fair (see Appendix 3) to recruit a massive armed force and establish a soviet government, but the plot was discovered. The provincial Guomindang government sent agents to the county, declared martial law, imposed a curfew, and with seven brigades of military police conducted a search and destroy mission against the county's party members. More than 600 were arrested and forced to confess; 40 were jailed; and on October 29, the leaders of the plot were summarily executed (DYSZ 1993: 533).

In 1937 agents were sent from Shanghai to reestablish the party organization and strengthen the anti-Japanese movement. In 1939, with Japanese armies advancing and Chiang Kaishek vacillating, the reestablished Dongyang county Communist Party committee held its first congress to discuss strategies in the anti-Japanese campaign. In the fall of 1939, party leaders once again used the occasion of lunar 8/13 and the Hu Gong temple fair, this time to organize a performance of a revised traditional opera to whip up anti-Japanese feeling and launch a demonstration, reaching the thousands of fairgoers with their message (DYSZ 1993: 543).

Dongyang was bombed by Japanese planes intermittently between 1938 and 1940, and in May 1941, 400 Japanese troops crossed the border from Yi Wu, and camped at Shang Lu village. On the following day, they bombarded the county town, and conducted missions in 11 northern districts, destroying homes and killing more than 160. By May of the following year, reinforcements of Japanese troops had crossed into Dongyang from Zhuji and Sheng counties, and exercised total control of the county. The Guomindang county government abandoned the county town of Wu Ning to the Japanese and established a government in exile, first in Hu Qi town, and then in the more remote town of Ma Zhai to the southeast.

During this period, the local population was subject to conscription by the Japanese army to improve and construct local roads, and villages were burnt to the ground for failure to cooperate. Communist forces carried out intermittent armed raids and sabotage on Japanese forces from party cells in Hu Qi and Pan An towns (Pan 1984: 563), and parts of the county were subjected to further bombing raids by Japanese planes.

It was from the period of the late 1930s that substantial migration from the county to Hong Kong began. According to local historians, a handful of Dongyang folk had already established themselves in Hong Kong beginning in the 1920s. Subsequently, Dongyang residents arrived in substantial numbers in four waves of emigration. The first was precipitated by the Japanese invasion of Shanghai in 1937 and the advance of Japanese troops toward Dongyang (fieldnotes, 5/3/89, interview with Hua Dehan). Mr. Guo Youxing was among this early group of migrants (see Chapter 5).

Later, when the Japanese took Hong Kong in 1941–42, many of these first wave migrants returned to Dongyang, some by foot in a long three-month trek covering more than 500 miles (see Chapter 3). Following the Japanese defeat in 1945, many of those who had fled Hong Kong returned to the colony, and new immigrants joined their ranks in a second wave. Mr. Wu Mantang moved to Hong Kong for the first time during this period, together with his brother who had settled in Hong Kong prior to the war.

The imminent and ultimately decisive Communist victory in the ensuing civil war against Chiang Kaishek's nationalist forces precipitated the third major wave of migration to Hong Kong. Even before the victorious forces of the People's Liberation Army reached Dongyang on May 8, 1949, many Dongyang residents, Mr. Zhang Mingyao among them (see Chapter 4), had made their way to Hong Kong in anticipation of their victory (Pan 1984: 563).

The fourth wave of migration occurred during the "Three and Five Anti Campaigns" in the early 1950s, when the Communist government instituted an all-out assault on the remnants of the urban private industrial sector still functioning on the mainland. Many Shanghai firms owned by or employing Dongyang expatriates responded by moving their operations to still-British-controlled Hong Kong at this time, and many of their employees followed (fieldnotes, 5/3/89, interview with Hua Dehan).

Nevertheless, the arrival of the People's Liberation Army and the cessation of hostilities in 1949 brought a modicum of stability back to Dongyang. In the course of the following year, bandit suppression brigades conducted mopping-up operations on pockets of remnant Guomindang resistance (DYWZX 1985: 100 ff.), as agriculture, commerce, and industry were reestablished on a cooperative basis.

Post-Liberation Dongyang: The Role of Rural Industrial Enterprise

In the early 1950s, peasant farmers, shop owners and craftsmen participated in the movement to *fanshen* (Xu 1986: 12; also see Hinton 1966), beginning new lives under the newly established Communist regime. Production revived as marketing co-ops were organized beginning in 1950. Co-ops had branches in all Dongyang villages by 1956. The earliest lower-stage agricultural co-op, called Fang Ru Xing—Agricultural Producers' Cooperative—was begun in April 1952, in Shou Ta Tou village of Huai Tang subdistrict, consolidated out of earlier mutual aid teams, and by 1954 lower-stage cooperativization was completed countywide. Higher-stage cooperativization began in 1955, emulating the experience of Tou Sui cooperative in Nan Shang Hu township, and by the end of 1957, there were 1,355 higher-level coops in the county encompassing 134,169 households, or 98.65 percent of all households.

During agricultural collectivization, rural workers employed in the "five skills"—the media of plaster, wood, bamboo, stone, and metal (*ni, mu, zhu, shi, tie*)—and those with skills in hand crafts participated in the formation of cooperative sideline enterprises, *fu ye*. With state encouragement, much of this activity was channeled into independent sideline brigades or teams, which kept their own accounts and were responsible for their own profits and losses. Paralleling the collectivization of agriculture was a series of socialist reforms carried out in industrial and hand craft industries.

By the end of 1957 in Dongyang county, six state-run enterprises had been started up, along with eighteen joint state/private enterprises, and 280 factories run by cooperatives. These enterprises employed 29,022 workers and produced an annual industrial production value of ¥14,950,000. In the early period of the people's communes, these became known as *she dui qi ye*—"commune/brigade enterprises" (DDZGZJ 1989: 266–67).

Dongyang's first people's commune was organized in September of 1959 in conjunction with the so-called Great Leap Forward, with Weishan town as its center. At a time when most people still had little idea what the word commune *(gongshe)* meant, the 1,355 higher-level co-ops in the county were organized into 14 "people's communes" by the end of the month. During the more than twenty-year regime of the communes, even with the unit of account dropped first to the level of the production brigade, and then to the level of the production team, agricultural productivity grew little if at all until collective agriculture was abandoned in the 1980s in favor of "household responsibility."

In conjunction with the Great Leap Forward in Dongyang, 176 new enterprises with 44,026 employees were established in steel smelting, construction materials, chemicals, fertilizer, medicinal herbs, agricultural tools, agricultural machinery, sugar refining, weaving, and paper production. Although these enterprises represented Dongyang county's first experiments in rural industry, by 1966, with the exception of the Qian Xiang electric generating factory, every one of these enterprises had closed down (Jiang n.d.d). Restricted in terms of the access of their goods to broad markets by a political atmosphere emphasizing commune self-sufficiency and critical of interregional trade, many were forced to rely on collective subsidies for support. In addition, the practice of rewarding workers and management regardless of performance, "eating from a common pot," did little to encourage efficiency (DDZGZJ 1989: 267).

The administrative and productive demands placed upon the communes combined with catastrophic weather conditions to provoke a national crisis in which the central government now acknowledges that millions of people died of famine. Bad as it may have been in Dongyang, my sense is that folks were not starving there during the Great Leap. That there was privation is indicated by anecdotal accounts by county residents that during the period attendees at wedding banquets had to bring their own food to consume at the affairs.

The small number of factories that remained in the wake of the Great Leap were engaged principally in the production of agricultural tools, repairing machinery and processing grain, and most of these required subsidies from the communes to function. In 1963, under directives of the Four Cleanups campaign, communes were required to function as *qingshui yamen* (uncorrupt, and by implication poor, administrative outposts). All economic activities in the villages (brigades) became subject to inspection in terms of how their organization reflected the interests of the working class. Evaluated in this way, many of the remaining commune and brigade enterprises were forced to shut down (DDZGZJ 1989: 268).

In 1966, to clarify the direction of rural economic development, party chairman Mao Zedong voiced approval of brigades running small collective factories when conditions were appropriate, but the Cultural Revolution intervened, and this instruction was not implemented until 1969 (DDZGZJ 1989: 268).

The Cultural Revolution

The central point of contention during the Great Proletarian Cultural Revolution in China (1966–76) was over how best to effect a transition to socialism. In short, while all parties to the conflict recognized the importance of developing the productive forces of society as a prerequisite to meeting the material needs of China's enormous population, fundamental differences of opinion existed as to the best means of achieving that goal.

Maoist forces argued that the role of ideology was central to the construction of socialism, that the development of the productive forces in itself was not enough. If development were to occur, it was necessary that the goals of socialism be reflected in the day-to-day functioning of the institutions responsible for fostering the development of the productive forces. Consistent with his essay "On Practice," Mao argued that it made little sense to build productive institutions according to capitalist principles of efficiency, and then expect socialism to emerge spontaneously when society had achieved a certain level of productivity. Rather, he argued, the construction of socialism required that institutions be built to reflect the ideals and goals of socialism in their daily practice. To organize an enterprise on the basis of principles of capitalist efficiency could only reproduce capitalist authority patterns, relations of production, and modes of thought, leading ultimately to a capitalist restoration or a socialism that was such in name alone. In other words, the politics of an enterprise could be read from its organization of production. That organization should be guided by socialist ideology. Generally hostile to private entrepreneurship and "petty capitalist" production, and confident in the state's ability to control directly the rural production process in the broader social interest, this strategy has been called the Stalinist strategy by some scholars (e.g., Nolan 1989: 34).

Mao's principal adversaries during the Cultural Revolution, Liu Shaoqi and Deng Xiaoping, came to stand for a position advocating the primacy of the productive forces. China was a poor country. The level of China's productive forces was low. Developing those productive forces required energy, investment, and risk, which apparently had lain dormant if not been suppressed outright under the collective agricultural and industrial regime. Above all else the productive forces of society needed to be developed. It made little sense to talk of socialist institutions in the context of mass poverty and privation. What was required was a massive effort in which any activity contributing to the advance of the productive forces would be deemed a positive step in the achievement of socialism.

Capitalist standards of profitability should be used to evaluate the performance of enterprises, and capitalist management techniques, insofar as they were the most advanced in the world, should be put to use and exploited for the benefits they would bring in the long run. If this led to increased income inequalities, contradictory relations of production, inappropriate individualistic attitudes, so be it. These would all be dealt with at a time when the material basis for establishing socialism was nearer at hand. For the moment, it was most important that any fetters on the development of the productive forces be removed. While recognizing the crucial function both of cooperation and appropriate state action, this approach is sympathetic to individual farming, entrepreneurial initiative, private accumulation, and to the positive role of market forces. It has been characterized as the Bukharinist strategy (Nolan 1989: 34).

Nowadays, it is difficult to find anyone in Dongyang with a good word for the Cultural Revolution or the Stalinist/Maoist position that was in ascendancy during that period. It is fairly clear that people found it difficult to live their lives with the political and ideological significance of their most minor activities (i.e., their "practice") uppermost in mind at all times, with an ever present and ever vigilant Communist Party enforcing political orthodoxy. The ideological issues at stake often became a vehicle for settling personal scores. Untold suffering and humiliation, not to mention needless loss of many innocent lives, created despair and disillusionment among large sectors of the population.

It was difficult to get details of how the national and provincial struggle between the two ideological lines—socialism and backsliding capitalism/revisionism—played itself out locally in Dongyang. It is clear, however, from Forster's work (1990) that the Cultural Revolution in Zhejiang province was a particularly complex and drawn out affair, with local interpretations of mixed signals emanating from Beijing and Hangzhou leading to near chaos in rural counties like Dongyang.

Armed clashes between the two factions, the Maoist "rebel" and Liuist "conservative" factions (called, respectively, the Revolutionary Rebel United Headquarters and the Revolutionary Rebel United General Headquarters), occurred from 1967 through 1969 in Dongyang, and revived again as late as 1974 when militia groups associated with each faction clashed on South Street in the county town (DYSZ 1993:

858–59), but the local issues and personalities that provoked the clashes were not shared with us.

The largest production unit in the county during the Cultural Revolution, with a large number of workers resident on the premises, was the Dongyang Woodcarving Factory (described in Chapter 7). It was among the production units of the county which felt the revolution's effects most dramatically. Its work force split into two factions, aligned with the factions of the county town. As elsewhere, there were ideological struggle sessions, but armed clashes in the factory's environs with homemade shotguns left two workers dead.

On East Street in the county town of Wu Ning, the elegantly carved "Flower Pavilion," *Hua Ting*, part of the former residence of Wei Zhongxian, an imperial eunuch of the Ming dynasty who ran afoul of court intrigue and retired to Dongyang as the dynasty was declining, shows signs of Cultural Revolution vandalism. The central hall, said by residents to have been the most sumptuously decorated with carvings in wood, has been demolished, but on the remains of the older Hua Ting structure, one can still see places where stone inscriptions over interior doorways were scratched out or defaced by Red Guards bent on destroying the "four olds" (old ideas, old culture, old customs, and old habits) (fieldnotes, 6/5/88, interview with Du Paiqing, Wu Ning city construction office).

During the Cultural Revolution period, some small enterprises were established in Dongyang as the result of efforts on the part of urban educated youth and cadres sent "up to the mountains and down to the villages" in 1969 under Mao's direction. Many of these relocated city folk are credited with using their urban connections *(guanxi)* and their own knowledge and organizational skills to help the brigades to which they had been assigned organize and run small factories and enterprises (DDZGZJ 1989: 268–69).

The overthrow of the so-called Gang of Four in 1976, and the subsequent repudiation of the Stalinist/Maoist position, resulted in a great collective sigh of relief, a relaxation in the conduct of life that one could literally feel on the streets. The Liuist position and the "openness" it called for, as applied in the policies of Deng Xiaoping, were met by most with a welcome embrace.

In 1977–78, governments at various levels throughout Zhejiang province began to emphasize the development of commune and brigade *(she dui)* enterprises, and a directive to "establish enterprises

Table 1.1

Production Figures for Rural Industrial Enterprises in Zhejiang Province

Year	Number of Enterprises	Workers (million)	% Rural Labor Force	Annual Production Value (Million ¥)
1974	35,000 *shedui*			¥857
1975	45,700			¥1,269
1976	51,000	1.240	8.9	¥1,450
1978	74,000	1.901		¥2,170
1983				¥7,734
1984	97,000 collective 93,700 cooperative and joint household	3.877	21.7	¥12,107
1985	345,000	4.650	27.6	¥22,370

Sources: ZSQGY 1986 and DDZGZJ 1989.

centering on and assisting agriculture" was put forward (DDZGZJ 1989: 270). In August 1978, the Zhejiang province Commune and Brigade Enterprise Management Bureau *(guan li ju)* was established, and at the end of 1978, there were 74,000 such enterprises employing 1,901,000 workers in Zhejiang province. Industrial production value stood at ¥2,170,000,000 (DDZGZJ 1989: 270).

Economic Reform

The Third Plenum of the Eleventh Central Committee of the CCP (TPECC), held at the end of 1978, set in motion a massive program of reform that, step by step, was to transform China's and Dongyang's rural institutions in the ensuing years. The rural people's communes, which for over two decades had been the basis of the rural economy, were to be dissolved, land apportioned to households, and rural industrial enterprises acknowledged as a positive force.

Such enterprises were now recognized as having a significant role to play in putting underemployed rural labor power to work, providing productive nonagricultural employment in the countryside, increasing rural income, reducing push factors in urban migration, filling lacunae in the planned state sector, and providing resources through local taxation for cultural and welfare facilities previously unavailable in rural areas.

The general strategy with respect to rural enterprise during the late 1970s was summed up in the phrase *"san jiu di"* ("according to locale in three aspects")—*"jiu di qu cai, jiu di jia gong, jiu di xiao shou"* ("employ local materials, employ local skills, and buy and sell in local markets." In other words, rural industry was seen as an adjunct to the state plan, and would develop only in its interstices in accord with local resources and talents to meet local needs (DDZGZJ 1989: 270).

Before long, the "three local" requirement came to be seen as too restrictive. In 1980, "economic adjustments" encouraged rural enterprises to abandon the policies under which their primary function was to "fill in the interstices" as a "junior partner to heavy industry," "avoiding the important, dwelling on the trivial." Policies were promulgated that granted tax holidays to new enterprises, relaxed restrictions on commodity transportation and sale, allowed greater flexibility in responding to market demand, lightened enterprises' obligations to the state, and guaranteed reinvestment of surpluses in enterprise expansion. Rural enterprises were thereafter encouraged to begin a process of structural transformation, strengthening internal organization, providing better service, improving their production and management systems, and implementing "more work, more pay"—*duolao, duode*—remuneration systems (DDZGZJ 1989: 270–71).

Under policies of "reform, openness, and securing livelihood" *(gaige, kaifang, gaohuo),* greater scope was accorded private entrepreneurial activity and individual accumulation, and this in turn led to a great outpouring of energy in pursuit of private gain. There clearly was productive work to which underemployed labor power in the countryside could well be put, and there was a substantial demand for the goods and services provided by private enterprise that was beyond the ability or desire of the state sector to satisfy with any regularity or efficiency. There were niches within the overall centrally planned system in which the creative deployment of resources by enterprising individuals could not only meet perceived needs, but simultaneously advance the development of the productive forces of society.

Through the late 1970s and early 1980s, as China wrangled with determining an appropriate mix of private and public enterprise in its overall economy under the newly introduced reforms, the phrase "socialism with distinctively Chinese characteristics" *(you zhongguo tese de shehuizhuyi)* gained currency. In effect, this formulation expressed a new flexibility with respect to the relative space that private, public, and foreign enterprises were to occupy in China's overall economy, in accord with the leadership's overwhelming concern to develop the productive forces of society.

The absorption of Hong Kong into the South China economy in 1997, in effect already under way in the late 1970s (Cooper 1979), would test whether a policy of "one country, two systems" was really viable. In the meantime, China was prepared to tolerate a high degree of entrepreneurial activity and personal accumulation on the part of its own citizens under the same banner as well.

In 1978 Dongyang county had some 2,852 rural enterprises employing some 40,542 employees, with an annual production value (APV) of ¥41,438,000. Of these, 492 enterprises were administered at the commune level employing 21,568 workers, with an APV of ¥20,130,000. The remainder were administered at the brigade level, of which woodcarving enterprises were most numerous. As a result of the efforts of a senior generation of elderly masters in the trade to guarantee the reproduction of the craft labor force in the early post-liberation period, a skilled work force was in place (see Chapter 2).

Woodcarving enterprises did not require much capital, and the homes of ordinary folk *(lao bai xing)* could be used as workshops. In the words of the assistant bureau chief of Dongyang's rural industrial bureau, these enterprises were characterized by a "handicraft workshop mode of production"—*shougongye zuofang shengchan fangshi*—relying on the old masters and their apprentices to function. The administrative requirements were quite simple, and the economic benefits and income were relatively substantial (fieldnotes, 7/4/88, interview with Lou Zhengzhi).

But the woodcarving industry was soon eclipsed in an increasingly diversified rural economy spurred on by the economic reforms. Building on the strengths represented by its traditions of artisanry, high levels of education, and expatriate experience, the county has witnessed development in more than thirty industrial lines including chemicals, electronics, machinery, electrical power, art craft objects, woven goods, clothing, food and drink, construction materials, printing, and tanning (Dongyang Tong Xiang Hui of Hong Kong n.d.).

In 1980, there were 85,000 Dongyang workers employed outside the county, mainly in the construction trades in Shanghai, Nanjing, and Hangzhou. With the further relaxation of restrictions on migration nationwide, introduced in the late 1980s, these numbers have increased dramatically. The relations *(guanxi)* deriving from Dongyang's traditions of expatriation have become an important factor providing opportunities for its residents in the context of the contemporary economic reforms. More recently, in line with national policies encouraging the export of the nation's most abundant resource—labor power—Dongyang workers have also manned construction teams working overseas in Southeast Asia, Europe, Africa, and the Middle East (Pan 1984; and Chapter 5 below).

In 1982, the Communist Party attempted to limit the number of employees that a private enterprise might employ to a maximum of two apprentices and five hired laborers, but this policy was soon relaxed, and by the mid-1980s, privately hired labor had expanded rapidly (see Nolan 1989: 14).

In 1982–83 there occurred a full-scale return to family farming. "Contracting responsibility to the household" (*bao gan dao hu*) became almost universal practice, and by the end of 1983, over 94 percent of rural households in China operated under this system (Nolan 1989: 8). This dismantling of the collective agricultural system, and the subcontracting (*cheng bao*) of the land into family leaseholds, seems to have liberated an enormous amount of energy not given vent under communal organization. In Dongyang, during 1989, it was said that the household responsibility system had ensured that most households had sufficient surplus grain to see them through three years.

With collective administration dismantled in favor of the household responsibility system, *she dui qiye,* or "commune brigade" enterprises, have become *xiang zhen qiye,* "subdistrict/township" enterprises, although *xiang zhen qiye* loosely refers to a great multitude of forms, from large state-run and collective enterprises employing hundreds of workers administered at the county and township levels, to smaller village administered and private enterprises employing no more than a handful of workers, some of whom may be kinsmen of their managers.

Cheng Bao—Changing Relations of Production

In the mid-1980s, major changes began to take place in the management of the enterprises of the collectively run sector, which, despite the expansion in numbers of private enterprises, were still the dominant form, in terms of both employment and total output in Dongyang. Instead of being run directly by the collective authorities, virtually all such enterprises, mimicking the subcontracting of commune land to individual households, operated under some form of subcontract *(cheng bao)* arrangement between the factory manager and the collective (Nolan 1989: 12). Generally, a village, subdistrict *(xiang)*, or town would subcontract the management of its collective enterprise to an individual, family, or management committee for a substantial fee. A formal contract was drawn up (see Appendix 4 for a translated specimen of such a contract), usually in the industrial office at the appropriate administrative level (county, township, district, subdistrict, village). The manager of the enterprise undertook to produce a certain quantity of goods and to return a percentage of its proceeds from the contracted production to its administrative unit. Production and profit beyond the contracted obligations to the village, subdistrict, or town that granted the enterprise its license to operate meant greater proportions to divide in bonuses between management and work force members, in accord with a variety of incentive schemes. Failure to meet contracted obligations resulted in rather stiff fines for management, and denial of quite remunerative bonuses.

The position of managers was thus altered substantially. Instead of lifetime tenure, by the mid-1980s managers were commonly appointed for a fixed term (usually three years) by the authorities administering the contract, and the criteria for appointing collective enterprise managers shifted decisively away from the political toward the technical. Generally, managers had become solely responsible for their enterprise's profit and loss. The manager's income was now determined by the enterprise's economic performance, with bonuses depending on the degree to which the enterprise overfulfilled contracted targets (Nolan 1989: 12).

By the mid-1980s, managers of these subcontracted "collective" enterprises had also greatly increased their autonomy to negotiate sources of supply, prices, and sales. According to statistics for 1985, in Zhejiang province, 60 percent of production value already relied entirely on market regulation for raw materials supplies and commodity marketing (DDZGZJ 1989: 281).

Managers were encouraged to adopt a strategy summed up by the following aphorism:

> what people don't have, I have; what people have, I have in excellence; what people have in excellence, I have cheap; when people have what I

have cheap, I move on to something new, always improving. (DDZGZJ 1989: 284)

Cheng bao (contracts) in Dongyang in 1989 generally described obligations of the contracting enterprise after tax obligations to the state were met. All rural enterprises must pay a profits tax of between 35 percent and 55 percent of their gross profit to the central government, depending on the overall size and output of the unit. There is a schedule of eight grades of which the highest rate of 55 percent is levied on enterprises with profits greater than ¥20,000 per year. Generally, the lowest rate of 35 percent is levied on small private *(geti)* enterprises, with the highest rate levied on large collective *(xiang-* and village-run) enterprises, but the correspondence between profits and level of administration is not perfect by any means.

Entrepreneurs may avoid the lump-sum payment at the end of the year by paying an assortment of surcharges and miscellaneous taxes (town construction taxes, education taxes, grain surcharges, etc.) together with a commodities tax and state tax assessed as a percentage of each sales transaction. The strategy adopted often depends on the level of sophistication of accounting skills in the enterprise. Smaller-scale enterprises usually adopt a simple lump-sum strategy, whereas larger collective enterprises with separate accounting staffs may opt to meet their various miscellaneous obligations separately on every invoice.

If an enterprise comes up with a new product serving the provincial market, it can avoid taxes for up to two years. If the new product meets the planning needs of the central government, the enterprise may be entitled to a three-year tax exemption. If the product is up to international standards, and may earn foreign exchange as an export, then the enterprise may choose to either avoid or reduce its tax obligation, or benefit from a surcharge of a specified percentage in the selling price of the product.

The balance of profits retained after tax obligations to the state are met is generally allocated as follows:

Of profit up to the *cheng bao* contract amount,

30 percent is paid to the responsible industrial office or village party committee;
20 percent is allocated to managers and workers in bonuses;
50 percent is reinvested in the enterprise.

Of profit beyond the amount contracted for,

30 percent is paid to the responsible *gong ban* (industrial office);
30 percent is allocated in bonuses;
40 percent is reinvested in the enterprise.

Industrial offices *(gong ban)* in the *xiang* have a certain amount of flexibility as far as the exact amounts to be contracted for in each category, but in general these percentages serve as rather strong guidelines. The cut of profit taken by the industrial offices have been the principal source of village, subdistrict, and township revenues since the mid-1980s.

In the late 1980s and early 1990s, industrial offices in the countryside began pushing the logic of subcontracting *(cheng bao)* arrangements to its limits, selling off previously subcontracted enterprises to their individual managers outright to create *si ying*—privately *owned* and managed enterprises—even assisting in the arrangement of financing through state commercial banks and local private mortgage companies.

But *cheng bao* contracts remain pervasive in the management of many Dongyang factories as well as in other walks of county life. The subdivisions of retail department stores are subcontracted to their managers on a *cheng bao* basis. And the sales and marketing sections of larger industrial enterprises are often "*cheng bao*ed" by their managers to individuals in the sales departments who undertake to dispose of an agreed upon output, and may win large bonuses for themselves by overfulfilling their targets. Even portions of the operations of state-run enterprises are often *cheng bao*ed to individuals with remuneration keyed to a percentage of output or sales.

The late 1980s thus witnessed a growing number of private contractual obligations in the management of a greater number of enterprises of all types, as well as the emergence of many more larger-scale private enterprises in the Chinese countryside. These arrangements generate profits and bonuses for their owners and subcontractors that dwarf by many magnitudes the "fortunes" for which "evil" landlords of the old society were submitted to revolutionary justice. Substantial fortunes make it possible, among other things, for some to flaunt population controls by paying the fines for having larger families with impunity, and this is among the more serious of the contradictions that rural industry has brought in its wake (see Nolan 1989: 33; fieldnotes, 5/16/88, interview with Wu Guosheng).

New Emphasis

Dongyang's rural enterprises received new emphasis in 1984, and many new factories in a greater variety of product lines were begun. In that year, the number of enterprises in the county expanded to 4,517, with 97,114 workers, producing ¥292,400,000 in APV, primarily in light industrial goods, clothing, machinery and electronics, construction materials, food and drink, and chemicals.

Still, in 1987 the woodcarving industry employed nearly 10,000 workers in more than 200 factories under various management forms (Zhou 1987a: 7). Eighty-two of these establishments were administered by the county Rural Industrial Bureau, while the balance were under the jurisdiction of the county Industrial and Commercial Bureau (fieldnotes, 3/14/89, visit to Rural Industrial Bureau with Li Zhijiang).

At the Thirteenth National Party Congress in 1987, Premier Zhao Zhiyang voiced official approval of the private economy, and the first session of the Seventh National People's Congress, held in the following year, amended the Constitution to legitimize the private economy, setting the stage for a rapid development of the private sector. It marked the ascension of a perspective that saw the private sector of the rural industrial economy as playing a role in restructuring the very foundations of the economy, transforming underemployed peasants into wage laborers through a massive penetration of capitalistic enterprises in the rural areas, encouraging those households or individuals that had become rich in past years to allocate a portion of their income to private investment in rural industries (Chen 1995: 143–44).

By the end of 1988, there were 9,737 enterprises operating in Dongyang with 100,688 workers, producing ¥918,200,000 in APV, and a precipitous increase occurred in the numbers of private enterprises.

In 1990, an economic downturn began and the number of enterprises dropped to 9,120 with a labor force of 102,722 workers, although APV continued to increase to ¥1,191,930,000. Losses and closings continued in 1991 when the number of enterprises declined to 8,885 with 104,757 workers, producing an increased APV of ¥1,632,950,000.

Nineteen ninety-two witnessed a resumption of expansion to 10,025 enterprises with 106,917 workers producing ¥2,732,690,000 in APV, and the bulk of the expansion was registered in newly organized private enterprises. Over the period of rural enterprise development in

Table 1.2

Dongyang Rural Industrial Enterprise Performance in 1988

Ownership	Number of Enterprises	Annual Production Value	Number of Workers
State	59	¥164,920,000	9,397
Xiang and above	624	¥455,230,000	39,576
County collective	120	¥143,510,000	11,203
Xiang/zhen collective	504	¥311,720,000	28,373
Village and below	9,234	¥462,970,000	71,587
village-run	1,016	¥109,780,000	16,722
joint capital	2,455	¥174,590,000	22,439
individual	5,763	¥178,600,000	32,426

Source: Jiang n.d.d.

Dongyang county since the implementation of the reforms, annual per capita income has expanded from ¥50 in 1978, to ¥480 in 1986, to over ¥1,000 in 1993 (Jiang n.d.g).

The reforms have also encouraged an opening to the world market, and increasingly Dongyang entrepreneurs have begun a scramble to earn foreign exchange, seeking outlets for their products on the international market. Where provincial export corporations previously controlled access to international markets, and generally took a cut, larger numbers of firms were granted export autonomy in 1989. Significantly, exports of the rural enterprise sector in Dongyang increased from ¥71,930,000 in 1988 to ¥199,240,000 in 1991 (Jiang n.d.g).

Dongyang has not been particularly well situated to take advantage of foreign joint venture capital, although county authorities are clearly eager to attract more. There was one substantial joint venture in the works in 1989 with a Hong Kong company called Xiao Gao Co., a manufacturer of plywood and veneers. In 1989, the equipment had not yet arrived from Singapore, but the enterprise was due to start up upon delivery (fieldnotes, 3/20/89). In 1994, a plastics extrusion factory was gearing up to begin production under a joint venture agreement with an American company, and a clothing manufacturer from southern California was operating a knit goods factory in Dongyang's new economic development zone on the western edge of the county town of Wu Ning.

Although the latter two enterprises involved no Chinese entrepre-

Table 1.3
Dongyang Rural Industrial Enterprise Performance for Selected Years

Year	Number of Enterprises	Annual Production Value	Number of Workers	Profits	Taxes Paid
1978	2,852 commune/brigade 492 commune-run	¥41,438,000 ¥20,130,000	40,542 21,568		
1984	4,517 672 *xiang* and above 1,954 village 1,411 joint capital 473 individual 4 joint household 3 bureau admin.	¥292,400,000	97,114	¥18,327,200	¥14,528,200
1988	9,737 504 *xiang* and above 1,016 village 2,455 joint capital 5,758 individual 4 bureau admin.	¥895,000,000	100,688	¥57,640,000	¥33,602,000
1990 1991	9,120 8,885 437 *xiang* and above 689 village 2,024 joint capital 5,785 individual	¥1,191,930,000 ¥1,632,950,000	102,722 104,757	¥85,190,000	¥66,610,000
1992	10,025 460 *xiang* and above 678 village 2,2,04 joint capital 6,683 individual	¥2,732,690,000	106,917	¥146,210,000	¥112,480,000

neurs, appeals to the "patriotic" impulses of expatriate businessmen occupy an important place in the promotional efforts made on behalf of rural enterprises by national, provincial, and local authorities. As China has progressively opened up to the international market, the call has gone out to its expatriates to invest in their native counties and villages *(lao jia),* and many have responded in pursuit of profit if not in fulfillment of altruistic "patriotic" motives.

An example of this transnational expatriate industrial investment in Dongyang is provided by the factory of Mr. Huang Lisan, which manufactures stuffed toys for export. In the late 1940s, Mr. Huang's family fled to Taiwan, where he earned his B.A. degree, and where his father became an official at the World Bank. Huang went on to earn his Ph.D. at the California Institute of Technology, and at present is the head of a high-tech engineering firm in Pasadena, California that designs and manufactures pollution-control devices.

Mr. Huang first returned to Dongyang in 1986, and his stuffed toy factory was begun shortly thereafter. His enterprise is the eighth largest in the county, employs 280 people, and earned ¥8,000,000 (about US$1 million) in profits in 1988 (fieldnotes, 6/27/89). His local factory manager keeps pressing him for additional capital to expand production, and Mr. Huang can be in instant touch with the enterprise after spending ¥25,000 to install a direct international phone hookup. However, for Mr. Huang the enterprise is really something of a diversion, not his principal source of income. Indeed, he has been thinking of using some of its proceeds to establish a school in his native village. Coincidentally, Mr. Huang's cousin, Huang Liren, runs an eminently successful woodcarving enterprise on a cheng bao contract from the subdistrict (xiang) industrial office that oversees his native village of Lou Xi Zhai.

In 1989, the county town was abuzz with the news that a Dongyang expatriate businessman in Taiwan, Mr. Wang Tiwu, had pledged US$1 million to establish a Dongyang university. Under negotiation in 1989, local officials were optimistic about the plans being realized within a few years and spoke with pride of the enhanced status the new institution would confer on the county's modernizing citizenry (fieldnotes, 4/26/89, Wu Ning). However, in the wake of the Tiananmen massacre in June of 1989, the pledged funds were reallocated for the establishment of two hospitals instead, one each in the towns of Wu Ning and Wei Shan. Some have suggested that it was the difficulties encountered recruiting qualified faculty to relocate to Dongyang that motivated the reallocation of funds, but it would also appear likely that government authorities became concerned that a university underwritten by funds from Taiwan might generate an inappropriate influence on local education and political ideology. The two hospitals were a less politically sensitive way for Mr. Wang to express his "patriotism," and still contribute to the county's development. If Dongyang can be said to have suffered any casualty as a result of the events at Tiananmen, the loss of its future university would appear to be the most grave.

Notwithstanding this setback, however, county authorities have redoubled their efforts in the economic sphere, and in 1992 they opened an economic development zone *(kai fa qu)* of 11 square km on the western edge of the county town. The zone is divided into specialized subzones housing facilities for industry, scientific research, commerce, construction, residences, and recreation; it offers a variety of preferential tax incentives to foreign and domestic entrepreneurs. It will also house a ¥40 million joint venture "three star" hotel, already under construction, a ¥10 million telecommunications building with a telephone system capable of handling 10,000 lines, and a 110 kilovolt electrical substation. A branch line of the Zhejiang–Jiangxi Railroad from Yi Wu to Dongyang is in preparation, linking up with the Hangzhou–Wenzhou and Jinhua–Ningbo public highways that intersect in the county, and diversifying the county's connections to the entire Hua Dong (East China) economic region. The development zone also expects to take advantage of its location just 20 km from the newly constructed airport in neighboring Yi Wu county, which has scheduled flights to and from Guangzhou, Shenzhen, Shanghai, and Xia Men. Both the plastics extrusion and textiles joint ventures mentioned above operated out of the zone, and county authorities were obviously hopeful for a broad influx of overseas capital, both from the country's own expatriates as well as from the wider international community of investors. Indeed, in the spring of 1993, the county hosted an "international business recruitment fair" *(guoji zhao shang hui)* to attract foreign capital to its new development zone.

The County Town

The reforms of the 1980s have led to a dramatic transformation in the economic and cultural life of the county town of Wu Ning. In 1986, the toilets in the best hotel in town, the Dongcheng Hotel, consisted of a bare tiled trough in the floor of a room in the hall, hosed out once a day. By late afternoon, the room was barely approachable. Within a year, the Nanyang Hotel had opened a few blocks away with modern flush toilets and baths in each room, and the following year, the Dongcheng, under obvious competitive pressure, opened a new wing with similar facilities. In 1989, the Dongyang Woodcarving Factory invested a considerable chunk of its profits and took on a massive burden of debt to construct a modern luxury guest house, the Yi Hai Bin Guan, obviously gearing up for an influx of larger numbers of upscale visitors and businessmen to the county (see Chapter 7).

One indicator of the county's recent growth and modernization was the change, in 1988, of telephone numbers in the county town from three to five digits, and the feverish construction of new housing and factory space in the southeast corner of town. The county has spent ¥50,000 in designer fees for an urban development plan whose details make it clear that the town is gearing up to both receive resources and send out finished product on an unprecedented scale (fieldnotes, 7/5/88, interview with Zhang Xiaoyang of the Wu Ning City construction office).

In 1988 and 1989, in accord with the plan, the main streets of the county town, Wu Ning West and Wu Ning East Streets, were being widened to 26 meters, and new piping for water and gas was being laid along their course. Traffic going through town on Wu Ning Street was limited to a single westbound lane, with eastbound traffic diverted north up to Huan Cheng Bei Road (see Map 5). Now complete, Wu Ning Street includes a central median with two lanes of traffic in each direction, two side medians, and two bicycle lanes. Through traffic does not pass through the city but proceeds along a widened Huan Cheng Bei—40 meters wide, 15 meters of which were to have been paved by the end of 1989.

Running nearly parallel to Wu Ning Street through the center of the old walled city, in 1989, East Street and West Street still represented the spatial understandings of an earlier age, at no more than three meters wide. Entering what was once the walled city through West Gate, one passed the stalls of dry goods shops, hardware shops, a writing brush shop, a ceremonial paper goods shop, a printing (silk screen) shop, and a couple of restaurants, as well as the narrow lanes branching to the north and south, leading to small workshops and private homes. Gradually one approached the post office and the com-

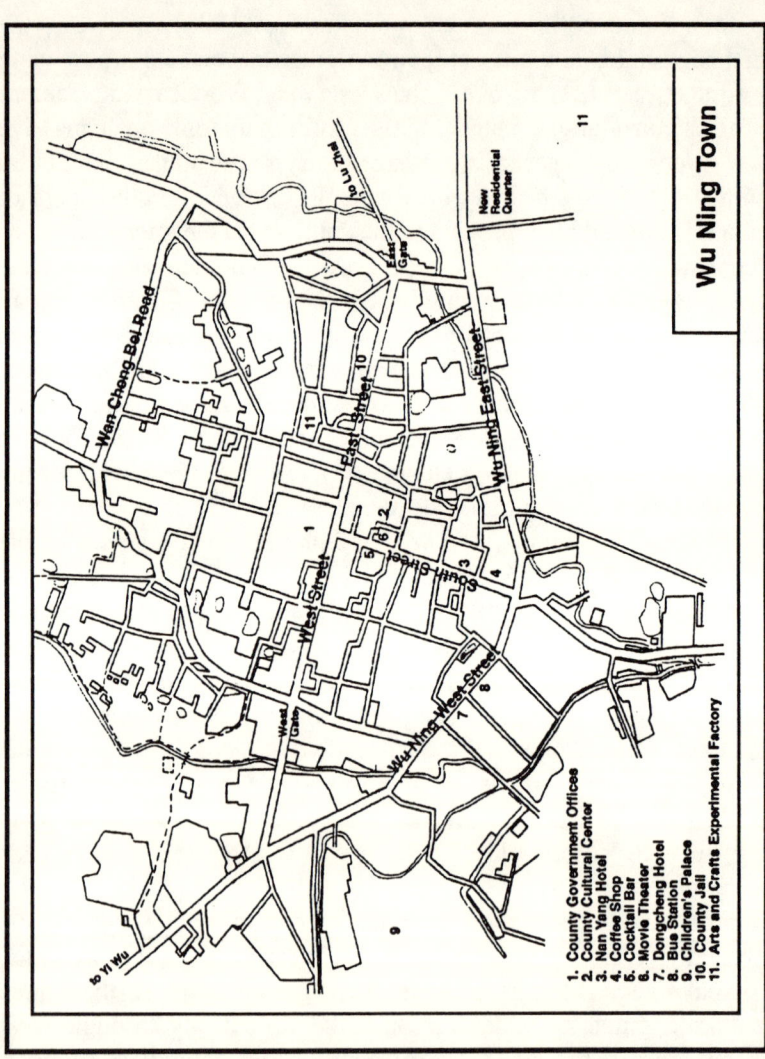

Map 5. Wu Ning town, showing principal roads and notable sites.

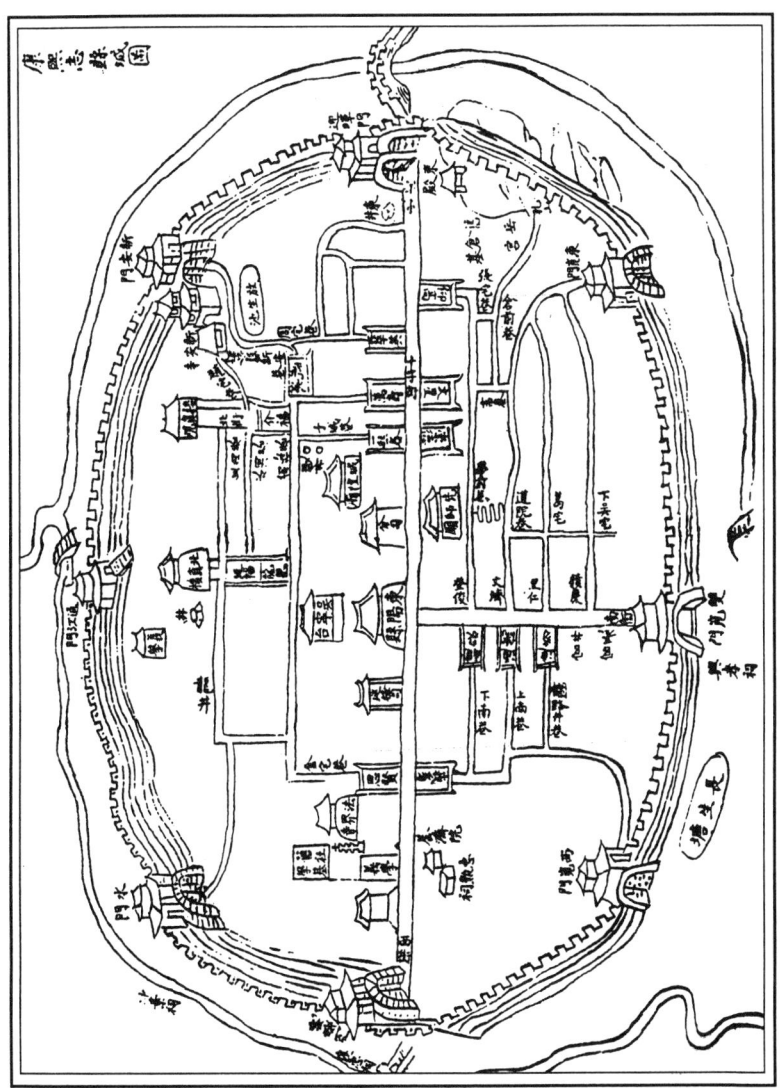

Map 6. Wu Ning town, from the Qing dynasty gazetteer, Kang Xi reign period (1662–1722).

Hardware stall on West Street in Wu Ning, the county town.

pound of the county government headquarters where West Street intersects with the broad modern avenue of South Street, the principal commercial street of modern Wu Ning town. The drainage system and sewers of South Street were scheduled for refurbishing under the urban development plan, and an associated water treatment plant was also to be built in the northwest corner of town.

Continuing along past the county government compound, on what has now become East Street, one passed the intersection of "Liberation Street" (formerly North Street), the widening of which to the northern border of town had been completed by 1987. Further along East Street, one encountered the previously mentioned Hua Ting, defaced during the Cultural Revolution, and almost immediately across East Street the Wu Ning *zhen* (township) cultural center. The center was the meeting hall, *dahuitang,* of the former Wu Ning people's commune. In 1989, it was under subcontract *(cheng bao)* as a theater to a proprietor who screened videotapes twice daily to the public for a ¥.20 admission charge.

Further east along East Street, one passed number 99—the county jail with a handful of uniformed public security officers usually posted

Looking west on West Street in Wu Ning.

just outside. Further along were several sheet metal shops, tool and sundries shops, and, as one approached East Gate, a Christian church—a building undistinguished from its neighbors but for the signboard outside announcing its function. East Street continues through what had once been East Gate to the outskirts of town and on to the suburban village of Lu Zhai where the Dongyang Woodcarving Factory is located (see Chapter 7).

Both East Street and West Street were widened to 16 meters under the urban development plan, the small commercial stalls on the south side of the streets having been razed, and modern brick and concrete structures erected in the early 1990s.

Beyond West Gate, West Street was also widened to 16 meters up to its intersection with Wu Ning West Street, which makes a dog leg to the north on the western edge of town (see Map 5). Houses and structures on the south side of the street were leveled. Wu Ning Zhong Street, which borders the old town on the west, was extended directly north to join a newly widened Huang Cheng Bei Road, running along behind the Plaited Bamboo Products Factory on the northwestern edge of town. People displaced by these construction projects have been housed in the newly constructed residential quarter *(ju min qu)* in the southeast of town, where one of Mr. Wu Mantang's nephews pur-

Figure 1.1 **Surname Distribution in Wu Ning.**

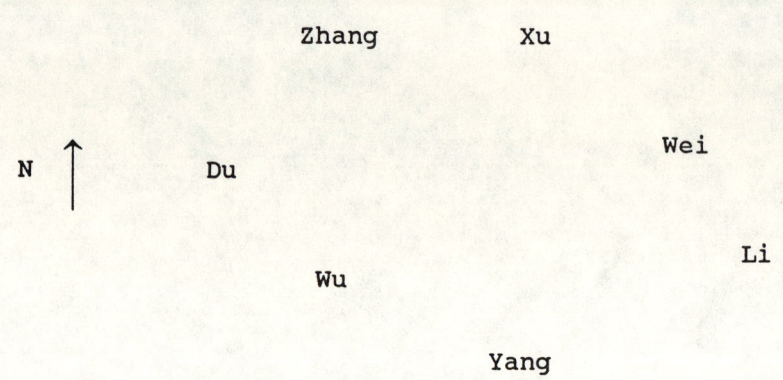

chased an industrial flat for his carved wood products factory, Three Stars Company (see Chapter 3).

In 1989, despite its feverish development and construction activity, spatial settlement in Wu Ning could still be conceptualized in terms of lineage and surname. Historically, the Wu, Du, and Zhang lineages occupied the western quadrants of town, whereas the Xu, Wei, Li, and Yang lineages were clustered in the eastern quadrants (see Figure 1.1).

One of the interesting institutions of reform-era China to appear in Wu Ning town in the late 1980s was the coffee shop. Such shops typically do not serve alcohol, and their coffee is usually of the instant variety (I drank this only when desperate), but tea and other soft drinks are also available, together with a variety of snacks. Coffee shops are places to relax, listen to recorded or occasionally live music, and in some such establishments, even dance. Although a ban on dancing was temporarily imposed on Dongyang coffee shops early in 1988, the ban was lifted shortly thereafter. In 1989, one of the larger of these establishments, whose premises are subcontracted to its proprietor by the state-run department store in town, had hired a live band to both attract and entertain customers on weekends. Under competitive pressure from a newly opened cocktail bar/nightclub (described below), the shop had also redecorated with mirrored ceilings, wallpaper, and new rattan furniture.

Although local public security operatives occasionally drop in to check up on the clientele, one's general impression of these shops is that they are somewhat off the beaten path, and outside the official "reporting" structures of the local government. That is, their proprietors are private entrepreneurs rather than employees of the government. The establishments are something of a haven from the otherwise ubiquitous government organs, and the proprietors are under no obligation to account to the government for their clientele. Such coffee shops, already a common sight in the provincial capital of Hangzhou, had also begun to spring up in some of the smaller market towns of Dongyang county in the late 1980s.

In early 1988, the above-mentioned cocktail bar/nightclub opened in the county town, upstairs from one of Wu Ning's more "classy" restaurants on the west side of South Street, just up from the county government offices. The bar is run by a Shanghai-based Dongyang expatriate, and clearly outshines all the other establishments in town. Its small bar and large dance floor are decorated smartly with wicker chairs and tables, and waitress service is provided. There is even a massive air-conditioning unit, regrettably if expectably on the fritz during one of my visits. But the place has the kind of look and feel that could only confirm the popular stereotype of the Shanghainese as au courant with the latest advances in modern entertainment. Loud disco music and strobe lights make it a haven of entertainment for both the local population of small entrepreneurs, and visitors to Dongyang from other parts of China. Several other such nightclubs had begun operation in Wu Ning in the early 1990s.

Other new centers of entertainment in the county town include videotape viewing parlors, which show taped selections of movies and operas to the public on conventional and occasionally widescreen TV for a modest admission fee, and video game stalls typically packed with youngsters bent on destroying the latest fleets of space invaders or super villains imported from Japan. There is also a Children's Palace, housed in a newly constructed modern circular building in the southwest corner of town. It contains a small library, a ping-pong room, billiard room, dance room, and music room, and in 1988 was displaying an exhibition of drawings, calligraphy, and photographs by young folks from children's palaces provincewide (fieldnotes, 5/30/88, Wu Ning).

In 1988, the Dongyang Cultural Palace, Wen Hua Gong, just off South Street in the center of the county town, was showing four different movies in its various auditoriums, one each from Hong Kong and Taiwan, as well as domestically produced flicks. The palace was also equipped with pool tables and ping-pong tables on the ground floor, and a dance hall on the fourth floor. On May 1, 1989, International Workers' Day, the palace sponsored a public dance, attended by some 200 young folks, with pop music and refreshments.

In the same complex of buildings is the county Cultural Center, which houses the offices of a variety of cultural officials as well as the county public library and reading room. The library's collection is primarily composed of well-known works of Chinese fiction, but also contains a host of technical and instructional manuals. The reading room is well stocked with up-to-date periodicals of which an exceedingly large number of new ones have emerged under recent "open" policies. On any given day, its fifteen or so tables are usually well occupied with anywhere from thirty to forty readers.

Several traditional forms of entertainment have begun to perambulate through the county town again since the economic reforms and open policies of the 1980s have come into effect. In March 1989, a traveling opera troop set up an elevated stage in a cleared-out area near the center of town and performed to great throngs of people. Such performances continue to be common just before the onset of the agricultural busy season, constituting a break for recreation before the hard work of planting begins (fieldnotes, 3/14/89, Wu Ning).

In 1988, a traveling circus from Anhui province set up its tent at the bus station across from the Dong Cheng Hotel on Wu Ning West Road. A performing bear paraded through the streets each day with cymbals clashing to attract customers to the shows in the evening. The huge tent was dimly lit, and its floor was wet and muddy. The audience, which jammed the wooden bleachers inside, consisted for the most part of ill-clothed country folk. The acts of the troop in this modest environment were really quite sophisticated, and included a variety of acrobats, a couple of magicians, a whip expert, an amazing balance contortionist who could twist her body every which way while holding a pile of assorted articles on her forehead, and so forth. Performing to the obvious delight of the crowd, this was a real people's circus, evoking scenes of the folk "up in the gods" of the "funambules" from Marcel Carne's classic film, "Children of Paradise" (fieldnotes, 5/14/88, Wu Ning).

In April 1989, a traveling performing family of motorcycle stunt riders set up their great barrel stage outside the Cultural Palace in the center of town. For a few *mao*, one climbed to a seat at the lip of the great barrel some thirty to forty feet above the ground, and watched as different combinations of family members performed stunts on their cycles, whirling around the interior surface of the barrel at great speed, taking advantage of the centrifugal force to climb the walls till their cycles were totally perpendicular. It was my privilege to have attended a show by the same family in the provincial capital of Hangzhou some months earlier (fieldnotes, 4/26/89, Wu Ning). While not, strictly speaking, a traditional form of entertainment, the show and its performers—an itinerant, family-based performing team—were clearly organized along very traditional lines.

At the west end of town a substantial commodities market, divided into scores of private stalls, does a brisk trade, mainly in women's and children's clothes, but also in dry goods, woodworking and construction tools, carving tool blades, and assorted knives, pins, watches, and so forth (fieldnotes, 5/30/88, Wu Ning). A daily vegetable and produce market has recently expanded on the east end of town near the newly developing residential quarter. South Street in the center of town boasts two department stores, a movie theater, and a great variety of retail stalls selling cloth, ready-made clothing, books, cassettes, electrical appliances and hardware, and a variety of comestibles. There is even, bless its proprietor's heart, a stationery shop with a xerox machine.

In the late 1980s and early 1990s, Wu Ning town was literally effervescing with activity. Its hotels held guests from Shanghai, Jinhua, Hangzhou, Wenzhou, Wu Han, Hong Kong, and Taiwan, in town on business. The hustle and bustle of new construction was everywhere. Its citizens spent their newly acquired wealth in the well-stocked shops of the town's private tradesmen and of the state sector. Recalling the transformation of the towns of Hong Kong's New Territories in the 1960s and 1970s, the county town of Wu Ning has been transformed from a sleepy, dusty, rural backwater into a modern industrializing economic center.

A core feature of that transformation has been the rural enterprises of the county, which have succeeded in raising the overall rural standard of living while altering the composition of rural income. They have played a role in enhancing the technical level of the rural work force, in loosening the bureaucratic constraints on the ordinary citizen, and in providing an overall brightening of economic prospects for those citizens.

While no one could be sure how the political suppression of the Beijing student movement in 1989 would affect foreign investment in or central government policies toward the private rural industrial sector, all indications from Dongyang are that those effects have been minimal. Political repression does not seem to have adversely affected the economic rights rural residents enjoyed throughout the 1980s, so much as it has reaffirmed the hegemony of the Chinese Communist Party politically.

The increasingly privatized rural enterprise sector has continued as the most vibrant and vigorous of Dongyang county's economy in the post-Tiananmen era of the early 1990s. China's rural industrial enterprises, private as well as collective, can be expected to remain an important part of what gives Chinese socialism its distinctive characteristics in the years to come.

Dongyang folk are poised to take a position in the emerging China–Hong Kong–Taiwan–overseas Chinese nexus, now commonly referred to as "Greater China," expected to be a strong influence in the future development of the so-called Pacific Rim (see, e.g., Overholt 1993: 347).

Chapter 2

Traditional Woodcarving and Its Revolutionary Transformation

The First Transition of Tradition

The woodcarving enterprises of Dongyang provided an important base on which the county's rural industrialization efforts were launched. That such enterprises existed in Dongyang in the late 1970s to be built upon was itself the result of a long history.

Traditionally, woodcarving in Dongyang was employed in the decoration of the walls and roof beams of homes *(minfang)* and lineage halls *(citang)* where auspicious animals and birds, lucky flowers, plants, and noteworthy mythical and historical characters appeared as motifs (FSZ 1985: 42–43; also see Knapp 1989; and Appendix 5 on the construction of the archetypal thirteen room house).

The carving of such images in Dongyang county is said to date from the Tang dynasty (A.D. 618–907). In 1963, in the county seat of Wu Ning, a pagoda known as Nan Si Ta collapsed, revealing a carved wood Buddhist image, 6.6 centimeters tall, in one of the walls, said to possess all the characteristics of latter-day Dongyang woodcarving style (Xu 1986: 12). Since Nan Si Ta was known to have been built in A.D. 961 in the second year of the Jian Long reign period of the Northern Song dynasty, the tradition of carving in Dongyang is said to have already been established at that time (DYMDBAO 11:2, March 5, 1988). However, since the carved image itself represents a specimen of what is a more or less fully developed carving tradition, local historical authorities argue that such a tradition must have developed over a period of some years. Thus, the origins of woodcarving in Dongyang county are regularly assigned to the latter part of the Tang dynasty. The Dongyang woodcarving tradition is therefore said to have "originated in the Tang dynasty, developed in the Song dynasty, and flourished in the Ming (1368–1644) and Qing (1644–1911) dynasties" (Xu 1986: 13).

There are those who doubt the validity of the claim for such an early date, arguing that there is no evidence that the Buddhist image found in the pagoda was actually produced in Dongyang (fieldnotes, 5/20/89; 5/24/89, interviews with Hu Zhonghe), but the belief in the more than thousand-year history of the carving tradition is a well established part of local folk wisdom.

There is evidence from Song dynasty documents that Dongyang carvers were commissioned to carve the printing blocks of the text of the Confucian classic *Xunzi* to commemorate the accession to high position of a local notable from the prefectural capital of Jinhua. Later, the four carvers so employed are alleged to have applied their considerable skills to preparing blocks for counterfeiting paper money (Xu 1986: 13).

In the southern Song (1127–1279) after the national capital was established in Lin An (modern Hangzhou), master craftsmen from all over the country gathered there. Hand craft industries flourished, and woodcarvers of Dongyang enjoyed a brisk demand for their skills in the construction of imperial quarters, towers, pavilions, halls, temples, and their interior decorations and furnishings. The great Buddhist image of Sakyamuni in the Ling Yin Temple of suburban Hangzhou, 19.6 meters high and carved from 26 tons of camphorwood, along with its incense burners and furnishings, are representative of Dongyang woodcarving of this period, although the temple itself is of considerably earlier date (DDZGZJ 1989: 382; Zhejiang People's Publishing Company 1985: 315–16).

As mentioned in Chapter 1, quite a number of specimens of domestic and temple architecture in Dongyang dating from the Ming dynasty attest to the development of the skills of woodcarving in that era. Su Yong Tang of Lu Zhai village is perhaps the most dramatic. Variously ascribed to the early or mid-fifteenth century, with some further additions made during the late Qing dynasty, Su Yong Tang commemorates the accomplishments of the Lu lineage of Lu Zhai, a suburban village on the eastern outskirts of Dongyang's county town of Wu Ning. For some 300 years during the Ming and Qing dynasties, every time the imperial examinations were held, at least one member of the Lu lineage passed to enter the ranks of officialdom. The success in the exams continued for ten straight generations. The nine receding chambers, *jin,* of the hall are said to represent the nine succeeding generations of scholarly success of the Lu lineage during this period (fieldnotes, 8/1/86, interview with Lu Xibing).

Su Yong Tang is significant for its elegant carved arches, pillars, beams, doorways, and window frames. While suffering neglect and vandalism during the Cultural Revolution, it is now on the national register of historically significant places, and renovation and restoration work was under way in the early 1990s. It demonstrates that by middle Ming times, there was a systematic relation between the skills of carving and architectural construction, and well-established understandings as to motifs, design, and execution in which elegant woodcarving was indispensable (Xu 1986: 13). In the late Ming, the repertoire of motifs represented in such carvings expanded, with greater attention given to the depiction of historical and mythological characters.

During the Qian Long reign period (1736–1796) of the Qing dynasty, it is said that some 400 Dongyang craftsmen were recruited to carve furniture, "dragon" beds, thrones, and lanterns in the Imperial Palace in Beijing (Zhejiang People's Publishing Company 1985: 383; Xu 1986: 16). The ensuing nineteenth century bore witness to a feverish construction of ancestral halls in Dongyang. Among the specimens still extant are Duan Ai Tang, constructed by the Li lineage of Xia Li Shu village; Wu Ben Tang constructed by the Wu lineage of Bai Tan village; Yi Jing Tang by the Lü lineage of Ma Shang Qiao village; Zhi He Tang by the Zhang lineage of Zhong Tu Jiang village; and Xun Zhi Tang, by the Lu lineage of Hu Tou Lu village (Xu 1986: 14).

The carvings in these halls are said to demonstrate the profound understanding of proportion, composition, and overall design achieved by the craftsmen of the period in the representation of natural and human figures both in the round and in relief. Advances were also made in furniture design and decoration.

During the Qing dynasty, decorative carving in homes and ancestral halls began to display themes from the stories of traditional operas. Operas were performed "for the benefit of the gods" at New Year's, at the opening of temples or during temple fairs *(miao hui)* in the spring and autumn, or during many of the festival observances of the lunar year. In addition, birthdays of the elderly, the birth of a son, the completion of a lineage genealogy, or the building of a bridge were other occasions for such performances. Performers were local amateurs or occasionally professional troupes, performing operas in the Jinhua

"Cow shanks" in the eaves of a traditional structure in Huai Lu village depicting immortal Lü Dongbin.

style *(Wu ju)*, Dongyang style *(Yue ju)*, or neighboring Sheng county style (JHFSZ 1984: 60).

Halls and homes built in the Jia Qing (1796–1820) and Dao Guang (1821–1851) reign periods, like Wu Ning's Xin Hua Ting (New Flower Pavilion), Wei Shan's Ding Feng Tang (Tripod Abundant Hall), Bai Tan's Fu Xing Tang (Good Fortune Rising Hall) and others, all display carvings of stories from traditional operas on the *niu tui* (literally, "cow shank"—refers to the beams protruding out from under the eaves; see photos 4 and 5), roof beams, or on the backs of the finest doors.

The association of carving with Dongyang traditional opera is apparent in two particularly distinctive examples of traditional architecture—the Shen De Tang and Shen Xiu Tang ancestral halls of Xia Cheng Li village. The former was built in 1828, and the latter in 1840 during the Dao Guang reign period (Chen 1989: 3).

It is said that when rabid opera fan Cheng Chunshe was preparing to

"Cow shanks" on a structure in Fang Jun town depicting a *qilin*.

build Shen De Tang, he hired ten opera troupes for the occasion to perform for three evenings each, so that the woodcarvers might see and hear the stories, and execute their carvings with facility and confidence. Twelve years later, his son Cheng Zuobu, also an avid opera fan, commissioned the building of Shen Xiu Tang. The junior Cheng took his workers to Suzhou, Beijing, and other places both to enjoy themselves and to observe the various opera styles of each locale, all to improve the artistic quality of their carving. Because of this, the carvings in Shen Xiu Tang are said to be even more lively and realistic. In any event, by Dao Guang times the rendering of operatic themes in carved wood decoration had been established and soon proliferated in Dongyang.

Even today there is a saying in Dongyang: "[One may] see a hall in one day, [but one] speaks of an opera for a year" *(shi ting yi ri, shuo xi yi nian)*.

During the Cultural Revolution (1966–1976), many specimens of operatic carving were destroyed as representative of the "four olds." Some were covered up with mud by the rural folk to protect them, and are preserved in original condition, but many carvings were vandalized and their figures lack heads or legs, or are otherwise defaced, with no way to restore them.

Another area in which woodcarving was historically employed was in the assembling of bridal dowries. For the women of powerful and wealthy families, as many as twenty carvers might be employed to produce the required items of furniture. A small dowry might involve six months' work, while a larger one could involve several years of preparation. Most characteristic of the dowry items was the "thousand work bed," *qian gong zhi chuang,* an elaborately carved canopy bed that was the jewel in the bridal trousseau, and the "eight immortals table," the construction of which was given careful attention as it was also employed in family rituals like "thanking the Buddha" on New Year's eve. On the day the bride was sent off and greeted by her in-laws, the length of her trousseau was an index of the wealth of her family *(kua haojing fu),* bringing honor and "face" to her family *(rong yao ti mian),* proportionate to its length (Xu 1986: 14).

By the middle of the Qing dynasty, Dongyang carvers were already plying their trade as expatriates in Hangzhou, Shanghai and other cities throughout the country (Xu 1986: 14), and with the establishment of foreign-dominated treaty ports at the end of the Qing, woodcarving began its transformation from a popular form of domestic architectural and furniture ornamentation carried out as an agricultural sideline to factory-based commodity production with an established export market (Xu 1986: 14).

For the Republican period we possess a report by Sowerby (1926) that describes how a style of furniture combining Chinese carved woodwork in furnishings of European design became popular in the expanding expatriate western community of late-nineteenth-century treaty ports, Shanghai in particular. The demand for original temple carvings by furniture makers producing for this market soon outstripped supply, as temples in and around Shanghai were denuded of original carvings.

Sowerby describes how furniture manufacturers in Shanghai had already begun placing orders with rural temple carvers for carvings of their own specifications, which not only ensured a supply of adequate carvings, allowing the manufacturer greater command over the design of the finished product, but also increased employment opportunities for workers in wood in the rural areas. Sowerby himself reports that the furniture makers of Shanghai had already begun hiring such rural carvers out of the villages and into their urban coastal furniture factories to assume full-time jobs in the hand manufacture of furniture (1926: 2). Sowerby does not identify the work regime as hand manufacture per se, nor does he seem aware of the fact that the county from which the large majority of these carvers came was Dongyang.

Contemporary historical materials available in Dongyang county (Xu 1986: 15) suggest that the enterprise Sowerby is describing was likely Ren Chang Co., a carved wood furniture shop begun in the early 1920s by Mr. Li Tiansheng, a Chinese Christian businessman from Dongyang's Nan Jiang subdistrict. It is reasonable to assume that Sowerby became acquainted with Mr. Li in the missionary circles they both moved in, and that the "new art craft" was discovered through their association. Sowerby is excited by his ability to observe "a new departure from the conventional" in "tradition bound China," and his article in the *China Journal of Science and the Arts* reads like an advertisement for the ingenuity of the enterprise.

In any event, the initial core group of some 30–40 Dongyang artisans originally employed by Li expanded in the early 1930s to some 300–400 as Shuang Hong Tai, Wang Sheng Ji, and Xu Hai Ji carved wood furniture factories opened for business. In Shanghai's English settlement, there were soon some 30–40 carved wood furniture factories, and Dongyang workers soon had a firm hold on jobs in an expanding industry.

Wang Sheng Ji Co. was the largest of the lot with more than 100 workers. Its proprietor, Wang Shengbin, before long opened his own retail outlet on fashionable Nanjing Road, counting Madame Chiang Kaishek (Song Meiling) among his customers. In 1956, after joint state/private management was introduced, the name of the factory was changed to Shanghai No. 5 Arts and Crafts Factory—*Gong Yi Wu Chang*—with Wang Shengbin staying on as private-side manager (Jiang n.d.e).

Both Shuang Hong Tai and Xu Hai Ji were among the larger enterprises to relocate to Hong Kong in the post–World War II period, operating under the English names J.L. George Co. and George Zee Co., respectively. The latter company figured in a labor dispute in the early 1950s reported on by the Hong Kong Labor Commissioner (cited in Cooper 1980a: 72), while the former company eventually established a branch showroom in New York City.

At the time of their move from Shanghai to Hong Kong, several companies of Dongyang origin were already in operation in the British Crown colony. Among these was Yi Hua Sheng Co. (Ngai Wah Xing), under the proprietorship of Dongyang native Zhang Hengxue (Cheung Honghok), said to have been one of the earliest Dongyang immigrants to Hong Kong.

Unbeknown to Sowerby, however, the "new art craft" he reports for Shanghai in 1926 had emerged at least ten years earlier in Hangzhou. There, Ren Yi Co. on Goat Market Street, Yangshi Jie, owned by an English Christian doctor who worked at Hangzhou's Xie He hospital, had a work force of some 200 Dongyang carvers participating in the hand manufacture of carved wood furniture well in advance of Shanghai developments. Three master carvers of illustrious reputation in Dongyang county, Du Yunsong, Huang Zijin and Lou Shuiming, were among the first group of carvers employed at Ren Yi Co., and the factory won a prize for its commodities in 1915 at the Panama Canal exhibition in San Francisco. In later years, the company moved to Shanghai in response to the broader foreign market there and many members of its labor force found employment in other Shanghai factories soon thereafter (fieldnotes, 5/3/89, interview with Hua Dehan aka Xu Wen).

The "invention" of carved wood furniture in Hangzhou for use by foreigners and for export abroad is occasionally also credited to Ma Youzhang, a carver of some repute himself, who lived in Hangzhou. He is said to have supervised the carving of the Buddhist images in Cheng Huang Temple in Hangzhou, and is said by some to have created the furniture style observed by Sowerby in 1926 in Shanghai, hiring rural temple carvers to produce imitation antique temple carvings for inclusion in his furniture, and to have been the first to export the product.

In 1937, when the Japanese invaded Hangzhou, Ma fled to Shanghai, and went to work at the Temple of the Jade Buddha, Yu Fo Si, in the English section of Shanghai on Jiang Ning Road. He worked for the temple and lived on West Beijing Street, where Guo Youxing of our target town of Guo Zhai bunked with him in the 1940s, by which time Ma was in his seventies.

A substantial community of Dongyang workers existed in

Hangzhou in the early 1920s, associated with the silk weaving and construction industries there. A Dongyang workers' same native place association was active in organizing an anti-Communist labor federation in Hangzhou during this period (Schoppa 1982: 182–83), and it is likely that among its members were workers in Ren Yi Co.

In addition, a woodcarvers' guild *(gongsuo)* is reported to have been active in Hangzhou in 1927, described as an association whose membership included both master carvers (employers) and journeymen, the goals of which were to "regulate and protect the trade or craft as a whole rather than the protection of the interest of one class, the laborers, against another class, the capitalists" *(Chinese Economic Journal* 1927: 223). Beyond a doubt, this woodcarvers' guild was a Dongyang organization, and the workers at Ren Yi Co. were assuredly among those described. It is noteworthy that a wage increase was announced by the guild in 1927 from ¥.60 to .66/day (ibid.).

In any case, the developments in production organization of carved wood furniture reported by Sowerby for Shanghai in the mid to late 1920s had clearly occurred in Hangzhou considerably earlier. While any connection between Ren Yi Co. of Hangzhou and Ren Chang Co. of Shanghai is denied by historical authorities in Dongyang, the common character *Ren* (benevolence) in the names of each company, as well as their mutual association with Christianity, is certainly suggestive of a relation of some sort.

Sowerby's account of the origins of urban hand manufacture of carved wood furniture in Shanghai is not otherwise at great variance with Dongyang sources (cf., e.g., Lu 1987: 3). These sources emphasize the transformation of a rural agricultural side-line occupation involving itinerancy in the countryside, to an urban factory-based production regime of hand manufacture, under stimulus of overseas markets and a growing commoditization of trade (Xu 1986: 15).

As one would expect in such a period of transformation, itinerancy in the countryside persisted as urban hand manufacture emerged in the treaty ports. Master craftsmen still made the rounds from door to door *(shangmen jiagong),* village to village, and town to town plying their trade to local rural householders during agricultural slack seasons, making furniture for bridal dowries and daily use, and decorating newly constructed houses. Earnings were crucial for the provisioning of their own households, a necessary supplement to meager agricultural incomes.

Labor force reproduction was achieved under these conditions by a term of apprenticeship, initiated by a ritual demonstration of respect for one's new master *(bai shifu)*. Preparations to *bai* one's master began with the invitation of a *da qiao ren*—"a bridge builder"—to serve as intermediary and arrange a first meeting. At the first meeting, the prospective apprentice offered his master a "first meeting gift," most commonly an axe head, employed as a mallet head in the process of carving. At the appointed time, the master asked a series of questions to test the boy's capabilities and temperament. If the master felt that the boy was clever and industrious, he would consent to take him on by accepting the axe head and would choose an auspicious day during the coming month for the boy to formally "pay respects to the master." If the master was not pleased with the boy, he would simply return the axe head (FSZ 1985: 21).

Before the ceremony, the prospective apprentice would light incense at the graves of his ancestors, and pray before Buddha, to request success in the venture. Afterward, if accepted, he would consume a bowl of "longevity" noodles. At the formal ceremony, he would light incense again, and perform the kowtow before an image of the craft founder Luban, before his prospective master, and his master's wife. Finally, he would host a banquet for his master and invited guests, and sign a contract guaranteeing his completion of the term, and absolving the master from all responsibility for any misfortunes that might befall the boy during his term (JHFSZ 1984: 28).

Generally the term lasted three years, during which the apprentice was "fed but not paid." The apprentice had to carry the chamber pot, wash the clothes, sweep the floor, care for his master's children, and perform other household duties and chores. He followed the master when he went out, and carried the luggage and tools. He fetched the water to wash his master's feet, and was scolded or beaten for the smallest shortcoming. He worked from dawn to dusk, working overtime by the light of an oil lamp. If he pleased his master, the apprentice might be given some pocket money for an occasional treat (Xu 1986: 15).

In order to "protect his own rice bowl," the master was usually very protective of his skills, and for the most part was unwilling to transmit them directly, or did so only grudgingly. A talented apprentice depended entirely on observing his master's performance, hardly ever getting any hand-to-hand instruction. Some masters even prevented their apprentices from looking closely at already finished carvings. Learning to independently design and execute a complete craft item by the time an apprentice had completed his term was by no means an easy task (Xu 1986: 15).

Being an apprentice was likened traditionally to being a new daughter-in-law (JHFSZ 1984: 28). One had to be able to withstand the bitterness to have a chance to dish some of it out oneself. An apprentice who failed to finish his term, who either returned home because the work was too hard, or was fired because he displeased his master, was called "a dried beancurd [thrown] back in the soup" *(hui tang dou fu gan* (JHFSZ 1984: 28).

When an apprentice completed his term, *man shi,* he was required to hold a "completion feast"—*man shi jiu.* He invited his master, and those people who were in attendance at his original "pay respects" ceremony. After thanking craft founder Luban, he would thank his master, his master's wife, and the other masters in the same craft. When an apprentice completed his term, his master generally made a lump-sum payment of some 14,000 copper cash in "back wages" for his three years of labor, enough to furnish the apprentice with a set of tools to begin practicing his trade as a journeyman (Xu 1986: 15). In that practice, he must not interfere with his master's earning a living, nor directly compete with his master for business. To do so would be highly unvirtuous behavior, "killing grandfather monkey" *(sha husun ye)* (JHFSZ 1984: 28).

In traditional times, journeyman status meant work for half wages *(ban zuo)* for another three or four years—"three years apprenticeship, four years journeyman" *(san nian xuetu, si nian banzuo).* Journeymen were paid out of a total wage bill paid to the master, from which amount the master allocated a portion in accord with their performance.

Under conditions of factory hand manufacture in the cities of Republican China, an apprentice could usually find a factory boss willing to pay him more than the *ban zuo* that his former master might pay him as a journeyman worker. If his former master was paying him ¥6, he might get ¥9 elsewhere. In the countryside there was little alternative. One usually had to spend at least another three years' *ban zuo* under one's master before one could formally graduate *(chu shi)* and strike out on one's own. But in the cities one could usually find other work (fieldnotes, 6/23/88, interview with Guo Youxing).

After completing three additional years of work as a journeyman in the countryside, most carvers worked within the borders of Dongyang or neighboring Yi Wu and Sheng counties, calling on customers at their homes or hiring out at market towns as itinerants. Some worked in their own homes making furniture for sale. Itinerant workers were generally fed by their employers, but money wages were very low. The end of a year of hard labor left little surplus, scarcely providing enough to eat or wear, and leaving little alternative but to rush about everywhere looking for additional work (Xu 1986: 15).

Traditionally, in hiring a master craftsman to work, there were three methods of remuneration:

gong fan dian ri (provide food, and wages by the day);
gong fan bao gong (provide food, and wages by the piece);
bao gong bao fan (provide only wages with the cost of food included therein).

But no matter what form remuneration took, the host had to provide the workers with a snack *(dian xin)* each afternoon. It was said of carvers, masons, and carpenters, "after [afternoon] snacks, their work can be counted upon" (FSZ 1985: 22).

The proprietor of a workshop or labor contractor usually hired workers at New Year's, or during Duan Wu and mid-autumn festivals. If the workers were already in his employ, it was at such times that he would decide whether to keep them on or let them go. The evening meal at mid-autumn festival was described as a "nervous feast" for all employees. Workers who had been with the firm for many years might be advanced their wages for the next period before the feast. Others would be informed of their employer's decision after dinner.

In the urban centers, opportunities for communication with craftsmen and artists in other expressive media such as landscape painting were somewhat greater than in the countryside, and the cross-fertilization between trades that resulted is said to have had a beneficial effect on the level of craftsmanship of the time (Xu 1986: 15). But life in the factories of the treaty ports was no bed of roses. Wages, although higher than those available in the countryside, were not especially so, and living expenses in the cities were considerably higher than in rural areas. In addition, most workers were obliged to generate a surplus of some kind to help support their families back in the villages.

Working conditions in the factories often bordered on the atrocious, and job security was nonexistent. Factory owners scrimped on meals for workers, and often cheated workers out of wages with claims of faulty workmanship. Medical care of any kind was simply unavailable (Xu 1986: 15–16). Nevertheless, life in the treaty ports was in many ways preferable to the alternatives in rural Dongyang in the 1920s and 1930s, and urban wage labor became an established supplement to rural household income.

Tradition in Transition

During the successive periods of disorder associated with the Japanese invasion in the late 1930s, what became World War II in the 1940s, and the civil war that continued in China until the Communist victory in 1949, the production, foreign trade, and export of Zhejiang province's hand craft products suffered a disastrous decline. Many folk craftsmen either returned to farming or sought employment in other occupations. For most, employment in craft occupations made up a deficit in their annual household subsistence budgets, and many became destitute and homeless as a result of the crafts' decline. In the period of the late 1940s just prior to Communist victory, the hand craft traditions of all of Zhejiang province were "withering on the point of death" (DDZGZJ 1989: 383).

For this reason, Dongyang woodcarvers in their fifties and sixties in the modern labor force are rather few and far between. The labor force consists mainly of 40+ year olds and their juniors, those trained after "liberation" in 1949, and 70+ year olds. Those in their fifties and sixties, born between 1929 and 1939, would have come up as apprentices during the Japanese War and the civil war when little training was done. Thus there is a gap in the demography of the carving population, on account of the interruption of training and labor force reproduction that occurred in the 1940s. Not much carved wood furniture was commissioned during war time (fieldnotes, 5/22/89, interview with Shen Fuxin).

Before the 1960s, there were very few women in the profession. The oldest women carvers began work as teenagers in the later 1950s. In traditional times, it was simply unacceptable for a woman to go out and about with a man to work on an itinerant basis. Girls of apprentice age (12–13 years old) were typically learning embroidery skills in the home to help in the preparation of their bridal trousseaus (Jiang n.d.e).

But after cooperativization in the 1950s, with the concentration of the labor force in collective factories, women were more easily accommodated in the labor force, and at present have come to constitute nearly 50 percent of the total. Nevertheless, there are still lingering prejudices against women workers among some employers and factory managers in Dongyang, who despair of women who leave the factories to have children just as their level of performance begins to mature (fieldnotes, 3/21/89, interview with Lü Weiqing).

In the first seven years following the establishment of the People's Republic, the Chinese Communist Party and the various levels of the new people's government in Zhejiang province instituted a policy to "protect, develop, and improve" traditional crafts (DDZGZJ 1989: 383). Newly established provincial handicraft management bureaus and cultural departments organized teams to carry out a series of surveys and investigations. Team members visited remote locales, called at the homes of older craftsmen for visits, recorded the history of the professions and the distinctive skills of the craftsmen, and assessed the degree to which skills had been preserved. The craftsmen were organized in a movement to return to their original professions, revive production, and reestablish the traditions in which they were trained.

Finally, the teams encouraged individual hand craftsmen and folk artists to follow developments in the organization of agriculture and opt for mutual aid and cooperativization in production. Once such co-ops were organized, small technical study groups were established in which views were exchanged and participation in activities to develop creativity encouraged. Provincial and local governments contributed capital and raw materials, supported the efforts of the craftsmen by placing orders for "labor added" *(jia gong)* services, and provided tax incentives to their enterprises. Within a few short years, the revived art craft professions in the province had trained more than 2,000 new practitioners, providing the basis for continuing and developing traditional skills (DDZGZJ: 383).

According to statistics for 1953, Zhejiang province had 95 craft professions *(hang ye),* 733,200 practitioners, with an annual production value of ¥515,000,000. This constituted 15.1 percent of the combined industrial and agricultural production value of ¥3,410,000,000 and 38.4 percent of the total industrial production value of ¥1,340,000,000 (DDZGZJ: 49).

In August 1953 the Zhejiang provincial government instituted a "simplified method of registration and management of hand craft enterprises" on an individual property basis, and began establishing hand craft marketing cooperatives with unified procurement of raw materials and unified sales promotion.

In 1954, in the aftermath of the Third National Hand Craft Production Cooperative Conference in Beijing, Zhejiang's cooperatives multiplied rapidly from 3,383 in 1953 to 7,453 in 1955; from 63,200 practitioners in cooperatives in 1953 to 489,600 in 1955.

In December of 1955, the Fifth National Hand Craft Production Cooperative Conference formulated a program for the socialist transformation of hand crafts, later promulgated by the central government as a report to the various localities. It called for the intensification of the pace of cooperativization of hand crafts, and insisted on the simultaneous achievement of cooperativization in hand crafts, agriculture, and what remained of capitalist industry and commerce.

In January of 1956, such calls climaxed in the demand for a high tide of agricultural and hand craft cooperativization. In Zhejiang, this meant pressing cooperativization more forcefully into the sphere of production. Where joint marketing cooperatives served individual property-based producers, now production was to be carried out in production cooperatives with collective ownership of production materials, shared labor, unified accounting, and remuneration according to labor. At the end of 1956, Zhejiang had 10,056 hand craft cooperatives, 3,335 of which were marketing co-ops, 6,919 of which were hand craft production co-ops. Together they employed more than 970,000 practitioners, more than 90 percent of the total labor force of hand craft practitioners. The cooperativization of hand craft production in Zhejiang was for the most part complete (DDZGZJ 1989: 50).

Given the relative stability in the countryside at this time, the production of hand craft goods expanded. In 1956, hand craft production value in Zhejiang was ¥590,000,000, more than double the ¥220,000,000 of 1949, and a healthy increase over the ¥390,000,000 of 1952, prior to cooperativization (DDZGZJ 1989:50).

Of the hand craft establishments in Zhejiang, there were 110 so-called art craft cooperatives, with specialized outworking practitioners numbering more than 500,000. In 1957, production value in the province's art craft industries was ¥24,600,000, 4.3 times that of 1950 (DDZGZJ 1989: 383).

The climax of the craft cooperativization movement nationwide was

Master carver Zhou Fangchun at his carving bench at home in Fan Jun township

the National Craftsmen's Congress held in Beijing in 1957. The Dongyang carving tradition was represented at the congress by two elderly master carvers, Du Yunsong (1884–1959) of Hou Shan Dian village and Lu Lianshui (1884–1961) of Tang Xi village. The work lives of these gentlemen began at the end of the nineteenth century, and their artistic works were exhibited nationally to great acclaim in the 1950s. Du Yunsong was known as the "emperor" *(huang di)* of the carvers in the southern townships of Dongyang county, and Lu Lianshui as the "emperor" of the northern townships (fieldnotes, 5/19/89, interview with Shen Fuxin, Hangzhou). Du was later listed in the National Historic Register of Distinguished Craftsmen, and Lu in the Zhejiang Provincial Register as a Woodcarving Craftsman of Renown *(Mudiao mingyi ren)*.

Mr. Hu Zhonghe, at present employed in the Arts and Crafts Research Institute in Hangzhou, was among those who participated in the post-liberation effort to locate masters in the woodcarving profession and encourage them to return and resume their past occupations. At the time, he recalls, master Du Yunsong was living in the village of Lou Dian. Du was distinctive among the many other craftsmen rediscovered during this period because of his ability to read and write, and his carvings are said to have been inspired by landscape painting. In 1954, Du was called to the Folk Arts Research Institute *(Minjian Yiren Yanjiusuo)* of the Provincial Academy of Fine Arts *(Meishu Xueyuan)* in Hangzhou to work with apprentices, and stayed for two years. In 1956, he returned to Lou Dian and assumed leadership of a craft cooperative *(hezuoshe)* there, which was to become one of the focal points for the reestablishment of the post-liberation woodcarving profession (fieldnotes, 5/20/89; 5/24/89, interview with Hu Zhonghe—Hangzhou). In July of 1956, four additional woodcarving small groups *(xiao zu)* from the towns and villages of Hu Qi, Xi Dui, Nan Ma, and Hu Tou Lu were consolidated into the operation, and in November of the same year, the cooperative established in Lou Dian moved to the village of Xia Qi Tan in Nan Shang Hu (a different Xia Qi Tan from the native village of Wu Mantang described in Chapter 3), where the cooperative occupied the more spacious premises of the De Fu Temple.

Among those recruited to the Lou Dian co-op was Master Zhou Fangchun (eighty-three years old at the time of our interview in 1989). Zhou had begun carving at the age of thirteen, apprenticed to Master Zhou Jinmu from Qing Tang village, whom he followed around the countryside of Fang Jun subdistrict and beyond, working in halls, temples, and houses. Upon completing his term, Zhou went to Jinhua where he worked for three years. He then set off for Shanghai, and worked in Lu Ji Co. for six years. At the time, he recalls, there were small companies all over Shanghai, and he worked for short stretches at many of them. Some time later he moved to Hankou for three years, and spent some time in the course of a year in Chungking, Chengdu, and Kunming. Zhou spent five months in Beijing, where he worked on the house of Cao Kun, former President of China just after the establishment of the Republic. There, he was introduced to Yuan Shikai, and met the famous opera singer Mei Lanfang, who came to watch him work.

Zhou worked in Tianjin for three years where he recalls conditions and wages were especially good. He wrote to friends in Shanghai, and some seventy to eighty masters came, all of whom were fellow Dongyang folk. In the end, the Tianjin factory burned down, and all returned to Dongyang.

In 1937, when the Japanese invaded, Zhou worked in the fields for more than ten years. After liberation he worked on a carving production team *(xiao zu),* and later on in Lou Dian he was involved in a research team *(yanjiu zu)* with several other senior workers studying and elaborating on traditional design in carved wood. Zhou moved to Xia Qi Tan in April 1956 with the other members of the Lou Dian post-liberation carving group, and later on to the Dongyang Woodcarving Factory, retiring in 1967.

Since then, he has continued to work at home on privately contracted orders, and since the early 1970s he has also been employed in a factory in Qing Tang village, teaching apprentices. Several of his former apprentices are at work in Guangzhou, and three of his grandsons are also there carving. Over the years Zhou gained recognition as an expert in rendering in wood the traditional stories of the *Romance of the Three Kingdoms*, *The Water Margin*, *Dream of the Red Chamber*, and other Chinese literary classics (fieldnotes, 4/2/89, interview with Zhou Fangchun, Fang Jun town).

In September–October 1958, the Xia Qi Tan cooperative was amalgamated with a similar cooperative established in the town of Wei Shan in the northeast of the county, and moved to Lu Zhai (Lu family village) on the outskirts of Wu Ning town. The new amalgamated co-op had more than 300 workers of whom more than 100 were newly recruited apprentices (NCNA 1972: 5278: 19). In December 1958 the amalgamated cooperative was transferred to state ownership and became a local state-run *(difang guoying)* enterprise, but in 1962 in the wake of the "three bad years" following the Great Leap Forward, the central government divested itself of responsibility for the enterprise, and it became a large cooperative *(da jiti)* factory run by the county *(xian ban de)* (fieldnotes, 5/2/89, interview with Feng Wentu). Now commonly known as the Dongyang Woodcarving Factory *(Dongyang Mudiao Chang)*, it is the largest production center of carved wood products in the county, employs upward of 1,200 workers on the premises, and serves as the distribution and collection point for the materials and products of some 2,000 outworkers in more than 60 subcontracting workshops *(jia gong dian)* (fieldnotes, 7/25/86, interview with Feng Wentu; also see Chapter 7).

Among the more illustrious of the senior generation of elder craftsmen were the so-called premier *(zaixiang)* of the woodcarving trade, Huang Zijin (1894–1981) of Huang Da Lu village, and the "imperial degree candidate" *(zhuang yuan)* of the trade, Lou Shuiming (1898–1983) of Heng Dian town.

Huang was known for drawing inspiration for his carvings from local operas. He worked with renowned carver Lu Lianshui on several collaborative projects, and Zhang Mingyao of Li Tang village (see Chapter 4) spent several years working in Huang's company. One of Huang's more distinguished apprentices was Feng Wentu, a member of the present management committee of the Dongyang Woodcarving Factory, and director of the factory's art craft vocational school.

Lou Shuiming's career is of particular interest since at the time of the Communist victory over the nationalists in 1949, Lou was in the British colony of Hong Kong working as a carver at Hua An Co. He returned to Dongyang in 1954 in the midst of the craft cooperativization movement, when most of the traffic was in the other direction. For this reason he has not only come to occupy a revered place in maintaining continuity with the great craft traditions of the past, but is also seen as a model of "patriotism" and loyalty to the motherland.

In 1956, after having been back in China for two years, Lou was sent by the central government to Ulan Bator in Mongolia to teach carving. While there, he studied the anatomy of horses, and after two years, he took the results of his study back to Dongyang where he is credited with having transformed the traditional representation of horses in the carvings of the county from "half pig, half donkey" to "fine steeds that appeared to move as in life" *(Zhejiang Gongyi Meishu* 1979: 16–18).

In 1958, Lou was called to Beijing and sent on a tour of Pakistan, Czechoslovakia, and the USSR for three months. He came back to Dongyang to the newly established Dongyang Woodcarving Factory where he stayed for the remainder of his days, except for a brief stint in 1968, when at the age of seventy, he studied painting at the Academy of Fine Arts in Hangzhou (fieldnotes, 3/29/89, interview with Lou Shunho, adopted son of Lou Shuiming).

His skills in design are renowned, and more than 300 products of the Dongyang Woodcarving Factory are said to have originated with him. One of Lou's carvings, "Spring at West Lake," was hung in the Great Hall of the People in Beijing in 1960, and in 1979 at the age of eighty-two, Lou was designated a "National Art Craftsman" *(guojia gongyimeishu jia)*. In the following year he served as representative to the Fifth National People's Congress, and in 1987, he was among twenty craftsmen honored (in his case posthumously) in a national exhibition of arts and crafts, held in the Hall of Nationalities in Beijing (fieldnotes, 7/5/87, interview with Lu Xibing). His former apprentice, Lu Guangzheng, is the head of the management committee of the

Worker inking motifs onto wood panel in preparation for carving

Dongyang Woodcarving Factory. Mention of the name Lou Shuiming in Dongyang evokes immediate recognition and even an air of reverence.

Somewhat paradoxically, the work regime to which Lou and his elder colleagues returned in Dongyang in the 1950s was one in which the division of labor characteristic of treaty port hand manufacture had become even further elaborated. While in the pre-revolutionary capitalist treaty ports like Hong Kong and Shanghai, it was the responsibility of a rough carver to determine the overall design of a carving with a few words of advice as to motif from the boss of the factory, in the new cooperative socialist division of labor, the tasks of design had become incorporated in a design studio (fieldnotes, 4/2/89, interview with Zhou Fangchun in Fang Jun).

In the design section, workers engaged in the rendering of drawings on paper to serve as standardized motifs for representation in carved relief on wood. The drawings were transferred to a heavy wax paper, and pin holes were then punctured along the lines of the drawing to prepare a stencil. The stencil was then placed over the planks prepared in the carpentry section of the factory and inked, leaving an outline of the entire picture to be represented in the future carving.

Thus, the rough carver received before him a board in which the motifs, characters, proportions, foreground, and background had already been established, and he was relieved totally of any design responsibility. His job was simply to begin the execution of the design created elsewhere. This he did, leaving off at the same point at which a rough carver in the pre-revolutionary treaty ports would have passed the carving along to the fine carving finisher; in socialist Dongyang, the fine carver completed the carving much as his counterpart treaty port fine carver would have—smoothing out the rough edges, finishing with care the faces of the characters, providing their clothing with appropriate trim, attending to detail and line work, and giving the piece its final flourishes.

In accordance with the principle enunciated by the nineteenth-century political economist Charles Babbage, incorporating the design function in its own studio had the effect of reducing the costs of labor force reproduction. In the case of woodcarving, this meant that a rough carver could effectively participate in production (execution) without necessarily possessing skills in design (conception). As Babbage noted, such specialization of function makes it possible to pay larger numbers of less generally skilled workers lower wages while still effectively turning out the product.

The presence of this heightened specialization in the socialist work regime represents something of a paradox since the separation of conception from execution is typically a phenomenon of the capitalist mode of production, associated with the alienation of the worker from his product (see Braverman 1974 for a discussion of Babbage's principle). One might expect that a socialist work regime would be organized to minimize such alienation, and yet this specialization and deskilling had proceeded further in socialist Dongyang and Shanghai than in the pre-revolutionary capitalist treaty ports, or for that matter in post-war British colonial Hong Kong. Furthermore, such specialization seems to have become consolidated in the generally over-organized and bureaucratized system of production and administration characteristic of the Chinese Communist state, and has persisted in the organization of larger collective carved wood furniture enterprises down to the present. Many rough carvers in the production end of such factories aspire to the "higher status" jobs in design.

Among those who, like Lou Shuiming, played a role in carrying forward the standards and understandings of traditional craftsmanship into the modern period, and establishing a basis for the post-liberation development of the woodcarving craft, was Master Zhang Zhengxi (eighty-two years old at the time of our interview in 1989). Zhang had two years of schooling before being apprenticed to Master Li Dajin at the age of thirteen in Zhuji county. When he turned eighteen, he married his master's daughter, Li Guizhen.

After three years as an apprentice, Shang went to Hu Zhou in northern Zhejiang, then on to Shanghai. In Shanghai at ages 18–19, he worked in a small shop in Jing An district, whose master was a Dongyang native. Zhang worked around from shop to shop, here one month, there another. At age twenty, he went to Hong Kong where his wife joined him shortly thereafter. He worked there as a carver for 11 years, during the last few of which he and a partner from Nan Ma town in Dongyang ran their own enterprise. When the Japanese invaded Hong Kong, he lost track of his partner, who he surmises has probably made his way to American by now.

Zhang was among those who participated in the three-month trek from Japanese-occupied Hong Kong back to Dongyang. His mother was still in the county, but the Japanese were there in Dongyang too, and there was little in the way of work. His family was forced to sell all their belongings—clothes, furniture, and so forth—just to eat. Times were really rough. Zhang stayed in Dongyang till just before the Communist victory, when he went to Shanghai and found a job in Yuan Li wood products factory.

After liberation, business at Yuan Li was poor, reaching a low point during the three-anti and five-anti campaigns. Zhengxi went off to Qingdao where he stayed half a year, and then returned to Shanghai, where he and several fellow workers organized a production team *(xiao zu)* in the course of the handicraft reform and cooperativization movement. The government provided relief *(jiu ji)* in the form of grain, and later the *xiao zu* was reorganized into a cooperative *(hezuoshe)*, and its organization formalized. Remuneration was changed from piecework to fixed monthly wages, of which the highest was about ¥80/month. A Communist Party branch was organized and a cooperative leader *(she zhang)* was appointed. Finally, in 1956, this cooperative, along with several others like it, was consolidated into the Shanghai No. 1 Carving Factory. Zhang knew Guo Youxing during his early years in Hong Kong, and they met again in the cooperative production team and the new factory when Guo returned to Shanghai in 1956.

Zhang worked in the No. 1 Factory until the Cultural Revolution decade was almost over. He retired in 1976, although after his retirement, he continued working in the factory for another two years. His official population registration *(hu kou)* is still in Shanghai, and his daughter occupies the family quarters there. She has worked in the Shanghai No. 1 Factory since just after liberation, having graduated from the Shanghai arts and crafts middle school *(gongyi meishu zhongxue)*. She retired from work as a carver at the end of 1988 at the age of fifty-two.

There have been carvers in Zhengxi's family for five generations. His father's brother, mother's brother, and mother's brother's son were all carvers, as was his wife's father, his former master. Apart from the daughter at the Shanghai No. 1 Factory, another daughter is employed at the Dongyang Woodcarving Factory. Zhang's only son is a carver, as is his son's wife, and their daughter (fieldnotes, 3/22/89, interview with Zhang Zhengxi, Hu Qi town).

Zhang has had many apprentices over the course of the years, both in Hong Kong and in Shanghai, and he is also skilled in carpentry and fine art painting. At present, he draws and paints at his home in Hu Qi town, but does not carve much anymore. He receives a pension from the Shanghai No. 1 Factory which supports him in his retirement.

As Zhang and his contemporaries advance in years, they represent in their apprentices both a continuity with the past, as well as a benchmark from which to assess the future. In their hands, an important transition was effected in the traditions of woodcarving. The reproduction of the labor force in the post–World War II period was secured through their efforts.

The process, of course, was not without setbacks, and serious ones at that. Immediately following the climax of the craft cooperativization movement in 1957, the Great Leap Forward was launched. With the self-sufficiency of communes proclaimed as a goal, the curtailment of market transactions and interregional and international trade was devastating to just the kind of recently cooperativized sideline enterprises represented by Dongyang's woodcarving shops. Such enterprises did not belong to the two sectors that received emphasis at the time—agriculture and steel production—and many craftsmen were forced to return to farming on a full-time basis. The creatively restored and revivified craft tradition, and the newly consolidated craft cooperatives, had little chance to show what they could do.

Provincial statistics for trade in art craft industries are predictably lacking for the Great Leap period. There are no figures for Zhejiang province's annual production value of such industries between 1957, when APV was reported as ¥24,600,000, and 1965 when the APV was reported as ¥34,000,000 (DDZGZJ 1989: 384).

Statistics from Dongyang county show that *exports* of the county's carved wood products stagnated from 1958 to 1960 at around ¥250,000/year, finally experiencing some growth in the mid to late 1960s, spurred on by the establishment of so-called multifunctional cooperatives under commune management, in which activities like the production of woodcarvings were once again reorganized. Under these new organizational forms, exports of carved wood products expanded to ¥361,100 by 1968, roughly paralleling developments in production value of art craft products at the provincial level (Jiang n.d.e).

But the recovery was short-lived, interrupted yet again by the Cultural Revolution during which the multifunctional co-ops were disbanded as "revisionist," and the fortunes of the woodcarving industry took another dive.

Tradition Under Siege—The Cultural Revolution

In 1966, the Cultural Revolution was launched against the very traditions the elder craftsmen of the senior generation of carvers had just succeeded in reconstituting. Art craft industries, and the subjects of their representations, became the object of criticism as manifestations of the "four olds" of the previous "feudal" system. Under ideological and physical attack from 1966 to 1970, production of art craft industries declined every year (DDZGZJ 1989: 385).

Despite the rhetoric of the Cultural Revolution regarding the oppressiveness of alienation deriving from increased specialization of function in the division of labor of capitalist industrial production, there do not seem to have been any attempts to deal with the manifestations of exactly that tendency in the division of labor of Woodcarving at the Dongyang Woodcarving Factory with its specialized design studio.

Nevertheless, the distinctive character of the craft products of the industry—part commodity, part work of art—gave them significance not only in fulfilling yearly economic targets, but in the expressive/ideological dimension of culture as well. Even with design functions isolated in a specialized studio, the execution of such designs in wood required the exercise of both manual and mental labor. Skill in the handling of tools was important, but a measure of inspiration and creative decision making was also indispensable, an aesthetic sense necessary to cope with the representation of each figure and motif as its qualities and the qualities of the medium demanded. In addition, these objects were inextricably bound up with the image that China presented of itself to the outside world.

The rationality of craft production thus included an expressive, creative component in on-line performance not present in most other industrial sectors, and subjected its practitioners to the same strictures of political line as were applied to intellectual, literary, and artistic pursuits in China during the Cultural Revolution. Products could not consistently overstep the boundaries of acceptable political discourse, and had to respond to changes in the volatile national and regional intellectual and political climate.

The execution of traditional designs, with their sometimes unsavory historical figures from China's past, or worse, with characters derived from China's wealth of "feudal superstition," clearly exceeded those boundaries. Indeed, we have already noted that many specimens of traditional carving in homes and temples were vandalized and defaced during the successive campaigns of the Cultural Revolution period. If, as a craftsman, one took recourse in portraying contemporary political figures, one had to be very careful lest a poorly executed or unflattering likeness subject one to labeling as a counterrevolutionary. Many masters went back to their labors in the agricultural collectives full-time, or into other professions, and few new apprentices were trained (fieldnotes, 5/3/89, interview with Lu Zhongxiao, factory head of Lu Zhai Woodcarving Factory).

Finding the tradition they had worked so hard to restore come under attack, many senior craftsmen like Lou Shuiming, who had sacrificed so much in the effort to restore that tradition, responded with anger. In an account that is surely exaggerated for dramatic effect, Lou is characterized as having been especially outraged by the destruction of painted scrolls, from which he had learned to take inspiration for his own carvings. He is said to have grabbed his pen and set about designing a grand screen, *"Shan hua lan man"* (Bright mountain flowers in full bloom), and accompanying wall hanging, *"Song He tu"* (Image of a pine and crane), with the following inscription:

> "Cut to death, the art of Dongyang woodcarving in the end will be like bright mountain flowers in full bloom, ever green like the pine and [long lived as] the crane." *(Zhejiang Gongyi Meishu* 1979: 17)

As the presentation below will confirm, Lou's words were indeed prescient, although not without a few twists and turns along the way. In the 1970s under Zhou Enlai's leadership, traditional crafts were absolved of being "reactionary and hateful" and were touted as important export items. In 1973, after the State Council promulgated a Ministry of Foreign Trade and Ministry of Light Industry "Report on Problems in the Development of Art Craft Production," expanded resistance to the leftist excesses of the Cultural Revolution ensued, and art craft industries revived. As foreign trade began to pick up, the woodcarving profession began to find avenues for expansion. Not only was the production of traditional articles revived, but a whole host of new articles began to be exported (DDZGZJ 1989: 385: fieldnotes, 53/89, interview with Lu Zhongxiao).

With commune and brigade enterprises *(she dui qiye)* making their appearance, and rural industry touted as an important element in China's development strategy, annual production value for Zhejiang province's art craft industries in 1978 reached ¥246,000,000—6.1 times the figure of 1965 (DDZGZJ: 385). Dongyang county exports of carved wood products expanded to ¥1,668,300 in 1976, ¥2,018,700 in 1977, falling back slightly to ¥2,000,600 in 1978 (Jiang n.d.e).

Post-Mao Reforms

At the Third Plenum of the Eleventh Central Committee in late 1978, the emphasis on rural industry was reaffirmed. As we have seen, controls on rural commodity trade were lifted, and in the ensuing years, ideological controls on the expressive arts, as well as controls on private accumulation of wealth and mobility of labor were progressively lifted.

This set the stage for the renaissance of the woodcarving tradition envisioned by Lou Shuiming. That tradition has been swept up in the rush to economic reform, increasingly bound to the international market, increasingly reliant on export, but also serving an increasingly wealthy local clientele.

In the seven years following 1978, more than 430 projects of basic construction and technical transformation were organized, and more than ¥230,000,000 invested in support of "backbone" enterprises producing craft items associated with distinct locales of Zhejiang province (so-called fist commodities), with an eye to enhancing earnings of foreign exchange. During this period efforts were made not only to protect and develop the distinctive traditions of art craft production, but also to acquire advanced technical equipment from outside the country to stimulate technical modernization and product improvement (DDZGZJ 1989: 387).

Early reforms revealed that due to the administrative structure under which exports were handled, factories had little information about the sales situation on the international market. Nor were foreign trade departments in the provincial capital Hangzhou well versed in the conditions under which production was carried out. Owing to this situation, in 1981, in the course of reform of the national foreign trade system, the Zhejiang province Art Craft Industrial Co. and the Zhejiang branch of the China Art Craft Products Import–Export Corporation of the Second Light Industrial Bureau combined to form the Zhejiang Art Craft Products Import-Export Consolidated Co. based in Hangzhou. Among the institutions which the Consolidated Co. had at its disposal to design prototypes to meet the demands of foreign customers was the provincial Art Craft Research Institute *(Gongyi meishu yanjiusuo)*. The Institute, which maintains a staff of skilled practitioners and designers in Hangzhou from among the diverse craft traditions of the province, keeps the company more attuned to the requirements and limitations of production, but may also generate new products on its own initiative, and test their marketability on the international market with assistance from the company.

The specialization and consolidation of marketing functions proved beneficial to practitioners in both production and marketing spheres. By 1985, production value of art craft products in Zhejiang province had doubled, and foreign trade export earnings had increased four times over 1981 (DDZGZJ 1989: 393). In 1985, the province had more than 1,804 enterprises producing art craft items (Zhejiang Rural Industrial Bureau 1986), with more than 54,000 associated specialist practitioners, more than 840,00 outworkers, and more than 1,145 creative design and technical design employees. Production value of the province's art craft industries in 1985 had increased 197 times over 1950 (DDZGZJ 1989: 388), accounted for 12.2 percent of all provincial foreign sales, and 10.7 percent of the entire nation's production of art craft products (DDZGZJ 1989: 381).

In 1987 the earnings of foreign exchange for the second light industrial sector nationwide were US$1,200,000,000, of which arts and crafts *(gongyi meishu)* accounted for one-third (DYMDBAO 11:2: 3/5/88 untitled).

Within the woodcarving profession there has been a proliferation of private enterprises that owe their existence to the investment of private savings and capital. Some of these enterprises function as "add labor shops" *(jia gong dian),* disembodied stages in the hand-powered portion of a production line of which outworkers' homes may constitute a part. They simply execute carvings on a putting-out basis according to designs created in the studios of larger collective sector factories.

The nature of the division of labor in woodcarving production encourages putting-out arrangements. These arrangements are not only manifest in the early experience of many of the enterprises, which began life as outworking shops for the Dongyang Woodcarving Factory and the Shanghai No. 1 Woodcarving Factory, but persist in the operation of contemporary township, subdistrict, village, and private enterprises that subcontract carving work to outworkers in smaller workshops or to individual workers in their homes.

In the larger enterprises from which the work is put out, wood is prepared by workers employing a bevy of modern carpentry machines, and the required designs are stenciled onto the wood. Carving of the panels is completed by the outworkers, after which the partial products are brought back to the central factory for assembly and varnishing.

But there is also a growing number of fully independent factories, owned and operated by private entrepreneurs and with commercial contacts in the domestic and international market; some of these began life as *jia gong dian,* later expanding to independent operation.

Some of the finer pieces turned out by county craftsmen are painstakingly created by individuals like Guo Youxing (see Chapter 5), who create the pieces from start to finish in their homes as sideline work. In such contexts, the regimentation, discipline, and elaborate division of labor that characterize factory work are completely absent, and carvings may take shape over many months, with the individual worker performing all the operations himself, from design, to rough carving, to finishing.

In Dongyang, the carved wood products industry remains one of the principal employers in the county. The development and diversification of the industry, building on the traditional skills of its labor force, has contributed to the enhancement of rural livelihood, even while the industry has been superseded in its overall significance to the county's prosperity as a whole by newer, more modern light industrial enterprises producing textiles, clothing, construction materials, and machinery.

While Dongyang's future prosperity probably depends to a greater extent on the success of these latter enterprises, its production of traditional hand-crafted wood carvings shows no signs of decline, indeed it may be said to be experiencing something of a renaissance. With their enhanced ability to maneuver in markets both domestic and international, the enterprises of the carved wood products industry display the marked dynamic characteristic of the economic life of the county as a whole, and seem likely to continue to contribute to the county's development on into the twenty-first century.

Chapter 3

Xia Qi Tan Village

Before the village, White creek [Bai Qi] runs by;
Behind the village, small mountain slopes encircle;
Below the slopes the creek forms a deep pool,
Whose water in the heat of the summer is jade green,
  clear, cold, and drinkable;
The village on the bank of this "summer creek pool,"
  thus takes its name Xia Qi Tan

Xia Qi Tan, the native village of Mr. Wu Mantang, is a single surname community inhabited by members of the Wu lineage, although a small number of non-Wu families have settled there since 1949. The village is situated on the north bank of White Creek *(Bai Qi),* and because of the sand and mud built up over the years along the banks, the soil is quite fertile (fieldnotes, 5/22/88, interview with Wu Changsheng).

The nearest market town, 1 km to the east, is Wu Liang, where prior to the Communist victory in 1949 the main Wu lineage ancestral hall *(citang)* was located. The intermediate market town of Zhang Cun, present center of the *xiang* government, is 2.5 km to the north of Xia Qi Tan, and 4 km to the west is the intermediate market town of Liu Shi (see Map 3).

Liu Shi has market days on the second, fifth, and eighth days of the ten-day market week *(chu er, chu wu, chu ba)*; Wu Liang has market days on the third, sixth and ninth days *(chu san, chu liu, chu jiu)*; and Zhang Cun has market days on the first, fourth, and seventh days *(chu yi, chu si, chu qi)* (fieldnotes, 5/18/88 Xia Qi Tan), meaning that Xia Qi Tan residents have access to markets nine days out of ten. This synchronization of market periodicity accords well with Skinner's findings (1964–65; 1977) regarding the regional marketing hierarchy in rural China, which our data on Li Tang village (in chapter 4) also serve to confirm.

Figure 3.1 **Founders of the Wu Lineage of Xia Qi Tan.**

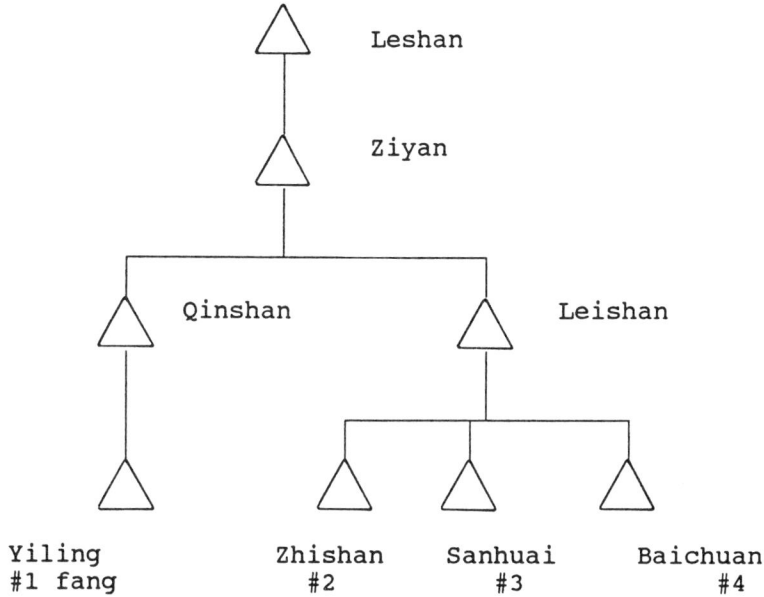

Settlement of Xia Qi Tan by the Wu lineage is said to date from the Jia Jing reign period of the Ming dynasty (A.D. 1522–1567). At that time, one of the nine sons of Wu Leshan, named Wu Ziyan, moved the short distance from Wu Liang market, established his residence, built a dike along White Creek, reclaimed rice fields and established the village. There have been some sixteen generations since Wu Ziyan, although the Wu genealogical poem, by means of which the generations of the lineage are marked, extends ten generations still further back (see Figure 3.1).

Ziyan had two sons, Qinshan and Leishan. Qinshan had a distinguished career as an official in Fujian province, and established a branch of the Wu lineage there. He was awarded the posthumous imperial title of Gong Hou Di and these characters decorate a memorial arch *(paifang)*, which still stands at the entrance to the present village senior citizen's center *(lao nian xie hui)*, formerly the Qinshan branch lineage ancestral hall. The descendants of Qinshan's son, Yiling, at present comprise the smallest segment *(fang)* of Xia Qi Tan village in terms of population, less than fifty households.

While Qinshan was off in Fujian, his brother Leishan was prosper-

Restored Leishan Ancestral Hall in Xia Qi Tan village.

ing. Holder of the *juren* imperial degree, he is said to have organized the construction of more than 200 houses in the village, and greatly contributed to its development. He had seven sons, three of whom settled in Xia Qi Tan—Zhishan, Sanhuai, and Baichuan. Together with Yiling, they comprise the four apical ancestors of the branches *(fang)* in which the Wu lineage of Xia Qi Tan is conceptualized (see Figure 3.1). A small temple honoring Leishan was recently refurbished on the far western edge of town after suffering destruction during the Cultural Revolution.

In 1988, Xia Qi Tan had a population of over 1,650 residents in 450 households. Its population farmed 800+ *mu* of irrigated fields *(tian)* and 1,200 *mu* of dry fields *(di)* (1 *mu* = .0667 hectares = .1647 acres). Some 1,000 *mu* of hill land *(shan di)* were unplanted, and the village also possessed some 150 *mu* of ponds (fieldnotes, 5/16/88) (see Map 7).

At present #1 fang contains about 50 households (12 percent), #2 fang contains about 100 households (24 percent), #3 fang contains 150+ households (38 percent), and #4 fang contains 100+ households (26 percent) (fieldnotes, 5/21/88).

Prior to the establishment of the People's Republic in 1949, most residents worked in agriculture. Some 20 percent of the population worked outside the village as masons, plasterers, painters, woodwork-

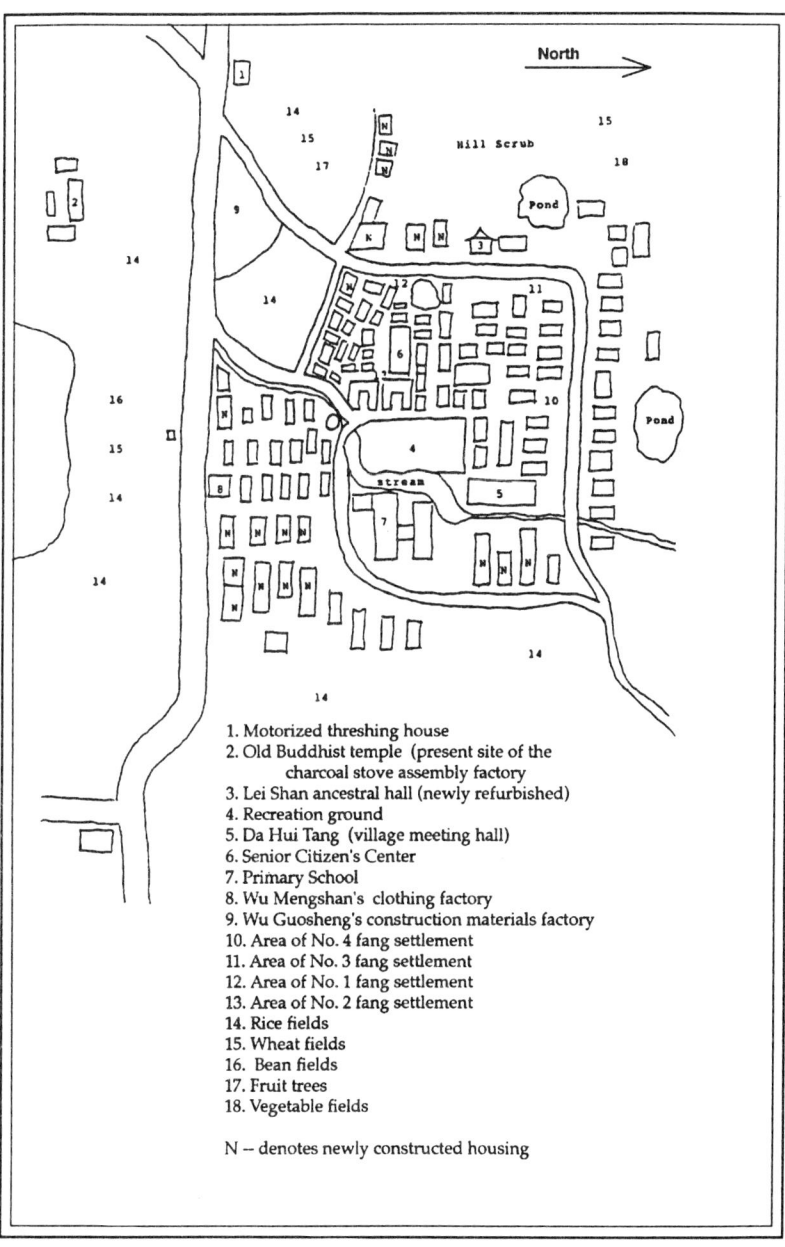

1. Motorized threshing house
2. Old Buddhist temple (present site of the charcoal stove assembly factory
3. Lei Shan ancestral hall (newly refurbished)
4. Recreation ground
5. Da Hui Tang (village meeting hall)
6. Senior Citizen's Center
7. Primary School
8. Wu Mengshan's clothing factory
9. Wu Guosheng's construction materials factory
10. Area of No. 4 fang settlement
11. Area of No. 3 fang settlement
12. Area of No. 1 fang settlement
13. Area of No. 2 fang settlement
14. Rice fields
15. Wheat fields
16. Bean fields
17. Fruit trees
18. Vegetable fields

N -- denotes newly constructed housing

Map 7. Xia Qi Tan Village.

ers, clothing makers (tailors), and small commodity traders (fieldnotes, 5/23/88, interview with Wu Changsheng). Many of the latter traveled south to buy ginger and *fen gan* (dried bean noodles) to be sold locally on itinerant rounds through the local markets described above (fieldnotes, 4/22/89, interview with Wu Guiyu).

Rice was the basis of agriculture, with corn, wheat, millet and potatoes also grown. Pigs were raised by most households, generally consumed during New Year's, but also preserved as ham (see Appendix 1). Chickens were raised for sale. Goats were kept and eaten as a winter treat. White radishes, cabbage, and sugar cane were also grown in small quantities. The diet consisted mainly of rice, vegetables and local pickles; meat was consumed only on ceremonial occasions.

Women spun and wove in the home, using some locally grown cotton, some bought in the market. The village was by all accounts very poor. Each year, every family was short about one or two month's grain. The "obliging need" to make up this deficit (see Cook and Binford 1990), was the primary stimulus to residents' seeking paid employment outside the village in artisan labor as Wu Mantang did in the 1940s (fieldnotes, 5/23/88, interview with Wu Changsheng).

Mantang emigrated to Hong Kong in 1947 accompanied by his brother, who had previously settled there, but who had returned to Xia Qi Tan during the Japanese occupation of the colony. Mantang had recently married, and he and his new wife settled on Fuk Lo Tsun Road in the Kowloon City district of Hong Kong. He had been apprenticed as a carpenter in Dongyang just outside of the market town of Liu Shi, and began his own furniture factory upon arrival in Hong Kong. My status as Mantang's former apprentice (see Cooper 1980a) made me something of a fictive kinsman of Xia Qi Tan residents.

Mantang emigrated to Hong Kong early enough not to have been classified by the victorious Communist authorities as a political refugee, and he and his wife still had claims on housing and property in Xia Qi Tan, out of which a nephew of Mantang's #2 fang at one time ran his country doctor practice.

After retiring from the carpentry business in 1980, Mantang slowed down considerably and, suffering from gout, always had a cane close at hand. His former factory premises were rented out to another entrepreneur, and the rent provided him and his wife with enough to support themselves in retirement. Several companies with whom they did business in years past still owed them money for goods delivered. Mrs. Wu

Figure 3.2. **Mantang's Segment of Xia Qi Tan #2 Fang.**

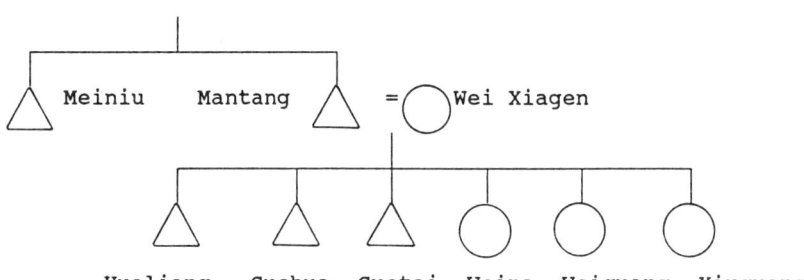

still has the invoices, and every now and then makes a renewed effort to collect.

The Wus' eldest daughter is married to the eldest son of one of Mantang's former business associates. The couple has settled in England where eldest daughter practices nursing and the son-in-law has a toy manufacturing business. Middle daughter lives in New York and works in a public library. Her husband deals in real estate. Youngest daughter is married, and was living in Meifoo Estates in Kowloon until she and her husband set out to seek their fortune in Kenya, from where her eldest brother had just returned in 1988. Eldest brother earned a degree in business from a Canadian university, and after recently returning from service as an accountant in an expatriate Chinese company in Nairobi, has taken up residence in Australia. Middle brother earned a degree in nuclear engineering from the University of Arizona, and recently quit his job as senior engineer in a large European firm in Hong Kong to take a new assignment in the Chinese Special Economic Zone in Shenzhen just across the Hong Kong border. Youngest brother has finished a degree in applied physics in England, but returned to Hong Kong to sell insurance.

In 1989, Mantang was involved in a car accident from which he never fully recovered. The energetic abandon with which he conducted his carpentry work in the past had left him, and under care in a nursing home, he passed away the following year.

Two years after Mantang's arrival in Hong Kong, the People's Liberation Army reached Xia Qi Tan village, and Guomindang (KMT) forces fled. A campaign to suppress counterrevolutionaries was carried out in the following year, during which political struggle sessions were mounted against a few functionaries of the former Guomindang government by the recently organized Communist Peasant's Association.

The land reform that ensued was relatively simple since there were no resident landlords in Xia Qi Tan. Those who owned land in the village owned very small amounts, and resided in the towns of Wu Liang and Zhang Cun. But there was very little private land altogether in the village. Eighty to ninety percent of village land was *ci tian* or *chang tian*—controlled by lineage ancestral halls both in Xia Qi Tan and outside. Rental income from the land supported lineage activities and ritual observances. Rents in Xia Qi Tan were generally paid in kind, consisting of 50 percent of the crop, either as contractually fixed rent or in perpetual lease usufruct arrangements *(yong tian quan)*.

The heads of each branch hall of the lineage kept the accounts for such land, and were responsible for the income it generated. It was they who sent agents dunning for rent payment at harvest time in Xia Qi Tan, and it was they who bore the brunt of the struggle sessions during land reform in 1950 when rent payments were suspended and land divided to the households. Each villager was allotted 0.6 *mu* of land (0.04 hectares or 0.1 acres).

Collectivization, although commencing somewhat late in Xia Qi Tan, followed patterns similar to those observed elsewhere in China (cf., e.g., Yang 1959; Hinton 1966; Potter and Potter 1990; Friedman et al. 1991). Mutual Aid Teams consisting of 7–10 households were organized in 1955. Land remained in private hands, and was worked with the assistance of team members. In 1956, four lower-level cooperatives were organized in Xia Qi Tan with an 89 percent participation rate.

Later in the year, these four cooperatives were consolidated into one higher-level cooperative under whose auspices draft animals, tools, and land were cooperativized. Earnings were accorded to households based only on labor performed by their members, with work points allocated according to the number of days worked. At the end of the year, the harvest was divided into per capita shares, and the shares assigned a value in work points. If the points earned by a household were greater than the work point value of their shares, the balance was made up in cash payments. If there was a deficit in work points earned against the work point value of their shares, the household had to return the difference in grain to the cooperative.

When the People's Communes were organized in conjunction with the nationwide Great Leap Forward, Xia Qi Tan village became one of fifteen brigades in Wu Liang People's Commune, which stretched along White Creek through the present subdistricts *(xiang)* of Liu Shi, Zhang Cun, and Huailu. When the communes were first established there were eight production teams of about sixty households each in Xia Qi Tan Brigade. But as with early communes elsewhere in China, Wu Liang commune was soon deemed too large and unwieldy. Its administration was overburdened with broad responsibilities in agricultural and industrial production, commerce, education, health, communication, transportation, and military preparedness. In 1961, in line with a general retrenchment in commune size nationally, Wu Liang commune was divided into three smaller communes—Zhang Cun, Huailu, and Liu Shi. Xia Qi Tan fell in the territory of Zhang Cun commune.

In 1981, the original 8 production teams *(xiao dui)* of Xia Qi Tan were reorganized into 16 production teams of 30 households each. In 1983, responsibility for agricultural and industrial production was subcontracted *(cheng bao)* to households, but the organizational structure of the communes was retained until 1985. In that year, it was dismantled altogether and replaced by a simplified *xiang* (subdistrict) government, with more limited functions (fieldnotes, 5/23/88, interview with Wu Changsheng; and 5/19/88, interview with Wu Fengde).

Just after the Communist victory in 1949, residents of Xia Qi Tan had made a move into cash crop production, growing watermelon, *sucai,* hot peppers, ginger, and especially tomatoes. Restrictions on local marketing introduced during the Great Leap Forward and stress on grain production during the Cultural Revolution stifled the development of this incipient cash crop economy, but the return to household farming in the 1980s has brought a return to cash cropping, and new income from the sale of watermelon, vegetables, pears, peaches, grapes, and tomatoes (fieldnotes, 4/22/89, interview with Wu Guiyu).

The Cultural Revolution began in Xia Qi Tan in the latter half of 1967. There were two factions of about equal size in the village, known as the *bao huang pai*—protect the cadres faction—and the *zao fan pai*—red guard or rebel faction (coinciding with Revolutionary Rebel United General Headquarters and the Revolutionary Rebel United Headquarters factions of the county town). There were struggle/criticism sessions, and several of the old "reactionaries" in the village were dragged out and paraded through nearby Wu Liang town on their knees, made to perform humiliating dances, and otherwise called to task again for their purported pre-revolutionary crimes and post-revolutionary subversion. Although directives called for the "destruction of the old and establishing the new" *(pojiu lixin)*, there was not much destruction in Xia Qi Tan. There was factional struggle, and big character posters were plastered up. There were frequent political meetings big and small, held separately by the two factions. But there was very little fighting, and nobody was killed in Xia Qi Tan. Residents emphasize that kin solidarity played a role in overcoming differences in ideology, which seldom resulted in violent confrontations.

The period of the most vigorous struggle was 1968–69. Every night there were struggle sessions to criticize Liu Shaoqi and Deng Xiaoping, "even during New Year's." Big character posters *(da zi bao)* voicing grievances against local leaders were everywhere. Red guards took over the party secretary's office, but after subjecting him to criticism he was allowed to remain in his post. There were no factories to go on strike. People simply worked the fields, ever aware that if there was no harvest, there would be nothing to eat. Thus, after struggle/criticism sessions, people ran to the fields to care for the crops on which their subsistence depended. According to the former party secretary of the village, the slogan advanced at the time by the central leadership, "make revolution—promote production," had genuine significance for rural folk, and agricultural production was maintained at pre–Cultural Revolution levels throughout the period (see Huang 1990: 285).

In 1974, the village was visited by the campaign to criticize Lin Biao and Confucius *(pi Lin pi Kong)*. Villagers were encouraged once more to struggle against the five bad elements—landlords, rich peasants, bad elements, counterrevolutionaries, right wingers. Community members who had been tagged with these labels during land reform, and subjected to humiliation during the earlier years of the Cultural Revolution, were once again dragged out and given the going over. Significantly, it was demanded of villagers that they overcome the intimacies they enjoyed with such folk deriving from their kinship relations—*"cheng xiong dao di"* (to be intimate and chummy as brothers/kinsmen)—and to cease referring to these people by their kin terms, adopting instead their counterrevolutionary labels (fieldnotes, 5/21/88, interview with Wu Fengde).

During the period of influence of the Gang of Four in the central government just prior to Mao's death in 1976, villagers claim to have been little affected. Their collective agricultural activities and responsibilities continued without interruption, despite the political intrigues going on in the national and provincial capitals (fieldnotes, 5/19/88, interview with Wu Fengde; also see Forster 1990).

Ploughing with a power tiller in Xia Qi Tan village.

Since the overthrow of the Gang of Four, and the implementation of economic reforms and household responsibility in agriculture, land has been subcontracted *(cheng bao)* to individual households. As in the original land reforms, each person was allocated 0.6 *mu*, with agricultural tax obligations of 20 kilograms of rice per 0.6 *mu* contracted for. No taxes were levied on the wheat crop, usually the third crop of the year after two rice crops were harvested. Minimum outputs of 1,250 kgs grain/*mu*/year are now common, with 2,000 kgs/*mu* considered quite a good yield, whereas in 1949, agricultural yields in Xia Qi Tan were on the order of 500 kgs/*mu*. In 1988, one year's rice harvest could support a household for two years (fieldnotes, 5/19/88, interview with Wu Fengde).

In Xia Qi Tan, as in most of Dongyang county under the economic reforms of the 1980s, residents have flocked to take up factory or construction work outside the village. As more and more of the younger men have sought jobs outside the village in the rural industrial sector, or begun their own enterprises, agriculture has been left in the hands of women and old folks. Those employed outside generally return during agricultural busy seasons *(nong mang)* to help with the harvest and planting for two weeks at a time twice a year, but remain absent for most of the rest of the year, returning again to celebrate the lunar New Year.

Where a parent or spouse is unavailable to tend to agricultural tasks, responsibility for one's land allocation may be subcontracted to a neighbor/kinsman. The latter, in exchange for meeting the state's compulsory grain purchase obligation, retains the balance of the crop. One older retired cadre in Xia Qi Tan works the land of four or five neighbor households. The weather has been good for the past few years, with rainfall timely, so returns to this specialized agricultural household *(zhuanye hu)* have been quite good.

Before the fall of the Gang of Four, when the commune structure was still in place, brigade members were not permitted to leave the village to work without special authorization. Those lucky enough to have found legal employment outside the village were required to remit a portion of the proceeds earned in outside work to the accumulation fund *(gong ji jin)* of the brigade to develop its own production, or forego their share of the brigade grain allocation at harvest time.

Since the implementation of the economic reforms, there are so many villagers working outside that Xia Qi Tan is experiencing a serious labor shortage in agriculture. With between 100 and 200 villagers working outside in construction jobs, it has become necessary to hire labor from outside the village to perform necessary agricultural tasks. Agricultural laborers, many from neighboring Jiangxi and Anhui provinces, earn ¥6–8/day plus food, cigarettes, and beer. By comparison, a worker hired to mix concrete in a construction crew earns ¥20/day. A skilled worker in a clothing factory can produce somewhat more than two Sun Yatsen style jackets in a day, at ¥5/piece or a total of ¥10+/day (fieldnotes, 5/16/88).

Unprecedented in the experience of most rural Chinese communities, such labor shortages could well be an important stimulus to agricultural mechanization, especially if combined with the consolidation of agricultural land in "specialized households" like that described above.

The rural industrial enterprises that have weaned so many away from the land began to appear in the area in 1973, when Zhang Cun commune began several collectively administered enterprises at the commune center. In 1975–76 brigades were authorized to begin their own industrial enterprises, and factories were begun in Xia Qi Tan producing clothing and construction materials. With the dismantling of the communal structures, these enterprises came under the administration of the village party committee, and more recently have been subcontracted *(cheng bao)* to individuals to administer for a contracted fee and a percentage of the profits remitted to the village (5/19/88, interview with Wu Fengde).

Xia Qi Tan's mayor, Mr. Wu Guosheng, is the proprietor of the Xia Qi Tan Cement Construction Materials Factory (Shuini Yuzhipin Chang). By far the largest enterprise in the village, it was begun in 1979 when three partners put together capital of ¥7,000–8,000 to begin. In that first year, they employed twelve workers, all from Xia Qi Tan, produced an APV of ¥30,000, and made a profit of ¥7,000–8,000.

In 1981, Wu Guosheng bought out his partners, who moved on to seek their fortunes in construction work as labor contractors *(bao gong tou)* in plastering and masonry. Between 1983 and 1986, Guosheng added five branch factories located in other villages to the enterprise, and in 1989 a sixth branch factory. In 1989, he employed more than fifty workers in the seven factories, most of whom were fellow villagers from Xia Qi Tan.

In 1986, APV was ¥600,000. In 1987, APV was ¥670,000. And in 1988, planned APV was ¥800,000. All the enterprise's products, which consist mainly of tubular reinforced concrete slabs (55–80 pieces/factory/day) used in the construction of walls and ceilings, are marketed within a 10 km radius of the villages in which the various branches are located.

It was common in the late 1980s for county residents to convert their cash savings into construction materials, even when their plans for building were in the remote future, as a hedge against inflation of the national currency (the RMB) and as a means of preserving value (official statistics put the annual inflation rate at 17.8 percent in 1989). Indeed, notwithstanding the 213 other construction materials factories in Dongyang countywide, Guosheng's six branch factories could not produce enough to meet the demand for their products.

No. 1 factory pays ¥6,000/year in taxes regardless of its output, and each branch factory about ¥4,500–5,000/year; 0.5 percent of APV is paid to the subdistrict *(xiang)* government in administrative fees. Workers in the enterprise are paid by the piece. Skilled workers can make ¥12/day, and each branch factory maintains a minimum of two skilled workers. Ordinary laborers make ¥6/day, plus year end bonuses/gifts. There are two ten-day periods each year when the factory closes during agricultural busy season, so that workers may return to their family farms to help out. They earn no wages during such periods.

Manager Wu Guosheng's new five-story house (or mansion rather) was receiving its final tile facing in 1988 and was all but complete, the tallest structure in the village, with an impressive radio antenna on the roof. Guosheng's business has continued to expand, although in 1992 the enterprise lost some ¥100,000 supplying materials to an unscrupulous construction contractor on the Sino-Soviet border.

Supplying Guosheng's enterprise with some of its raw materials is the Xia Qi Tan Steel Reinforcing Wire Drawing Factory (Gang Jin La Si Chang), just down the road. Guosheng's lineage cousin, Wu Xinglong, the factory head, had worked as a carpenter in the construction of a new airport in Guiyang, Guizhou for seven years, earning about ¥10,000/year. In 1988, he returned to Xia Qi Tan and invested about ¥40,000 in the new enterprise, of which half was borrowed. Two machines were purchased in the latter part of the year, and production started shortly thereafter.

The factory is housed in a single room where steel wire is drawn for the manufacture of Guosheng's reinforced concrete. The wire itself is purchased from a privately run company in Hangzhou for about ¥1,500/ton, and occasionally from a firm in the county town of Wu Ning, but prices from the latter are higher. Xinglong can generally process one ton of wire in an eight-hour day, or about 300–400 tons/year. He can sell each ton of processed wire for about ¥1,630 for a gross profit of ¥130/ton. The enterprise uses a lot of electricity to run its two wire-drawing machines. Indeed, it uses so much that Xinglong is not permitted to operate during daylight hours. His machines buzz along from 10 P.M. to 7 A.M., and he is fined ¥20/kilowatt if he runs them during the day. In any event, when production expenses are deducted, Xinglong can make about ¥70/ton of processed steel, and figures to earn between ¥15,000 and ¥20,000/year, of which about ¥10,000 can be saved. He has recently built a modest new house of two stalls and two stories, costing about ¥10,000, in which he lives with his wife and two school-age sons. Xinglong has given up agricultural production for full-time work in his enterprise. His brother farms the land allocated to Xinglong's household.

Lineage cousin Wu Mengshan was the proprietor of the Xia Qi Tan Clothing Factory (Fu Zhuang Chang), one of the more successful of the village's several clothing manufacturers. Mengshan had spent five years working in a bamboo/rattan weaving factory in Wu Liang town from 1976 to 1981, earning ¥100/month. In 1981, he put together his own savings with some money borrowed from friends and relatives, managing to scrape together some ¥2,000, roughly half of the start-up capital of the partnership he entered with Wu Desheng in the clothing factory. In the following year, Mengshan bought out his partner, and the factory was subcontracted (cheng bao) to him to operate by the village Communist Party committee.

The factory employed ten workers when it first opened. Their most successful year was 1984–85 when APV was ¥400,000 and they made some ¥30,000 in profit. Mengshan left at the end of that year to take an administrative position in the subdistrict industrial office *(gongye bangongshi)* in Zhang Cun, and profits fell off. While Mengshan earned a salary of ¥2,000/year for the execution of his subdistrict duties, these duties kept him from giving full attention to the operation of the enterprise.

Notwithstanding the distraction, Mengshan's wife took over the day-to-day running of the factory, and APV in 1987 was ¥160,000 with profits of ¥16,000. The factory paid 0.5 percent of APV to the subdistrict industrial office in administrative fees *(guanli fei)* each year, and paid another 0.5 percent of APV in administrative fees to the village. Five percent of APV was paid to the state in taxes *(guojia shui)* each year.

In 1988, nine workers were employed in the factory, earning from ¥70/month to as much as ¥130/month on a piecework basis. Workers used their own sewing machines on the factory premises. An additional twenty workers were employed on an outwork basis performing embroidery in the home, for which a highly skilled worker could make as much as ¥10/day.

Workers who came to work from other villages were provided with lunch each day; and twice a year, once each in summer and winter, all workers were treated to a one-day factory outing to a scenic spot or place of historic interest in the area at factory expense.

Since Mengshan and his wife have abandoned their own agricultural activities and earn no income from agriculture, during agricultural busy season from June to August and in November, when workers returned to their own homes to help with the harvest, Mengshan would close down the factory and the family would take a vacation. In the past, they have traveled to Guangzhou, Guilin, and Huangshan (in neighboring Anhui province) at a cost each time of some ¥3,000.

In 1985, Mengshan built a luxurious three-story dwelling at a cost of some ¥90,000. The factory was housed on the ground floor, and the family of four—Mengshan, his wife, and two sons—lived upstairs. The second floor was really well appointed with carpeting and stylish lighting fixtures. In 1988, rooms on the third floor had just been plastered and painted in preparation for occupation by the family, and were still unused. Mengshan donates ¥1,000 to the village school each year, and he and his wife have savings of upward of ¥50,000.

Since our initial visit, Wu Mengshan has left his administrative post in the subdistrict, closed down the clothing factory in Xia Qi Tan, and opened a large metals shop *(wu jin shangdian)* in neighboring Yi Wu county.

One of Wu Mantang's grand nephews, Wu Pinju, runs an eminently successful woodcarving enterprise, Three Stars Co. (San Xing Gongsi), in Dongyang's Economic Development Zone outside of the county town Wu Ning. In 1968, Pinju began his apprenticeship as a woodcarver at the Dongyang Woodcarving Factory (see Chapter 7). He was among the first from Xia Qi Tan village to study carving, although village residents had worked traditionally in carpentry and masonry. Pinju was one of four apprentices sent to the Dongyang Woodcarving Factory by the then Xia Qi Tan rural production brigade.

His master in the Dongyang Woodcarving Factory was Ying Qinqi, one of the elder generation of carvers who began work at the Dongyang Woodcarving Factory when it opened in 1958. Physically disabled from the waist down from birth, Ying won first prize in a Chinese nationwide arts contest for the handicapped, and he was sent by the central government to represent the nation in an international arts exhibition of works by the handicapped held in Colombia, South America, in 1985. In that capacity, he traveled together with the son of national leader Deng Xiaoping, who was crippled when pushed from a window during the Cultural Revolution, and has since become a national spokesman on behalf of the disabled.

Pinju's wife, Wu Yaping, started carving at the Dongyang Woodcarving Factory as an apprentice in 1982, having been assigned there by the county labor bureau. The couple had been acquainted before Yaping entered the factory, and married several years later. Pinju worked at the Dongyang Woodcarving Factory from 1971 to 1984, whereupon he left the factory to start Three Stars Co. in Lu Zhai village, in the shadow of his former place of employ, with an initial capital investment of ¥5,000 the couple had saved. His wife retained her position at Dongyang Woodcarving Factory into the 1990s, from which the family retained a variety of benefits, including a regular monthly salary, state subsidized health care, the promise of a pension upon retirement, and so forth.

In each successive year of Three Stars' operation, the couple reinvested some 30 percent of their profits, distributing only very small bonuses to their otherwise well-paid workers. Although Pinju is reluctant to take on too many apprentices, since their low level of skill requires too much supervision, a lineage nephew—Wu Chaohui—from Xia Qi Tan, was learning the craft from Pinju in 1988 and 1989, and one of Pinju's older brother's sons—Wu Chaoping, a former apprentice—still worked in the factory.

In the spring of 1988, Pinju and Yaping, after two rather successful years, moved their enterprise and household to a new "high rise" block on the southeast end of Wu Ning, the county town, where they purchased a five-story building for ¥45,000. In 1989, after having received final authorization from the county Rural Industrial Bureau, Pinju, wife, and daughter moved into the fourth and fifth floors of their new premises, with production proceeding on the three lower floors. The labor force expanded from 13 workers to 23 workers, and already Pinju was feeling the need to rent still more space from neighbors next door. But Yaping was very excited about their new self-contained kitchen, equipped with bottled gas, since in their former home in Lu Zhai she had to prepare meals on a charcoal stove on a cramped and exposed second-floor terrace.

During one of our visits with Pinju, a group of outworking carvers arrived on the premises from Bai Yun subdistrict, west of Wuning, bringing a batch of rough carved pieces, carved in their homes, for Pinju to look at, and presumably purchase at roughly one-third of their finished sale price. They would be fine carved and varnished by Pinju's workers, and would help to fill his orders for friendship stores and urban retail outlets.

In 1993, Pinju was employing more than sixty workers, and Yaping had left her job at the Dongyang Woodcarving Factory to oversee the finances of the business at home. Pinju's products had won several prizes, and the magazine *Shanghai Yishu* (Shanghai Arts) published a brief feature article on the success of his enterprise. In the same year, Pinju and Yaping sold their five-story building on the eastern end of Wu Ning town, spent ¥200,000 to acquire two *mu* of land in Dongyang's new Economic Development Zone *(kaifa qu)*, and in the following year invested ¥500,000 in the construction of a six-story free-standing factory to house their rapidly expanding enterprise.

There are several other enterprises in Xia Qi Tan village—a metal bottle cap factory, which in 1987 manufactured 1,000,000 bottle caps and earned ¥20,000 in profit; a workshop in which charcoal cooking stoves are assembled; a household that specializes in the raising of ducks whose flock of 500 produces three broods per year, and earns the household ¥10,000/year.

There are also four small retail shops in Xia Qi Tan, two of which are run as private enterprises. One is a small stall in the center of town selling cigarettes, soft drinks, and sundries. The other had just opened on Bei Jie (North Street) and sold very much the same kinds of products.

There is also a pork shop that is subcontracted to its proprietor by the subdistrict *(xiang)* government, and a state run sundries shop housed together with the village post office across from the senior citizens' center *(lao nian xie hui)* near the northern edge of the village.

Xia Qi Tan village also supports its own primary school, begun in 1967. Up to 1981, there were five classes in the primary section and two middle-school classes. In 1981, the middle school was moved to Wu Liang town, and in 1983, a kindergarten was added to the primary school. Today there are 211 students and 7 teachers. The latter earn ¥64/month base pay and some ¥50/year in bonuses. Senior teachers make as much as ¥170/month.

Primary school graduation is nearly universal in Xia Qi Tan, with 95 percent of its youngsters graduating. Some 60 percent of its youth finish lower middle school, and 20 percent graduate from upper middle school. Xia Qi Tan has produced ten college graduates over the years, and in 1987, four students went on to higher education either at universities or teacher's colleges. More than ten middle-school teachers from the village are teaching in other nearby villages and towns.

The current vitality of the local primary school is closely tied to the success of industrial enterprises in Xia Qi Tan and the villages in its vicinity. Increased income and improvement in general livelihood of the residents of the region have meant significant annual contributions from village entrepreneurs to the school's budget, and make higher levels of education affordable for larger numbers of youngsters.

An index of the changes wrought by economic reforms in the 1980s is evident in a comparison of income figures for the pre-and post-reform periods. During the pre-reform period, roughly 60 percent of village households were deemed "needy," earning only ¥200–300/year. The most well-off households, those with the greatest number of agricultural workers earning work points, earned the equivalent of ¥1,000/year.

In 1989, about eighteen well-off households (4 percent of village households) had incomes exceeding ¥30,000/year, and those deemed needy (with incomes of less than ¥8,000) accounted for only 30 percent of village households. While a certain polarization is clearly evident, the number of needy households has been halved. The wealth introduced into the community by rural industrial enterprise has made it possible for 90 percent of households in Xia Qi Tan to build new houses since the implementation of the reforms. In the early 1980s, a two-story house could be built for ¥7,000–8,000, a three-story house for somewhat more than ¥10,000. But only ten households in the village had sufficient resources to build new houses during those years, and those built at that time are no longer considered very desirable. In 1989, a comparable three-story house would cost ¥60,000–70,000, which has done nothing to stop the accumulation of construction materials and the boom in housing construction in the village. What has done more to slow it down are state concerns about conversion of agricultural land to housing, and state-imposed limits on new housing construction in the village to 1,000 square meters of space per year. All such new construction requires authorization by the subdistrict government (fieldnotes, 5/20/88, interview with Wu Guosheng).

Fortunes of Xia Qi Tan villagers have taken them to all corners of the globe, from Hong Kong to Nairobi to England to the United States to Australia. Local entrepreneurs have extended the horizons of village life while amassing substantial fortunes for themselves, providing supplementary wage labor for their family members, neighbors, relations, and employees. Under the economic reforms, petty capitalist enterprise has reestablished itself as "China's motor" (Gates 1996), providing Xia Qi Tan villagers with a means of meeting material needs with unprecedented success and security.

Chapter 4

Li Tang Village

Li Tang, the native village of Mr. Zhang Mingyao, is a single-surname community less than a kilometer's walk up toward Turtle Mountain (Wu Gui Shan), immediately to the north and east of the market town of Hu Qi (see Map 3). Li Tang is nestled in the lower slopes of the mountain along a formation called "Daoist Priest Covers His Mouth" (Dao Shi Wu Kou), also known as "Rat [Coming] Down the Mountain" (Xia Shan Laoshu). In the early spring, the countryside is lush, and the *li zi* (plum) blossoms explode in sprigs of white all over the surrounding hills.

Local elders of the Zhang lineage say their habitation of Li Tang goes back 9 or 10 generations, probably 200 to 250 years, when a group of Zhangs migrated up into the foothills from Lu Zhuang, a village in the valley that has now been absorbed into the town of Hu Qi. The Zhang lineage, according to the poem by which the generations of its genealogy are reckoned, extended some eight additional generations back in time to the founding ancestor, Zhang Tangyi, who settled in Wu Ning town, the present county seat, 17–18 kilometers to the northwest as the crow flies. The Li Tang branch of the Zhang lineage is itself conceived of as consisting of four *fang,* established during the third and fourth generations of settlement in the village.

The origins of the Zhang lineage of Li Tang are described in the romantic tale of "iron broom" and "iron scoop." As narrated by two village elders, the account runs as follows:

In a neighboring village called Da Tang, there was a peasant household, surnamed Yao, with a daughter who was very ugly. Among other characteristics, she is said to have been bald, and at the age of thirty she was still unmarried. One day, shortly after harvest, a tax collector of the Zhang lineage came through Da Tang village on his rounds. As was customary in the area, the family's grain had been stored up in the

Figure 4.1. **Founders of the Zhang Lineage of Li Tang.**

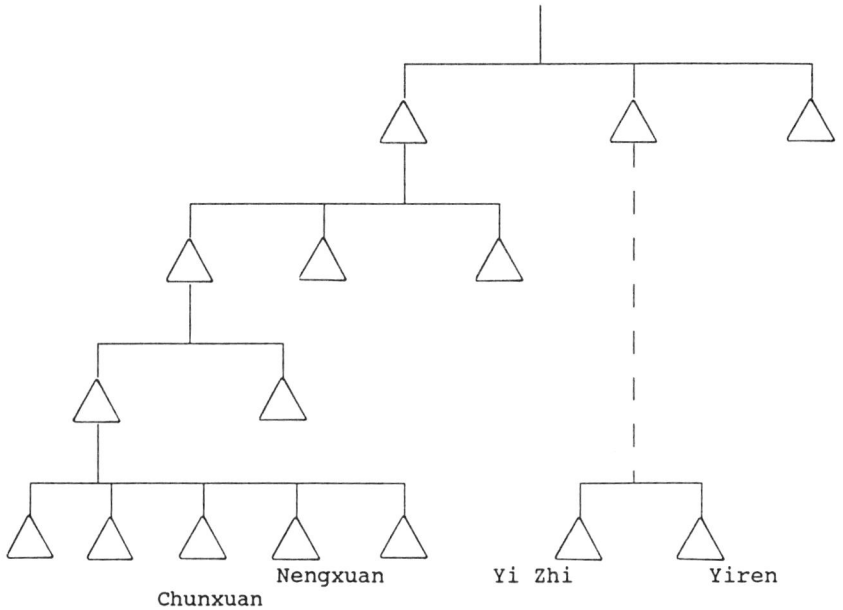

Figure 4.2. **Li Tang Genealogical Poem.**

康寧 祭仁

聖義忠 和

孝友睦淵

任恤禮樂

射御書 教

```
康 is the generation of the lineage founding
聖 is the generation of the move to Lu Zhuang
孝 is the generation of the move to Li Tang
```

attic, and the girl was up in the attic tending to the grain when Mr. Zhang arrived at her home. Ashamed to show her face, she poured the family's tax allotment of grain through a crack in the ceiling into the collector's container. Tax collector Zhang was amazed that not a single grain of the rice spilled anywhere but in the container. A bystander asked if the tax collector was still single. When he replied that he was, the bystander informed the tax collector that the clever woman upstairs was still unmarried. Although he had not yet laid eyes upon her, tax collector Zhang thought out loud to himself, "Such a talented girl I would certainly like to marry." She came down from the attic and agreed to the match. The tax collector's home was in Tuo Tang, one of the constituent communities of the county town of Wu Ning, and as was customary, he sent his relatives to fetch her in a sedan chair on the appointed day. But the girl refused to go.

Her father had for years scolded her for her ugliness and at one point had threatened to "take a broom and sweep her out of the house" if she could not find a husband. Before she would mount the sedan chair, she demanded her father give her a broom. When he at last produced one and gave it to her, she took it with her as she stepped into the sedan chair, and proceeded on the journey to her new husband's home. Along the road, her hair miraculously began to sprout. In Nan Shan Lin (South Mountain Woods) she demanded that the bearers stop. She stepped out, and swept the ground three times. With this action, she took revenge on her father whose village remained small (only thirty households until today), whereas she and her tax collector husband prospered. He was known as "iron scoop/dustpan"—Tie Benji—because he was so good at collecting taxes, and she was known as "iron broom"—Tie Saoba. Hence they were a well-matched pair. She bore seven sons, and the couple adopted another. The sixth son was an official at the court in Beijing during the Ming dynasty and retired to the neighboring subdistrict of Nan Jiang. He had many wives and many sons. One of those sons settled in Lu Zhuang, and it was one of his descendants six generations later who settled in Li Tang village. The Zhangs still go to Da Tang village to pay respects at their ancestral "wife's mother's village" *(wai po jia)* (story told by Zhang Shengliang and Zhang Xinghua).

Li Tang village overlooks the town of Hu Qi, which lies on the northern bank of Dongyang's South River. The town is inhabited by 900 households, of which some 800 are surnamed Zhang. Markets are

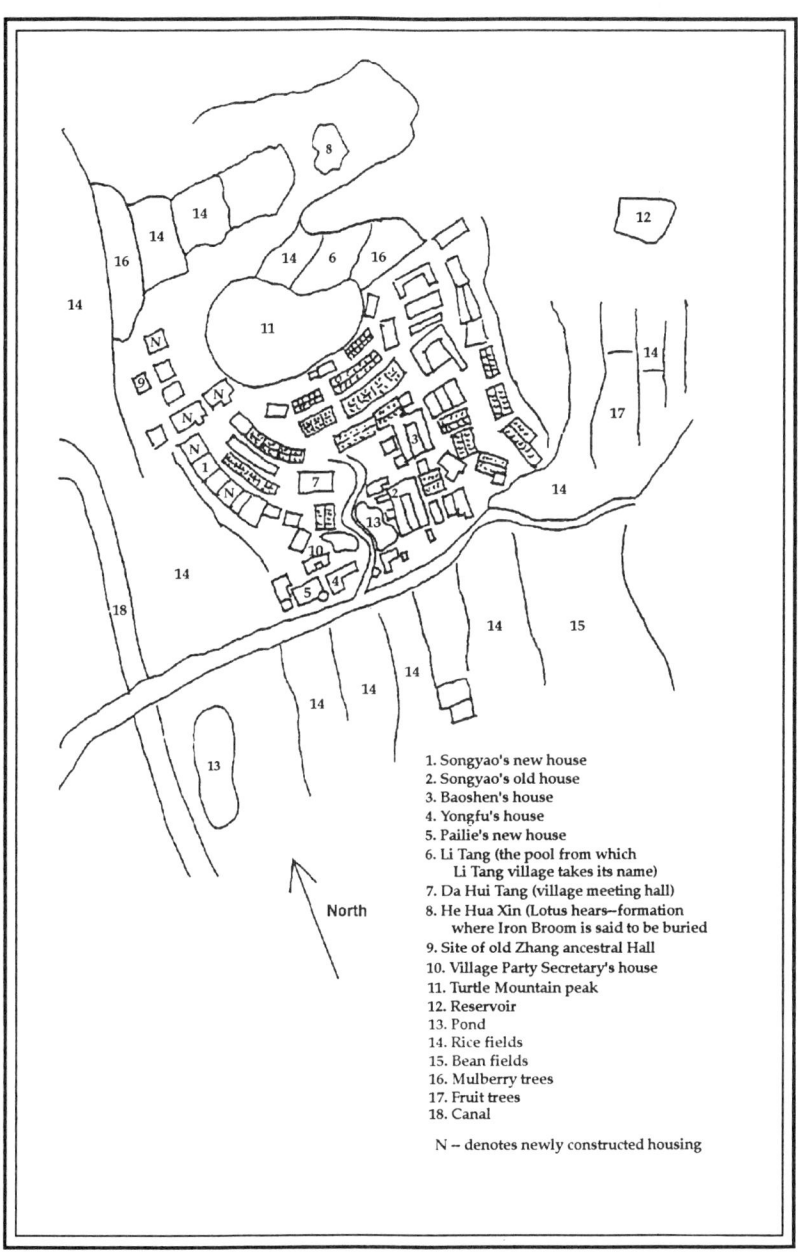

Map 8. Li Tang Village.

held in Hu Qi on the first, fourth, and seventh days of the ten-day market week *(chu yi, chu si,* and *chu qi),* and this is the market most often patronized by Li Tang residents. However, villagers occasionally patronize the market in Guo Zhai town some 4 km to the north, which is held on the second, fifth, and eighth days of the ten-day market week *(chu er, chu wu,* and *chu ba),* or that of Heng Dian town some 6 km to the east, which is held on days 3, 6, and 9 *(chu san, chu liu,* and *chu jiu).* Like the villagers of Xia Qi Tan, Li Tang villagers may get to market on nine days of the ten-day market week.

Hu Qi township was traditionally a center of silk production in Dongyang county, and Li Tang residents produced cocoons in pre-liberation days, although they have produced very few since. Still, a portion of village land is devoted to mulberry tree cultivation (see Map 8), and mulberry leaves are marketed in town to villagers in the area who still raise the worms.

Li Tang village was never well off economically. Its lands were marginal mountain slopes, and village elders recount their memories of destitute village families selling their infant sons into temples as "orphans" for money to survive.

In 1949, when the People's Republic was established, there were 46 households in Li Tang, with a population of 130. In 1988, there were 85 households and a population of 283. An additional 110 lineage members are known who have settled outside the village in Nanjing, Shanghai, Hong Kong and Taiwan. Among these was Zhang Mingyao, who left for Hong Kong in 1948, and presently lives in a new high-rise housing estate in the New Territories.

When I knew Zhang in Hong Kong in the 1970s, he was among the premier carvers in the colony (see Cooper 1980a: 125 ff.). His carvings were of such grace and elegance that he was able to earn a living independent of the factory-organized work regime that prevailed in the woodcarving line. His backlog of privately commissioned pieces extended several years into the future, and he was never at a loss for work.

Mingyao left Li Tang for the first time at the age of twelve to be apprenticed as a woodcarver in the northern Zhejiang county of Hu Zhou. After completing his apprenticeship in 1930, he returned to Dongyang to work with one of the county's illustrious carving masters of the senior generation, Huang Zijin (see Chapter 2). They worked together for two years as itinerants *(yi jia yi hu),* before Zhang went back to Hu Zhou for two to three years. When the Japanese invaded in

1937, production ceased, so Zhang returned home to Dongyang. After the Japanese defeat he went to Shanghai to find work and stayed from 1945 to 1948, whereupon, with Communist victory imminent, he fled to Hong Kong. He worked for several factories owned by Dongyang natives, among which was Yi Hua Sheng Co.

Zhang Mingyao was acquainted with master Lou Shuiming of nearby Heng Dian town, who was in Hong Kong in the late 1940s and early 1950s. Indeed, they played Mah-Jong together. When Lou later returned to Dongyang to great local acclaim, helping to reestablish the post-revolutionary carving industry on the Communist Mainland, Zhang remained in Hong Kong.

For most of his life, Zhang has been hostile to Communism and the Communist regime in Beijing. Indeed, the "patriotic" Woodwork Carver's Union of Hong Kong, affiliated with the pro-Beijing Federation of Trade Unions, considered Zhang a "troublemaker." But in the late 1980s, with the reform policies of Deng Xiaoping replacing the ideologically charged policies of Mao Zedong, Mingyao has become a frequent visitor to Li Tang, and he has even entertained younger brother Songyao on a visit to Hong Kong. Mingyao now looks forward to returning to Li Tang to retire and live out his remaining days in his native village in the countryside.

From about 1971, Mingyao worked independently out of his home in Hong Kong. At one point, he was commissioned to carve a reproduction of the imperial dragon throne in Beijing for the presidential palace in Taiwan. Upon completion, many people in Taiwan, including President Lee Teng-hui himself, invited Mingyao to come live and work in Taiwan, but he declined. In the end, the Taiwan government awarded him an honorary doctorate for his contribution.

In recent years, Zhang's eyes have begun to fail, and he has taken on less work. His five children, raised in the single room of a Kowloon resettlement estate, are grown and earning a living of their own. Mingyao's youngest daughter is a clerk in a medical equipment company in Hong Kong, and his eldest daughter is married and raising a family. Middle daughter has been studying chemistry and, more recently, computer science at Michigan State University. Eldest son works as a fireman for the Hong Kong government, and youngest son was just entering the job market. When at last the Hong Kong government condemned the old resettlement estate in which they lived, Mingyao and his wife qualified for new Hong Kong government hous-

Figure 4.3. **Mingyao's Segment of Li Tang #2 Fang.**

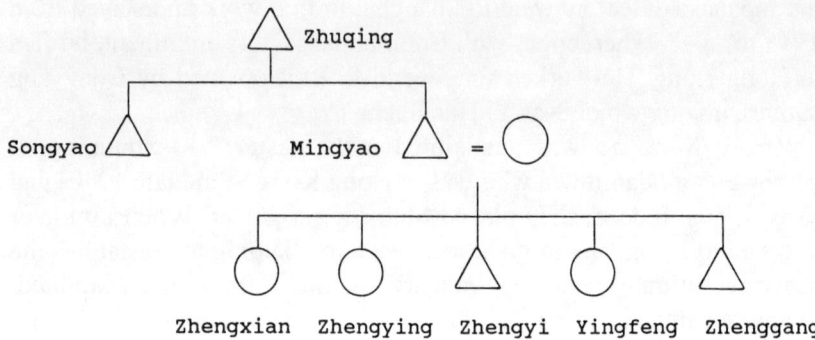

ing in Shatin in the New Territories, and were allocated a luxurious three-bedroom apartment.

The present population of Li Tang village consists of 129 men and 154 women in its 85 households. Thirty-five villagers work outside Li Tang, most of them in masonry *(ni gong)* and carpentry, but return to the village during agricultural busy season. Mingyao's younger brother Zhang Songyao spent most of his work life as a carpenter in Fujian province, and since retiring, continues to work as a watchman for a large construction firm in the suburbs of Shanghai for most of the year. Forty-four Li Tang villagers are employed in enterprises in the town of Hu Qi and walk to work each morning; another forty, mainly older folks, work the fields and/or perform cottage work in the village itself.

Li Tang has 162 *mu* of irrigated fields *(tian)* on which rice is grown, and 28 *mu* of dry fields *(di)* on which three principal crops are grown in succession each year—one crop each of wheat, white bean, and dry rice—the latter replacing the corn or sweet potato grown traditionally. Some 60 *mu* of hill land *(shan di)* are planted with fruit trees, mulberry, tea, sweet potatoes, tobacco, and other dry field crops.

Seven *mu* of irrigated land are devoted to growing the medicinal herb *yuan hu,* and vegetables are grown on another 14 *mu. Yuan hu* has been planted since 1960 when some 10–20 *mu* were set aside for its cultivation by the collective production brigade then in existence. At that time, one *mu* of the stuff could produce 3 *dan* of the herb (1 *dan* = 100 *jin* = 50 kg). At ¥80/*dan,* or ¥240/*mu,* it was an important supplement to collective income. Since the division of land to households in 1983, much less has been planted. The herb severely depletes the soil, which

Figure 4.4. **Agricultural Cycle of Li Tang Village.**

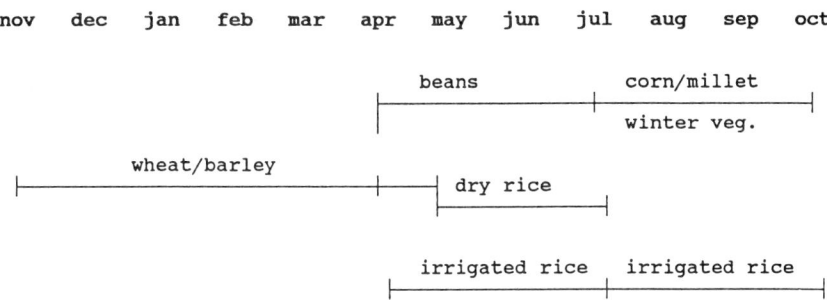

cannot be planted again for three years, and under household farming is not cost effective. The rest of the irrigated land in the village is planted in two rice crops per year, followed by one crop of wheat.

Before liberation in 1949, villagers grew mainly corn and wheat. Irrigation was ill-developed, and the fields of Li Tang relied exclusively on natural rainfall. In the spring rainy season, rice and wheat were planted. In the dry fall, they planted corn and wheat. The second wheat crop often meant the difference between having something to eat and going hungry in the spring. Its failure could mean disaster.

In the 1950s Li Tang villagers harvested only one crop of rice per year, of about 250 kg/*mu,* but in the late 1950s and early 1960s they began getting a second crop of rice from fields newly irrigated under intensification policies associated with the Great Leap Forward. Unfortunately, it was not very good quality grain, and yields were quite low, only 100 kg/*mu*. In the late 1960s and early 1970s new strains of rice with a shorter growing season were introduced, and they now get 400–500 kg/*mu* from the first crop, plus another 500+ kg/*mu* from the second crop (6/15/88, interview with Zhang Guimu, party secretary).

Li Tang village at present pursues the following planting and harvest schedule: Wheat/barley, planted in dry fields at the beginning of November, is harvested in early to mid-May. Beans, interplanted in the wheat in early April on dry fields, are harvested in early to mid-July. Rice is planted in early April in irrigated fields, and again in mid-May in dry fields earlier planted in wheat. Both rice crops are harvested together in late July. Rice is then planted again in late July in irrigated fields, and harvested in mid-October. With minor variations of a week or two one way or the other, this schedule is characteristic of most villages in Zone 2 of Dongyang county.

Land reform began in 1950 in Li Tang. At the time, roughly one-third of the land in the village was owned by those who cultivated it. About one-third of the balance of village land was *chang tian*—land controlled by lineage ancestral halls *(ci tang)*, the majority of which was held by lineages other than the Zhangs. The remainder of village land was owned by two absentee landlords, one in Xi Zhuang village surnamed Jin (metal) from whom the majority of land was rented, and another, also surnamed Jin, from Tian Li village whose holdings in Li Tang were much smaller. In those days, one *mu* of land produced a first crop of 200 kg of rice of which 50 percent was owed in rent. Tenants in those days paid no rent on the second crop, usually wheat.

At the time land reform was instituted in 1950, only one household in Li Tang was classified as a landlord family, that of Zhang Baoshen. Everyone else was classified as a middle or poor peasant. Baoshen owned only 5 *mu* of land, and was not really all that well off, but he was one of two officials native to the village who served in the KMT government.

Baoshen began his career in the Jiangxi soviet, and served in the Red Army of the Communist Party. When the Communists abandoned their Jiangxi base area and embarked on the "long march," Baoshen fled and ultimately joined the KMT to become a military policeman *(xian bing)*. He was later appointed county head of Sui An county, and ended his official career in Yong Jia county near the coastal city of Wenzhou, first as a county head and then as a low-level administrative commissioner. He retired to become a middle-school principal in Shanghai, but he was sought out and arrested by Communist forces, and sent back to Wenzhou where he was executed around 1955 (fieldnotes, 3/25/89, interview with Zhang Fude).

Modern villagers stress that Baoshen was not an evil man, and that the fortunes of modern entrepreneurs in Li Tang dwarf by many magnitudes the meager resources for which "uncle" Baoshen was submitted to revolutionary justice. While his house was larger than most, parts of it remained unfinished for years due to lack of funds. Indeed, Baoshen was often strapped for cash, borrowed money from his poorer cousins, and, being literate, wrote letters for the folk in Hu Qi town as a way of earning a little extra money. Among his contributions to the village was the planting of peach and plum trees on the hillsides around the village, for which a broad local market developed, and organizing the construction of the road from Li Tang to Hu Qi town (fieldnotes, 6/15/88, Li Tang).

During land reform, Baoshen's property and land were confiscated and sections of his house were apportioned to poorer village families who continued to call him uncle or grandpa, but that indulgence was cut short by his subsequent execution.

One of Baoshen's protégés, Zhang Ronghai, began a thirty-five-year period of hardship at this time. Having been introduced into the Guomindang (Nationalist Party) by his uncle, Ronghai rose through the ranks of the army to become a bodyguard of Chiang Kaishek. Having failed to escape to Taiwan with other Nationalist forces in 1949, Ronghai was undergoing "reeducation" at a branch school of the Communist Government Military University in Sichuan province during land reform in Li Tang. He was apparently not diligent enough in his efforts to convince the Communist authorities of his loyalty to the new regime. Therefore, rather than being assigned a new job, he was bound and sent back to Li Tang where he lived for three years under house arrest, assigned a room away from the rest of his family. His brothers disavowed him, and his wife was thrown out of their house. The family had nothing to eat, no clothes, no belongings.

After three years as an outcast in his native village, he was sent for two years of labor reform *(lao gai)* in the county, and was later assigned to a labor reform camp in Jinhua city. There, there was nothing to eat. The inmates ate grass, bark, frogs, snakes, insects, anything they could find. They were beaten regularly. Many of his fellow prisoners died during the ordeal. Others were taken out and shot. He recalls having spent long hours cangued in stocks. Upon release from camp, he continued to "eat bitterness" for more than twenty years (see below), somehow managing to survive. His case was reheard in 1980 at the behest of his brother who traveled to Beijing to request a reversal of verdict. In the end, the county government, under instructions from Beijing, approved a reversal of verdict on him in 1983, and the document authorizing it is hung framed on the wall of his original house reassigned to him and his wife. Having had his citizenship restored, he now receives a state pension of ¥116/month.

During land reform, each person (including children) was allotted 0.5–0.6 *mu* of mainly dry fields *(di)*. Soon thereafter, in 1951, mutual aid teams were organized, varying in size from 3–4 households to as many as 10 or more. Membership in the teams was voluntary.

In 1953, collectivization began. Teams joined together into co-ops, membership in which was also voluntary. Some mutual aid teams continued as teams. In 1956, high-level cooperatives were organized in which membership was compulsory. In Li Tang, there was no strong opposition. The co-op organizers were sent up from Hu Qi as there was no party branch in the village.

In 1958, in conjunction with the Great Leap Forward, Li Tang became a production team in Hu Qi brigade of Hu Qi commune. The commune was centered in Hu Qi town and was roughly the same size as present-day Hu Qi subdistrict *(xiang)*. It consisted of twenty-four brigades. In 1962, Li Tang became a production brigade, composed of four production teams, in a smaller Hu Qi commune.

In 1966 the Cultural Revolution reached Li Tang, and the slogan of "destroy the four olds" was promulgated. There really was not much left in the way of "old" in Li Tang. Some old paintings, old books and genealogical records were destroyed, but there were no temples, or elaborate ancestral halls or other symbols of the old society left. The movement was really pretty simple in Li Tang. There was no factional struggle, no organized pro–Liu Shaoqi faction. Villagers "struggled" with the descendants of Zhang Baoshen, his sons and grandsons. One of the latter was working in a coal mine in Jiangxi province. Villagers were going to bring him back to answer for his and his grandfather's "crimes," but his performance at the mine was excellent, and his unit *(danwei)* refused to let him go.

For lack of other suitable objects of struggle, "reactionary" Zhang Ronghai was subjected to another installment of "bitterness." He was dragged out again and beaten, made to kowtow to Mao Zedong, forced to make daily reports of all his activities and conversations to party authorities. His wife, overwhelmed by the new stream of vitriol directed against her family, asked for a divorce, but finally decided not to go through with it. As mentioned above, Ronghai survived to see his verdict reversed, and lives on in modest if bitter retirement in Li Tang.

Big character posters *(da zi bao)* denouncing the village head, Zhang Shujin, and the party secretary, Zhang Chunyuan, were put up by *zao fan pai* rebels. Other posters inquired accusingly "Who stole trees from the hillside?" and "Who's been stealing vegetables?" Villagewide meetings were held attended by leaders from the commune government, but they never saw the People's Liberation Army in Li Tang. Villagers kept up planting lest there be nothing to eat. There were no real serious issues at stake in Li Tang, and the big character posters are said to have exaggerated the mistakes of local cadres "10 times or 100 times." According to local residents, the distinctions between the two lines (capitalist and socialist) were very blurry. For them, the "two line struggle" had no empirical referent.

At one point, a thief was brought over from the neighboring township of Guo Zhai by the militia. Among his other crimes, he had stolen money from Zhang Mingyao's father before finally being apprehended. Villagers held struggle/criticism sessions against him, and he was returned to Guo Zhai to be dealt with.

People with family members in Hong Kong or Taiwan, who often suffered discrimination in other regions of China during this period, were unaffected in Li Tang. Many Taiwan-based relatives were not discovered until the 1980s, and those with relatives in Hong Kong were never subjected to any harassment on that account in Li Tang (3/25/89, interview with Zhang Fude).

In 1983–84 land was subcontracted *(cheng bao)* to households under the economic reform policies. Li Tang brigade was dissolved and Li Tang village was recreated. Several village ponds were converted to irrigated fields at the time. Each person received 0.6 *mu,* the same as the allotment during the land reform of the 1950s. All the land in Li Tang has always been ploughed by oxen and cattle, and continues to be so today. Since the subcontracting of land to households, land parcels became too small to make machinery efficient, even if increased wealth might have made power tillers accessible. There are a total of three cows in the village that plough all its land at a cost to households of ¥18/*mu* paid to the owner of the cows, Zhang Baoshan, agnatic cousin of Baoshen.

In 1984, the second year of household responsibility in agriculture, one *mu* of irrigated land *(tian)* produced 859 kg of grain. Weather was particularly good, and rainfall especially timely. It was their best year ever, and they did not equal such yields in the four subsequent years. However, current yields still represent a considerable improvement over those obtained during the collective period.

As Li Tang is too small to support a school of its own, its youngsters attend primary and middle school in Hu Qi town. Since the late 1970s, more than 90 percent of village youngsters finish primary and lower middle school, with 40 percent graduating upper middle school. Two Li Tang youngsters are at present studying at a university, and several are preparing to take the entrance exam.

Li Tang had no traditions of business or entrepreneurship. While there was work outside the village in construction, this was mainly wage labor or contract work in carpentry and masonry. The village's first enterprise was a metal factory begun in 1978–79 just after the economic reforms of the Third Plenum of the Eleventh Central Committee of the Communist Party (TPECC) went into effect. The factory went bankrupt after two or three years.

Today, there are no enterprises located in the village itself, but one of its residents, Zhang Rongfu, is the manager/proprietor of a substantial wall covering factory located on the southern outskirts of Hu Qi town south of the river. This enterprise, the Dongyang Wall Covering Factory, was begun in June 1977 as a commune-run enterprise. The buildings went up in the course of the year, and production began in December. When the communes were dissolved, responsibility for production reverted to the township *(zhen)* of Hu Qi, with Zhang Rongfu appointed as manager.

The enterprise is centered on a single machine that laminates paper onto the back of home-loomed hemp, and sometimes straw fabric. The paper is then dyed, dried, trimmed of its rough edges, rolled up, and packed for export. A separate enterprise on the factory grounds produces woven silk brocade on a bevy of old Jacquard looms, but the silk fabric is unaccountably not used in the production of what might be very attractive wall coverings.

Original capital for the enterprise was ¥100,000, of which state loans accounted for ¥40,000, loans from the brigade *(da dui)* accounted for ¥40,000, and credit from the factory that provided the machinery accounted for ¥20,000. The enterprise remained a collective enterprise, and its workers continued to "eat out of a common pot" *(chi da guo fan)* until 1987, when the enterprise was subcontracted *(cheng bao)* to Rongfu. According to Rongfu, business had fallen off since 1985, and in 1988 wages were rising and raw materials were increasingly expensive. Nevertheless, the factory overfulfilled its first *cheng bao* contract in 1987, so bonuses were generous.

The factory employs 87 workers on the premises who earn average wages of ¥1,500/year/worker, paid on a piecework basis *(duo lao duo de)*. In addition, there are some fifty-five looms in surrounding village homes, including Li Tang, where hemp and straw cloth to be laminated on the wall covering paper is woven. Each loom can produce 6–8 meters/day, depending on the closeness of the weave required. Work at the loom is often performed in brief periods of respite from other chores. A fifteen-meter roll of closely woven cloth pays its weaver ¥76, and can generally be completed in two days of full-time work. The factory pays ¥52,000/year in wages to village workers in their homes. Ninety percent of the factory's wall coverings are exported, mainly through the Zhejiang Provincial Art Craft Import–Export Corporation in Hangzhou, to markets in America, France, Belgium, and West Germany. In 1987, the factory employed eighty-seven workers, and earned ¥140,000 in profit (fieldnotes, 6/15/88).

One-half of 1 percent of the factory's APV is paid to the rural industrial bureau in administrative and licensing fees *(guanlifei)*; 45 percent of the enterprise's gross profit is paid to the state in profits tax. Of the remainder after taxes, 30 percent is allocated to worker bonuses in four grades in accord with workers' skill, attitude, and so forth, with ¥1,200/year for grade one workers, and ¥300/year for those in grade four. The factory manager earns considerably larger bonuses for fulfilling contracted production targets. Forty percent of after-tax profits are allotted to reinvestment in enterprise production. The final 30 percent is clawed back by the township *(zhen)* government in *cheng bao* fees.

In 1989, factory manager Zhang Rongfu bought the wall coverings factory outright from the township for ¥860,000 and the factory became a privately owned and managed enterprise *(siying qiye)*. Rongfu borrowed most of the money: ¥300,000+ from banks, ¥200,000+ from the county foreign trade office *(wai mao ju)*, ¥200,000+ from the provincial foreign trade office, and ¥60,000 from Hu Qi township.

Township *(zhen)* authorities insisted that Rongfu pay ¥60,000/year to rent the premises. Rongfu was holding out for an arrangement in which he would rent only half the premises, but the township government insisted he pay for all the space. In addition, the factory had a car and a truck which the township authorities seized when the factory was sold, and were insisting on payment of an additional ¥150,000 from Rongfu if he wanted them back. When we left the county in 1989, Rongfu was still wrangling with township authorities over the conditions and obligations of the respective parties to the final settlement with respect to the land, buildings, and machinery of the enterprise.

The internal organization of the factory remained the same in the transition to private ownership, and the contracted APV for 1988 was the same as in 1987—¥1,600,000. In fact, the factory cannot make enough to meet its orders, so fulfilling their contractual obligations should be no problem.

Zhang Rongfu is among those villagers of Li Tang with family in Hong Kong. His father, a carpenter named Zhang Xingde, moved to Hong Kong in 1947 and lived there for most of his adult life, keeping in close touch with his fellow villager, Zhang Mingyao. It is unclear from the family history why Rongfu never moved to join his parents, but in recent years he has traveled to Hong Kong twice to visit the family. The family suffered a loss last year when Rongfu's father was killed in an automobile accident.

Rongfu's widowed mother lives on in a flat in a Hong Kong government high-rise housing estate in Kowloon together with Rongfu's younger brother and sister. The flat is decorated with family photos, including those of Rongfu's past visits, the marriages of his two younger brothers, and the imperative funerary picture of his father. Rongfu's mother hailed originally from the town of Guo Zhai (see Chapter 5), and is well connected in the Dongyang expatriate community in Hong Kong.

One of Rongfu's sons is a driver at the wall covering factory and earns ¥120/month plus ¥300/year in bonus wages; another works repairing machinery at the silk weaving factory on the wall covering factory grounds and also earns ¥120/month plus a similar bonus; a third farms the family's 3 *mu* of irrigated land and 1 *mu* of dry land. Rongfu's household raises two pigs, some chickens, and harvests 2,700 kg of grain each year. Rongfu's wife is a technical assistant at the factory and earns ¥120/month plus ¥300/year in bonuses. Rongfu earned a salary of ¥200/month as factory head, and ¥2,000/year in bonuses for his enterprise's performance in 1987.

The family spends roughly ¥1,800/year in subsistence expenses, and ¥1,000/year entertaining guests during festivals and at New Year's, and claims a yearly surplus conservatively estimated at ¥2,000.

Rongfu's new house, a truly impressive L-shaped structure of seven stalls and two stories, was begun in 1984 and took four years to complete at a cost of ¥44,000. Of that, ¥32,000 was provided by his father in Hong Kong. Another ¥4,000 was borrowed. Interior decoration work on the new premises required a full year to complete. When the house was finally finished, there was the obligatory housewarming for relatives and friends, expenses for which were more than ¥2,000.

In the past, the family relied on remittances from relatives in Hong Kong to purchase its food, so Rongfu's present circumstances represent quite a change. Around the town of Hu Qi, he is referred to by his associates and friends as "Big Capitalist" *(da zibenjia),* and in 1993, the newly privatized factory was doing well with expanded export markets in West Germany and Japan.

Rongfu's lineage brother Zhang Zuming runs a much smaller operation out of Li Tang village, marketing dyeing materials. Zuming served in the army for five years from 1980 to 1985. After leaving the army, he worked for two years as a salesman on a commission basis for a leather clothing factory in Dongyang River subdistrict, where with bonuses he earned ¥200/month. In 1987, he worked for a year in a clothing factory in Hu Qi township in commission sales, again earning some ¥200/month. Later in the year, with the experience and contacts established in his career as a salesman, he began his own private *(geti)* enterprise.

The enterprise entails no actual production. Zuming serves as a middleman, soliciting orders for dyeing materials, while making a circuit of Dongyang county on his motorcycle. His company maintains an office in the provincial capital of Hangzhou, manned by his sister's son, and together, they seek out materials nationwide to meet their local orders. In 1987, the enterprise made a profit of about ¥10,000; 1988 figured not to be as good as the previous year since the materials market had become more competitive. However, during our visit with Zuming, he had just received a telegram offering ¥380,000 worth of dye from a new factory in Manchuria, and he figured that in turning it over he could make ¥50,000 (fieldnotes, 6/20/88).

The enterprise is privately run, and was established with an initial capital investment of ¥30,000, some of which was borrowed. As owner of a private enterprise, Zuming may elect one of two methods of tax payment, either 3.3 percent of APV according to receipts, or 10 percent of profits, both of which he finds excessive.

Zuming's enterprise supports him, his wife, and their three-year-old daughter. The family farms 1 *mu* of irrigated fields from which it harvests 750 kg of grain a year, and 2 *mu* of dry land from which it harvests 500 kg of fruit and subsidiary crops a year. They raise one pig a year, valued at about ¥300, which the family slaughters and consumes during New Year's. The family has planted a portion of their dry land in plum trees, and earns about ¥50/year from the fruit. Their household expenses include ¥2,000/year for subsistence, and some ¥400–500/year in festival observances and ceremonies. The dyeing materials company nets a surplus of ¥10,000/year.

Zuming is at present constructing a new house of four stalls, two of which will be two stories, and two of which will be three stories. It has cost ¥30,000 so far, and will probably cost about ¥60,000 when finished. His present premises are half a stall of three stories.

There are several construction contractors *(bao gong tou)* who operate from Li Tang village, of whom the most successful is Zhang Pailie. Employed in Shanghai as a team leader in the Dongyang Construction Co., he is said to have made ¥90,000 last year in bonuses for fulfilled contracts alone, first among contractors in the company, and another ¥30,000 in sales of machinery to other factories. Those who know him say he is good for a minimum of ¥30,000/year, although the surplus his family reported to us was only ¥3,000/year.

Pailie's only son works with his father in the construction company as a mason and earns ¥2,000/year; elder daughter is an upper middle school graduate presently preparing for the entrance exam to university; younger daughter is still in middle school.

The family farms 2.5 *mu*, and harvests 1,750 kg of grain/year, worth about ¥1,000 on the private market. Fifty kg are owed to the state in taxes. They raise a pig, consumed at New Year's, and earn some petty cash from fruit trees. About ¥200/year are earned weaving cloth for Zhang Rongfu's wall covering enterprise, and wage labor earns the family about ¥5,000/year to which they admit. Household expenses include ¥1,200/year for the family's subsistence, and another ¥1,800/year to maintain Pailie in Shanghai. Some ¥500/year are expended in festival celebrations, and another ¥220/year in school fees for the girls. About ¥200/year is spent on fertilizer, and another ¥24 is paid to the village for the privilege of caring for a portion of its fruit trees.

Pailie is in the midst of building a new house of three stalls and three stories, which remains unfinished. The construction proceeds as they get materials. It is genuinely grand, with an impressive cylindrical tower in one corner, the most dramatic structure first visible as one comes up the road to Li Tang from Hu Qi (fieldnotes, 6/21/88).

Another enterprise of Li Tang worthy of note is the carpentry shop of Zhang Zhongsheng. Zhongsheng makes furniture, window frames, and coffins to order for villagers and townsfolk. His enterprise is run out of his home as a household sideline *(jiating fuye)* from which he earns ¥2,000/year.

Zhongsheng's two sons are both employed in construction, the elder in Shanghai, the younger still an apprentice in Hangzhou. The family farms 3 *mu* of irrigated land and 0.5 *mu* of dry land, harvesting 2,000 kgs of grain/year. Pigs, chickens, and silk sideline work bring in ¥1,500/year. Household expenses included ¥1,800/year for subsistence, and ¥300–400 in festival observances, mainly New Year's, leaving the family a surplus of about ¥1,500–2,000/year. Approval for the construction of Zhongsheng's new house is still pending in the subdistrict office. He is ready to begin building on approval, but will need more money to complete it (fieldnotes, 6/21/88).

The town of Hu Qi is also the site of one of the more distinctive woodcarving enterprises of Dongyang, Ai De Artcraft Products Factory. Manager Zhang Wanlong was originally apprenticed in a commune-run enterprise of more than eighty workers in Hu Qi that has since closed down. Wanlong left the factory in 1980, and went to the famous pottery center of Jing De Zhen in Jiangxi province where he worked as a woodcarver for two years. He returned to Dongyang where he worked as a carver in the Plaited Bamboo Products Factory in Wu Ning town for 6 months and the county Arts and Crafts Co., Gongyi Meishu Gongsi (the former craft marketing cooperative), for 6 months.

Zhang began planning his present enterprise, Ai De Artcraft Products Factory, in 1985 and commenced production in 1988. The enterprise produces carvings exclusively on Christian themes. Zhang's father had converted to Protestantism in pre-revolutionary times and in 1986 provided Zhang with an introduction to attend the Second National Christian Conference, organized by the China Christian Association and the China Christian Patriotic Committee in Nanjing, at the Jin Ling Consolidated Theology Institute.

Dongyang county had been missionized beginning in 1920 with the arrival of the Honorable Shen Kunhua, who established Catholic congregations in Heng Dian, He Zhuang, Qian Shan He and Weishan. Catholic priests Lorne McFarland and John Kelley preached in the county in the early 1940s, and Thomas Morrissey and Guo Mutian in the mid and late 1940s. Between the Japanese defeat in 1945 and the Communist victory in 1949, Dongyang was among the more heavily missionized of Jinhua prefecture's constituent counties with seven functioning Catholic churches, more than any other Jinhua county (JHWSZL 1987: 152).

Both Catholic and Protestant congregations were located primarily in the larger towns in Dongyang county—Wu Ning, Wei Shan, Liu Shi Kou, Hu Qi, Heng Dian, Nan Ma, Fang Jun, and Huang Tian Fan. Beginning in 1949, missionary activities were severely restricted by the new Communist authorities, and during the Cultural Revolution, strictly forbidden. But with guarantees of freedom of religious practice implemented after the Third Plenum of the Eleventh Central Committee in 1978, Christianity has revived, and converts are on the increase. In some places, the demand for Sunday services is so great that three shifts are held, and each shift is full to overflowing. This is quite unprecedented in Dongyang's history, and the unity of spirit, group loyalty, and warmth of feeling among parishioners is remarked upon by their neighbors (Jiang n.d.d).

At the National Christian Conference in Nanjing in 1986, Zhang Wanlong had the opportunity to see many examples of Christian arts and crafts from many countries in the West and other parts of the world, and began to formulate the idea of employing Dongyang woodcarving techniques in the execution of Western Christian themes. He received encouragement and advice from several important dignitaries at the conference including Ding Guangxun, the bishop of China; Han Wenzao, the assistant head of the Zhejiang Province Christian Society; and Lin Yixuan of the Theology Institute. During the lunar New Year in 1987, he took some samples of his new Christian-inspired carvings to a party at the bishop's house. Bishop Ding presented them to the teachers and students at the Institute as a fine example of "China's Christian Crafts," and the praise inspired Zhang to continue his efforts.

At the end of the year, teachers and students at the Theology Institute invited Zhang to their Christmas party which was attended by more than 500 foreign guests. A West German television crew came to the institute and took some footage of Zhang and his newly designed Christian carved wood articles. As a result of the exposure, he received still further support and encouragement from Christians in China and abroad.

In the summer of 1988, Mr. Zhang and his wife made trips to Christian churches in Hangzhou, Shanghai, Nanjing and elsewhere seeking orders for their new enterprise, and in September of 1988 they formally applied to the Industrial and Commercial Bureau to open Ai De Factory. The factory is a private enterprise with 13 workers, not necessarily Christians themselves, 11 carvers, 1 carpenter, and 1 painter/varnisher. Counting Mr. Zhang and his wife, who both carve, there is a total of 15 workers. There are also 20 or so outworkers in workshops in Wu Ning town and neighboring Pan An county to whom he turns for outwork services when his orders outstrip his small labor force.

Zhang has a repertoire of more than 100 products, all of which are inspired by Christian themes and biblical stories, and all of which are of his own design. During our visit, he was working on a carved wood diorama of a nativity scene. Most of the enterprise's products are marketed in China, primarily to visiting westerners, but Zhang is already in contact with American and Japanese Christian groups abroad and hopes to expand his export market. Not surprisingly, his best season for business is around Christmas time, and most of his wares are marketed in Nanjing, with Shanghai, Suzhou, and Hangzhou taking smaller quantities. The town of Hu Qi in which the factory is located also has a small Christian community but is not a significant market for his goods.

More significant is the domestic market for cremation urn boxes decorated with Christian motifs for the relatively small but still substantial community of China's urban Christians, among whom Zhang's distinctive wares are appreciated. Like urban residents throughout China, Christian Chinese in the cities must be cremated upon death, and Mr. Zhang's enterprise is probably the only producer of urn boxes with Christian decoration in the country. There is surely enough work in this market niche alone to keep his 15 workers continuously occupied into the indefinite future in meeting the demand.

Mr. Zhang is proud of his "departure from the tradition that all the others follow," and of his "union of Eastern and Western traditions." In operation for less than a year, the enterprise did not make a great deal of money in 1988, but Zhang planned an APV of ¥200,000 in 1989, and in 1993 he was busy receiving foreign delegations of Christians from Australia and the United States to discuss export possibilities. He attributes the results he has already achieved to the state's "open" policies, especially with respect to the free practice of religion. His enterprise could not exist otherwise (fieldnotes, 3/22/89).

The example of Mr. Zhang's enterprise is interesting for a number of reasons. For one thing, the discovery of his enterprise occurred by chance and had not been prearranged by our county hosts. The Christianity of his enterprise also represents something of an ironic twist since the commoditization of carved wood furniture production for export from the treaty ports of Hangzhou and Shanghai in the early twentieth century was initiated by entrepreneurs who were also Chinese Christians (Xu 1986; and Chapter 2 above). Although these early entrepreneurs did not produce Christian articles, Mr. Zhang's enterprise cannot help but evoke thoughts of their early efforts in the line. It is almost as though his "departure" from tradition also represents something of a "return" to tradition, to a later inflected, commoditized, missionized, colonial tradition of the early twentieth-century Chinese treaty ports.

But the Dongyang Christian community of which Zhang is a member may also give us pause to reflect on its revival in a context of proliferating commodity production and wage labor in the Chinese countryside under the reforms. Marx, after all, has written that "for a society based upon the production of commodities, in which the producers in general enter into social relations with one another...whereby they reduce their individual private labor to the standard of homogeneous human labor..., Christianity with its *cult* of abstract man... is the most fitting form of religion" (Marx 1967: 79).

Perhaps it is not so surprising to find that alongside the revitalization of traditional folk belief and ritual, the Christian churches of Dongyang, whose activities were forcibly suppressed during the Cultural Revolution, have reestablished sizable congregations with many new worshipers.

In any event, Li Tang villagers have taken advantage of the opportunities afforded by the economic reforms to accumulate substantial fortunes in several cases, and to secure comfortable subsistence in most households. Political relaxation has been welcomed, and overseas as well as domestic economic connections revitalized. Like Xia Qi Tan, day-to-day agricultural tasks are carried out by the women and the elderly, with substantial employment outside the village supplementing the harvest. Residents return during New Year's and during the planting and harvest seasons to help out, but remain absent most of the rest of the year.

Again, like the people of Xia Qi Tan, Li Tang's residents have become agents in the creation of flexibly organized petty capitalist enterprises, snatching start-up capital from Hong Kong relatives for local enterprises, elaborating world market links for local village looms, expanding Dongyang county's expatriate networks in the construction trades, performing contract work for the Taiwan government. Even world Christianity is nearby, both in the form of a new congregation and a "traditional" woodcarving enterprise turning out Christian products in Hu Qi town.

─────── Chapter 5 ───────

Guo Zhai Town

It is said of Guo Zhai Town that it has three precious things;
No grass grows in its lake.
Birds do not nest in the paifang *of its ancestral hall.*
Beggars do not loiter about its Xiang Hou temple.

Some four to five kilometers due north of Li Tang is the market town of Guo Zhai, literally the "residence of the Guos," from which Mr. Guo Youxing emigrated to Hong Kong in the 1930s.

The founding ancestor of the Guo lineage, Guo Ziyi, lived during the Tang dynasty in Fen Yang prefecture of Shanxi province. Later, he took up residence in Tian Tai county in Tai Zhou prefecture where he fathered four sons. The Guo genealogical poem records thirty-five generations from Guo Ziyi to the present day.

The descendants of Ziyi lived on in Tian Tai for seven generations until the Southern Song dynasty (A.D. 1127–1278) when descendants of the fourth son, Guo Ai, arrived in the present area, and settled in Ma Zhai, literally surrounded by Ma lineage families. The Guos gradually came to outnumber the Mas, and finally the name of the town was changed to Guo Zhai.

In the years that followed the initial settlement by the Guos, the town developed commercially, and a great "road of ten *li*" (5 km) was constructed housing shops and homes along its length, stretching from Tong Keng village to Hu Yi village, the latter now known as Guo Yi, one of the modern administrative divisions of Guo Zhai town (more below).

In generation 14, the town was looted and burned to the ground by bandits, to be rebuilt under the leadership of Guo Zhenbao of the 15th generation. Zhenbao is said to have had six sons, yet the six extant branches of the Guo lineage nevertheless derive from two of

Figure 5.1. **Guo Genealogy.**

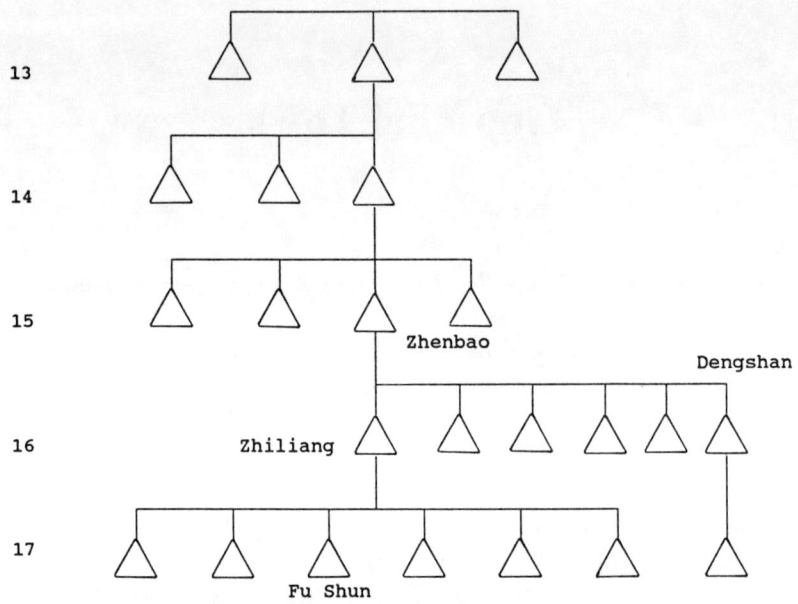

those sons, Zhiliang and Dengshan (6/25/88, interview with Guo Zhigen and Wang Wenfa, see Figure 5.1).

It is said of Zhiliang that he was taken away and imprisoned as hostage to his family's unpaid taxes. Leaving a wife and four sons behind, he was taken to Shanxi province and locked in a dark, crowded prison with other tax debtors. Somehow, he managed to survive the harsh treatment and atrocious conditions, while others died around him. The jail keeper thought this miraculous, and sized up Zhiliang as no ordinary mortal. He offered his daughter to Zhiliang in marriage. The marriage took place, and Zhiliang sired eight more sons.

Meanwhile, Zhiliang's mother prayed constantly for her son in the local temple in Guo Zhai, offering to construct two giant candles to illuminate the temple in Buddha's honor if only her son might be returned to her. During this time, Zhiliang's brother Dengshan was mistreating his nephews in their father's absence, prompting Zhiliang's oldest son to leave home in search of his father. After many years of wandering, he tracked his father down and urged him to return. Zhiliang took two of his sons by his second wife with him and returned to his place of birth in Guo Zhai where his four sons by his earlier marriage still resided. Five of his sons produced offspring, who, taken together with Dengshan's one son, constitute the founding ancestors of the six branches *(fang)* of the Guo lineage of Guo Zhai town. Since the foundation of the six branches there have elapsed some 17 generations with an 18th well on the way.

Commencing with Zhiliang's return to Guo Zhai, the giant candles (some three meters high and nearly one meter across) promised to the Buddha by his mother were produced each year, and lit at Yuan Xiao festival (lunar 1/15). Each year, new candles were ritually greeted by the townsfolk after a grand parade, with the candles carried at the head, in front of an image of Hu Gong, a patron official of Dongyang (FSZ 1985: 101; also see Appendix 3). All the shops along the route set off fireworks, and the atmosphere was extremely animated. After the parade, the candles were housed in the Xiang Hou temple honoring Hu Gong (on the road to Qian Qi village, once again in use), and the candles burned continuously until the following year, honoring the vow of Zhiliang's mother. Each year, the tradition of making new candles was continued until liberation in 1949. From that time, the ceremony was banned as "superstition" until 1988, when controls on such activities in the countryside were loosened, and the production of the candles each year has since resumed.

Guo Zhai town is known for the famous Stone Cave Academy (Shi Dong Shu Yuan), located some 2 km from town in a village called Xia Jie Tou. Siu (1989) has characterized the activities of such academies in the following terms:

> [County academies were] started as gentry led institutions to promote local education, [and] became centers for political networking among the subcounty elites and between them and imperial officials. Their organization closely resembled that of the lineage, and their activities confirmed the ideals of lineage, territory and literati culture. Together, they made explicit a system of authority diffused in the everyday social life of both elites and peasants. (1989: 67)

The Stone Cave academy of Dongyang county was constructed during the Song dynasty in the Shao Xing reign period (A.D. 1131–1163) in a particularly scenic setting meant to inspire intellectual contemplation. The Song poet Lu You taught classes there on two different occasions, and wrote more than twenty poems set in its environs.

Song neo-Confucian scholar Zhu Xi, whose commentaries on the Confucian classics became the state-sanctioned orthodox interpretation, came to teach four times, and thus the Shuyuan attained a certain notoriety. Indeed, Guo Zhai became a pilgrimage site for the educated and cultured Confucian gentlemen of the region in traditional times, who came to honor and sacrifice to master Zhu each year during the ninth lunar month. An image of Zhu Xi hung in the hall, over which there was a poem in the master's own hand:

Cang yan yi shi shi nian qian;
Ba jing hui kan yi chang ran.
Fu po lin shen liang wu ji,
Qie jiang yu ri fu can pian.
[Already ten years since hair and skin have turned;
Looking in the mirror in memory I feel sorrow.
Shoes wear thin, I am on the point of profound understanding,
I must use what days are left to attend to my texts.]
(DYWZX 1985: 71)

In 1989, the Academy was not open to the public, but plans were afoot to effect its refurbishing and renovation as a historic landmark *(wenwu dian)*.

Guo Zhai is a market town, older, larger, and more genealogically ramified than either Xia Qi Tan or Li Tang. It consists of some 1,500 households with a population of about 5,000 residents. Markets are held on the second, fifth, and eighth days of the ten-day market week *(chu er, chu wu,* and *chu ba),* as noted above, synchronized with the markets in Hu Qi (days 1, 4, and 7) and Heng Dian (days 3, 6, and 9).

In 1955, Guo Zhai was divided into four agricultural producers' co-ops—San sheng (Three victories), Xin jian (Reconstruct), Zhong he (Central harmony), and Zeng feng (Increase prosperity). These were reorganized into three production brigades during the Great Leap Forward in 1958, when Guo Zhai became the administrative center of Lamp Pagoda (Deng Ta) people's commune. These brigades have become three administrative "villages" since the dismantling of the communes in the 1980s, although Guo Zhai remains a largely single-kin community.

The three villages are:

Guo Yi (Guo No. 1) village, described by locals as the residence of the Tian Guo (heaven Guos). It is the largest of the three constituent administrative units with some 600 households. The ancient Road of Ten Li ran through the territory of Guo Yi.

Zeng Feng (Increase Prosperity) village, described as the residence of the Di Guo [earth Guos], with four hundred households, encompasses the territory of the earlier cooperative of the same name.

Hu Shan (Lake Mountain), described as the residence of the Ren Guo [people Guos], encompasses the section of town from which Mr. Guo Youxing originally emigrated in the 1930s, and to which he has returned in semiretirement since 1978.

One of four of his mother's thirteen children to survive the rigors of traditional childbirth, Guo Youxing was apprenticed at the age of fifteen to a Hong Kong factory owner from Guo Zhai, who had sent word back to the countryside that a couple of apprentices were needed. It was 1937 and times were hard in the county. The Japanese had already invaded China, and their armies were expected in Dongyang before long. Youxing's parents decided to send their son, and somehow scraped together the necessary ¥5 for the boat ticket from Shanghai. With only the clothes on his back, Youxing set off for Hong Kong. His master-to-be was waiting for him at the pier, took him to buy a set of new clothes, some socks and shoes, got him a haircut, and then took this "country bumpkin" off to the factory to begin his career as an apprentice.

Upon completing his apprenticeship, Youxing worked in Hong Kong briefly until the Japanese armies reached the British colony. Thereupon, he fled to Shanghai where he worked as a carver in the suburban county town of Jia Xing for a few years, returning to his native Dongyang for several months until the Japanese defeat in 1945. He returned to Shanghai and worked in a small factory for a year or so before moving on to work at George Zee Co. (Xu Hai Ji), one of Shanghai's larger carved wood furniture factories (see Chapter 2). In 1949, when the Communist government came to power, proprietor Xu Guoxiang moved his enterprise to Hong Kong, and Guo Youxing returned with him to the environs of his former apprenticeship, where he worked until 1952. He then returned to China, and took up work in Guangzhou at the New China (Xin Zhong Hua) furniture factory for three years before returning home to Dongyang. Guo moved to Shanghai in 1956, where he worked for a spell in a recently organized cooperative production team, later amalgamated with several others into the Shanghai No. 1 Woodcarving Factory. Guo worked there until retirement in 1979. Guo's perambulations were typical of woodcarvers of his generation.

Somewhat atypically, however, Guo was among the small number of craftsmen who returned to Communist China in the 1950s, and participated in the craft cooperativization movement, in Guo's case in both Guangzhou and Shanghai. Along with other experienced masters, he worked at training a new generation of apprentices, and getting the post-war, post–civil war industry going again.

Later, in retirement, his knowledge and skills were called upon to help organize and launch the Arts and Crafts Factory of Heng Dian town in 1978, where his daughter and son-in-law both worked for several years before starting their own small private carved wood enterprise in 1988–89 (see Chapter 6). In recognition of the early assistance he rendered to the Heng Dian enterprise, the factory provides Youxing with all the wood he requires to design and execute such creations as he might fancy in his retirement.

Indeed, since retiring, Youxing continues to work at home on privately commissioned carvings, which the recent economic reforms have encouraged. Many of his past apprentices, of whom he has had more than 100, have urged him to open a factory of his own under the reforms, but he has thus far declined. He earns ¥86/month in retirement pay and another ¥20/month in subsidies that pretty well cover his immediate subsistence needs. In 1988, the Handicraft Import–Export Corporation of Guangzhou had commissioned him to carve a large dragon boat peopled with figures from the classic Chinese novel *Dream of the Red Chamber,* for which he would receive ¥3,000 upon completion. Most recently, he traveled to Zhu Hai Special Economic Zone in Guangdong province where one of his sons is employed, to serve as an adviser/consultant to a carved furniture factory there, earning ¥800/month for several months' work. For Guo the prospect of getting rich is simply not worth the aggravation of running his own enterprise. Demand for his technical skills and organizational experience are sufficient to maintain a reasonably comfortable existence for him and his wife.

Something of a renaissance man, Guo Youxing is also an expert in the Shao Lin martial arts tradition. Up at 5:00 A.M. each morning, he practices his skills on a hill just outside of Guo Zhai, and is in excellent physical shape. He teaches martial arts during summers to young people in the town of Hu Qi for a fee of ¥150/month, and he finished second in a provincewide martial arts competition for senior citizens. He is also an accomplished Mah-Jong player, having learned the skills in Hong Kong, and makes mincemeat of the competition in the Guo Zhai senior citizens' center *(lao nian xie hui)*, where playing the game is once again permitted.

In traditional Chinese fashion, Youxing has already made provision for his "future home," having acquired the land on which his grave will be sited in a geomantically favorable location on a hill overlooking an orchard just outside of Guo Zhai.

Hu Shan "village," in which Youxing resides, has 791 *mu* of land of which 750 *mu* are irrigated *(tian)*. Its 510 households grew rice, wheat, and corn for their own subsistence in traditional times, although the corn crop has, as elsewhere in the county, been replaced with an additional dry rice crop. Roughly 70 percent of Hu Shan residents trace their descent to a branch of the Guo lineage descending from Guo Fushun, or what residents refer to as branch or *fang* #3.

Some thirty-odd non-Guo families settled in Hu Shan in the late 1950s when Heng Jin reservoir, seven kilometers east of town, was constructed during the Great Leap Forward, inundating several villages in the neighboring subdistrict. Some of the residents were settled by county authorities in Guo Zhai, and several have been quite successful in entrepreneurial endeavors since the initiation of the economic reforms (see below).

Since the economic reforms, some 300–400 town residents have taken up work outside the community; among them is Guo Youxing's eldest son Wuliang. Wuliang works as a carpenter in the No. 4 Construction Company of Zhejiang province in the provincial capital of Hangzhou. The company built and decorated the ultramodern International Mansions Hotel in Hangzhou. In 1982, Wuliang signed on to a work team sent by the company to Iraq for two years to build and decorate mansions of the ruling elite. He returned to China, stayed for a year, and was sent off to Kuwait on a similar project for two years thereafter.

The Iraqi project was organized by Japanese contractors who hired a crew of 300 Chinese workers. Wuliang and his cohorts worked twelve-hour days, with two days off each month. They earned 10+ Iraqi Dinars/day, (about ¥130+/day, the equivalent of a month's wage in China). Of this total, the workers received 10 percent in wages (¥13/day × 28 days = the equivalent of ¥364/month in foreign exchange), with the Chinese state clawing back the other 90 percent. But families at home continued to receive the workers' regular monthly wages while the workers were also paid at the workplace in Iraq. An additional "hardship" stipend for living expenses away from home was also included in their remuneration. If one was frugal, one-third of the stipend could be saved, and this surplus in addition to one's overseas wages could be redeemed in foreign currency certificates good for purchase of fancy imported foreign goods upon return to China. Each overseas worker received a card authorizing him to legally use the restricted access outlets in China that deal in such products. In addition, the crews had some time for recreation on the way to the work sites when they stopped briefly in Thailand, and on the way back to China when they stopped briefly in Pakistan. During each of his years abroad, Wuliang returned home with upward of ¥10,000.

A portion of Wuliang's overseas earnings have been invested in a bathhouse in Guo Zhai (four stalls in which one can shower in private with hot water and soap), and the business, managed by his wife, is brisk. Wuliang has considered giving up his job in Hangzhou to work full-time at the bathhouse. Indeed, his father, keen to have his oldest son nearby, has urged him to, but thus far he has refrained. Wuliang's son was trained as an apprentice in the craft of woodcarving by grandfather Youxing, and is now at work in the profession.

Youxing's two younger sons, Xingliang and Weiliang, are also carvers. Weiliang took advantage of a state policy in effect for many years that allowed a state-sector worker upon retirement to pass his position on to a descendant (so-called *ding ti* arrangements). For several years, Weiliang occupied the workbench from which Youxing retired at the Shanghai No. 1 Carving Factory. Weiliang later left the factory to seek greater fortune in the special export processing zone of Zhu Hai in Guangdong province.

Many other Guo Zhai residents work far from town in factories and in the construction trades of carpentry and masonry. As elsewhere, these are mainly younger menfolk, who return to help with the harvest during agricultural busy season *(nong mang),* and for Chinese New Year. Others work nearer to home in various parts of the township in clothing factories, woodcarving enterprises, restaurants, and shops.

The construction of two hundred rooms of new housing by individual households since the start of the reforms, and the installation of running water to households in the town in 1983, at a cost of some ¥60,000–70,000 for each constituent "village," are signs of the vitality that the reforms have brought to Guo Zhai. Guo Zhai also sports its own primary school built on the site of the old ancestral hall *(zong ci)* of the Guo lineage, and a new middle school is under construction. The Senior Citizens' Center *(lao nian xie hui)* is a beehive of activity, as well as a rich repository of historical knowledge and local lore.

Hu Shan "village" does not administer or license any "collective" factories or enterprises, although there are some seven privately run *(geti)* enterprises within its borders—two construction materials factories, one brick factory, and four clothing manufacturing workshops. Most of the collective enterprises in Guo Zhai town are administered by the township government. But the management of these collective enterprises has now for the most part been subcontracted *(cheng bao)* to individual factory managers, and all that remains of their collective heritage are the administrative fees and *cheng bao* obligations paid to the township government by their managers.

Among Guo Zhai's enterprises are several substantial, export oriented factories, as well as many smaller firms that market products or provide services domestically and locally.

Among the larger enterprises is the Dongyang No. 6 Knitting Factory Zhen Zhi Liu Chang, located in Qian Qi village, 2 km to the east-northeast of town. Begun in 1984, it presently employs 265 workers, who operate knitting machines, dye the knit cloth, and manufacture high-quality underwear and jogging suits. Ninety percent of their product is exported to Japan, France, Czechoslovakia and other countries, through the provincial foreign trade corporation in Hangzhou. The corporation also provides some raw materials—principally cotton, which comes from outside the province.

The enterprise began with a start-up capital investment of ¥1,500,000, of which ¥1,200,000 was borrowed from the state bank. Interestingly, each of the 200 or so workers originally hired paid ¥800 to secure his or her job, contributing ¥160,000 to the original start-up capital. Shares valued at ¥140,000 were also sold publicly to the local citizenry. Worker and citizen shares pay a dividend of 0.7 percent/year, the same interest as that paid by state banks. The factory was begun as a large, collectively run *(xiang ban)* factory, but was subcontracted to its manager in 1987, when the factory earned a profit of ¥430,000 on the basis of an APV of ¥5,000,000. Projected APV for 1988 was ¥10,000,000.

The factory pays 5 percent of APV to the state in taxes, and 1 percent of its profits to the Rural Industrial Bureau in administrative fees *(guanli fei.)* Workers' average wages were ¥87/month, with bonuses of roughly ¥23/worker/month awarded for speed and quality (fieldnotes, 6/27/88).

Another substantial enterprise run by Guo Zhai residents is the Pan An Electric Lightbulb Factory, located in neighboring Pan An county. Pan An was at one time within the borders of Dongyang county but became an independent county in 1985. The factory has the distinction of having qualified to become a local state-run enterprise *(difang guoying qiye),* which means that its production, supplies, and raw materials, as well as the wages and benefits paid to workers, are included in the national economic plan. Workers enjoy security of employment as well as a variety of perks and privileges, retirement pensions, and state-subsidized health care, which their co-workers in the private and collective sectors do not enjoy.

The enterprise was begun in 1981 in Bai Shui Kou village, Dong Men *xiang,* by its proprietor, Guo Zhongyun, with start-up capital of ¥50,000 borrowed from the bank, his sister's husband, and family. In 1982, production was moved to Hu Shan in Guo Zhai town, but in 1984 it was moved again to Pan An town to get better market exposure. In 1987, performance was deemed impressive enough, and their commodities important enough, that the factory was integrated into the national plan as a local state-run enterprise *(difang guoying qiye).*

In 1988, Zhongyun's elder sister's husband, Guo Zhongxiang, undertook sole responsibility for managing the factory under subcontract *(cheng bao)* from the Pan An county government. Zhongyun undertook to handle the marketing end of the business under a similar contract. The *cheng bao* contract for 1988 called for ¥5,000,000 in APV, and projected profits of ¥470,000—the same as in 1987. If they fulfill the contract, each brother-in-law earns ¥10,000 in bonuses. For 1989 APV was projected to be ¥8,000,000 APV, with profits of ¥600,000. Fulfilling the contract would earn each ¥11,000.

Zhongyun makes a wage of ¥265/month. If he and his brother-in-law fail to fulfill their contract, not only does he lose out on his bonus, but he is also retroactively docked $200/month, leaving him with a basic wage for the year of ¥65/month.

The factory employs more than 200 workers, who earn an average wage of ¥140/month. Of these 200 workers, 100 are employed in three associated branch factories: a glass factory employing 50+ workers, a metal factory employing 30+ workers, and a bakelite factory employing 20+ workers. Bonuses of ¥1,000/worker/year are awarded if the *cheng bao* contract is fulfilled.

The enterprise pays 5 percent of its APV to the state in commodities tax, 1 percent of APV to the subdistrict *(xiang)* in education tax, 1 percent of APV to the subdistrict in construction tax, and 10 percent of gross profits to the county economic committee *(jingji wei yuan hui)*. Twenty percent of the enterprise's net profits are reinvested in production.

Although Guo Zhongyun still lives with his wife in the household of his father and mother, materials have already been purchased for the construction of a new house for himself and his wife, consisting of two stalls and three stories at a cost of ¥30,000. Zhongyun's wife also works in the electric light bulb factory and earns a wage of ¥100/month.

The family farms 2 *mu* of irrigated land and harvests 2,500 kg of grain a year. They raise two pigs a year, which they consume themselves at New Year's, valued at about ¥600. Zhongyun earns more than ¥10,000/year at the factory, and his father and mother earn ¥2,000/year and ¥1,000/year, respectively.

Family expenses include ¥2,400/year for subsistence, and ¥1,000/year for New Year's celebrations. Blessed with five daughters, household expenses for Duan Wu festival when daughters return home amount to ¥250. In any event, the family's annual surplus was between ¥10–15,000 (fieldnotes, 6/27/88).

Of the smaller enterprises of Guo Zhai is the Xiang Shan Paper Products Factory run by Wang Wenping. It was begun in 1978 as a private *(geti)* enterprise. Prior to 1978, Wang worked in a collectively run printing factory. Work was farmed out to workers in their homes and most of their business was printing labels for a fertilizer factory in the county town of Wu Ning.

His present operation makes cardboard boxes and printed paper wrappings. He employs six workers who earn an average wage of ¥100+/month. The enterprise is organized on a *lai liao jia gong* basis, with customers providing raw materials that are processed for a fee. Wang made a ¥10,000 profit in 1986, and again in 1987 on an APV of ¥70,000 each year. He pays 8 percent of APV to the state in taxes, and ¥60/year to the County Industrial and Commercial Office *(gong shang chu)* in administrative fees.

Not a native of Guo Zhai, Wenping moved to the town along with some thirty other Wang families from one of the villages inundated by the construction of Heng Jin reservoir in 1958. His is a four-member household, consisting of himself, his wife, and two sons in primary and nursery school. The family farms 2 *mu* of irrigated land, and harvests 2,000 kgs of grain per year. Without extensive kin networks in town, Wenping hires help to plant and harvest his land allocation. He raises two pigs a year, consumed by the household at New Year's, valued at ¥600. His factory nets him about ¥10,000/year. Family expenses include ¥3,000/year for subsistence, ¥700/year in ceremonial expenses for New Year's, and ¥500/year in ritual observances and gifts.

Wenping began building his new house of three stalls, three stories in 1985 at a cost of ¥30,000. It is indeed a very lovely house, beautifully decorated and furnished. Wenping has already purchased the land to build a matching house of three stalls, three stories directly across from the present structure. The land cost ¥2,400, construction has already been approved and the foundation already laid. It would to cost ¥80,000 to complete.

One of the more interesting and successful enterprises in Guo Zhai is that of Xu Xinghuo, proprietor of Xi Wu Orchards. In 1981, Xinghuo arranged with subdistrict authorities to have 200 *mu* of hill land *(shan di)*, including a pond which serves as a local reservoir subcontracted *(cheng bao)* to him for the purpose of beginning an orchard. At the time there were no fruit trees on the land, but he set about planting them himself. His orchard has become very well known, and visitors come from the county, the subdistrict, and elsewhere to look it over and study his methods. Xinghuo's biggest problem is getting enough fertilizer. He uses some 2 tons/year. He claims to have been ¥6,000 in the red in 1987 due to purchases of new saplings and fertilizer, and in part because of the expense of two funerals in the family. He expected to clear ¥10,000 from the sale of fruit in 1988 as prices were on the rise. Xinghuo also plants trees for lumber at a cost of ¥0.35 each. After four years, he sells them for ¥40 each for plywood manufacture.

From 1981 to 1988 Xinghuo has invested ¥30,000 in his orchards. He borrowed ¥2,000 from the bank initially, the rest having been borrowed from friends and relatives. He pays back the loans as he sells his fruit. Indeed, he often gives his creditor friends and relatives fruit in repayment of their no-interest loans.

He hires up to 20 workers at ¥3/day when he needs them, as he does in the early summer when he harvests 10,000 *jin* (5,000 kgs) of plums at ¥32/100 *jin* (¥3,200), and 4,000 *jin* (2,000 kgs) of peaches at ¥35/100 *jin* (¥1,400). Friends and relatives also come to help.

Xinghuo avoids taxes due to his improvements to the land, and his tax holiday appears to be indefinite. The township government has encouraged his efforts, and officials *(ganbu)* from all over the country have come to inspect his operation.

Xu Xinghuo was another of the folk who moved to Guo Zhai when the Heng Jin reservoir was constructed in 1958. However, he was in the army until 1964, and therefore did not take up residence in Guo Zhai until then. He married a local woman, Guo Lamei, and resided in the household of her father, agreeing to have their children take the Guo name. His is a four-person household consisting of himself, his wife, and two sons. The elder son has worked as a mason in a construction team, but at present helps his father in the orchards. Younger son is still studying in middle school.

The family farms 5 *mu* of irrigated rice fields under the care of his wife, in addition to the fruit trees, and harvests 5,000 kgs of grain a year (valued at about ¥2,000). They raise pigs, which net a cash income of ¥1,000/year. The orchards net about ¥4,000–5,000/ year, and Xinghuo also raises fish in the pond on his *cheng bao* land, which brings in about ¥2,000–3,000/year.

Family expenses include ¥1,680/year for subsistence, ¥400/year in New Year's observances, and ¥400 in festival observances and gifts. Two funerals in the past year for Xinghuo's wife's father and mother cost a total of ¥3,000, and the marriage of his son Guo Lixin in the coming year is expected to cost ¥6,000. Xinghuo plans to build a three-stall, one-story house in Hu Shan at a cost of ¥10,000, but construction had yet to begin in 1988.

In the center of town is the photography studio of Guo Xinhua. Begun in 1986, it is a private *geti* enterprise that nets its proprietor ¥4,000/year. Xinhua's household consists of four persons—himself, his wife, and two small daughters. His wife's father was the proprietor of a photography studio, so she knows the business, and has a hand in managing the shop. Xinhua was a construction contractor *(bao gong tou)* in masonry *(nigong)* in the provincial capital of Hangzhou. He worked on his own soliciting contracts, and still does some technical advising in construction from time to time, earning about ¥130/month for such work. But at present the photography studio secures subsistence for the family, and all the equipment and accessories are in place.

Xinhua is not looking for big money, and is more or less content with his life as it is.

The family farms 1 *mu* of irrigated land every other year. In alternate years, the land is sublet to an acquaintance who undertakes the tax obligations for the plot. Family expenses include ¥2,400/year for subsistence, and ¥600/year in New Year's and festival observances, leaving a yearly surplus of about ¥1,000/year.

The land for their new three-stall, three-story house cost ¥3,200 in 1983, and was awarded to Xinhua on the basis of his having submitted the highest bid. The house was completed in 1985 at a cost of ¥30,000. The photo studio on the ground floor opens out onto one of the town's main streets, convenient to its customers who include schoolchildren, workers, and officials requiring photographs for their identification and work cards, as well as those needing recreational snapshots processed and developed.

Just around the corner from Xinhua's photography studio is the woodcarving processing shop of Mr. Xu Wenxin. Wenxin studied carving with master Guo Wanlong, former factory manager of the subdistrict-run woodcarving factory in Guo Zhai town. Master Guo retired in 1978 and moved to Hong Kong.

After completing his apprenticeship, Wenxin worked in the subdistrict factory for thirteen years. He met his wife, Li Maofang, also a carver, while she was apprenticed at the factory, and they were married in 1982. Her father worked at Shanghai No. 1 Woodcarving Factory as a carver, and her older brother is presently employed there. An older sister works at the Dongyang Woodcarving Factory.

The couple live in Gao Tang village, some 5 km from Guo Zhai town, and their little privately run processing shop was begun in 1985. At present, they rent the quarters in the center of town for ¥15/month. Two additional workers are hired at an average wage of ¥200–300/month. The enterprise pays 10 percent of its APV in taxes to the County Industrial and Commercial Bureau *(gongshang ju)* and that is the extent of its obligations to the state.

Xu purchases his own raw materials in the lumber market in Hu Qi town, and sells mainly to hotels in Shanghai and urban arts and crafts retail outlets *(fu wu bu)*. During our interview, Xu was working on a relief carving depicting a scene from the White Snake Chronicle, to sell for ¥240. In 1987, he and his wife earned about ¥4,000/year from enterprise profits, and wages the enterprise paid to each as carver workers.

The Xus still farm their household land themselves, 2 *mu* of irrigated rice fields allocated to them after the breakup of the communes. They harvest 3,000 *jin* of grain to support themselves, their son, and Xu's mother and father, and raise two pigs each year. They recently purchased an older single-story dwelling of three stalls in Gao Tang village at a cost of ¥2,500 (fieldnotes, 6/25/88).

The economic reforms have brought new prosperity to residents of Guo Zhai. From the upper reaches of the "petty" capitalist sector, the No. 6 Knitting Factory increasingly markets its goods abroad, and the Pan An Lightbulb Factory enjoys a national market. Guo Zhai residents have undertaken contract work in the Middle East, sojourned in the special economic zones of the south, and participated in the creation of new enterprises in the neighboring town of Heng Dian (see Chapter 6). Like their fellow Dongyang residents of Xia Qi Tan and Li Tang, they have taken full advantage of the market reforms to transform their lives in ways unimaginable a decade before.

Chapter 6

Heng Dian Town

In the previous chapter we noted that in the course of his woodcarving career, Mr. Guo Youxing had helped establish a woodcarving enterprise in the town of Heng Dian, some eleven kilometers to the southwest of Guo Zhai. Guo's daughter, Guo Shifang, began her own woodcarving career in that factory, the Heng Dian Woodcarving Arts and Crafts Factory (Mudiao Gongyimeishu Chang). She met her future husband there, and the couple has since gone on to establish their own woodcarving enterprise in Heng Dian town (more below).

Heng Dian happens also to have been the native town of Master Lou Shuiming, and a center of the Dongyang woodcarving industry from very early on. It still counts several elderly retired masters among its residents, and the town is rich in the lore of the carving trade.

The Heng Dian Woodcarving Arts and Crafts Factory is still in operation. Its roots lie in a Heng Dian production brigade–run enterprise begun in 1971, which brought together workers of several small shops from villages in the suburbs of Heng Dian town, but ceased production in 1978. Most of its 38 workers sought employment elsewhere, but a short time later 12 of those workers reorganized, with advice and assistance from Guo Youxing, Ge Zhangde, and other master carvers, and the encouragement of the Heng Dian Township Industrial Office *(gongye bangongshi)*. The factory was one of the Office's early efforts at organizing rural enterprises under the economic reforms, based as it was on locally available traditional skills. Up until 1981, the factory worked on a "bring materials add labor" *(lai liao jia gong)* basis, but in 1982 began producing finished products on its own. Under the dynamic leadership of factory manager Wu Chuwei, the enterprise has prospered.

Manager Wu Chuwei was born in 1949 of a landlord family, and thus suffered many disadvantages from the start under the new communist government. He was apprenticed rather late at the age of twenty, and studied with two different masters. The first was Master Guo Songlin for whom Wu worked at home. As a result of restrictions placed on people like Wu of "bad class background" during the Cultural Revolution, his master was not allowed to bring Wu into the workshop with him. Wu would bring his finished work to his master, who corrected it, made suggestions, and sent his apprentice back home.

When Master Guo Songlin died of ill health, Wu was introduced to Ge Zhangde of Nan Jiang subdistrict who was making bridal furniture on an itinerant basis in the countryside of Pan An. Wu completed his apprenticeship with Ge beginning in the early 1970s, spending five years with Ge altogether. Ge now helps out instructing apprentices in the Heng Dian Woodcarving Arts and Crafts Factory (more below).

At age twenty-eight, Wu Chuwei went to Yong Kang county to manage a subdistrict enterprise. After a year, Heng Dian township called him back to manage the Arts and Crafts Factory, and he has been factory manager ever since. With the onset of the economic reforms, the Communist Party has begun expanding its recruitment of managerially competent personnel, and despite his bad class background, Wu has been admitted to the party, and is also a member of the county People's Political Consultative Conference (Zhengzhi xieshanghui) (fieldnotes, 3/27/89, interview with Ma Jinpin). Wu earned the honorary title High Class Craft Master *(gaoji gongyishi),* producing a written thesis in the context of a correspondence course that was published in the newspaper *Gongyipin Xinxi* (Art Craft Product News) in late 1988.

In 1986, the old factory premises were clearly overcrowded, with workers all jammed together workbench upon workbench. One room was occupied by some thirty apprentices crowded together working on relatively simple pieces, and carpentry was carried on in a separate premises with a battery of heavy machines. All were awaiting completion of a new building under construction, a somewhat smaller version of the massive Dongyang Woodcarving Factory—smaller in scale, similar in style. They would add fifty workers when the new quarters were completed in 1988.

In 1987, ¥90,000, or 47 percent of profits, was reinvested in the enterprise. Under the *cheng bao* contract that year, 30 percent of profit was paid to the Heng Dian Industrial Company *(gongye gongsi)* and the balance of 23 percent was divided among the workers and management in bonuses.

Table 6.1

Production Figures for Heng Dian Woodcarving Arts and Crafts Factory

Year	Annual Production Value	Profits	Workers	Taxes Paid
1980		¥1,000>in debts	12	
1981	¥35,200			¥16,600
1982	48,000			26,000
1983	135,000	¥15,326	110	37,200
1984	240,900	25,186	144	52,000
1985	364,200	35,200	152	68,000
1986	1,351,900	142,000	186	122,000
1987	1,684,000	189,730	238	176,000
1988		252,000		272,000

Nowadays apprentices in Wu's factory must pay a fee of ¥200 for their first six month's training. Since the implementation of the economic reforms, the freeing up of the labor market has made it harder to keep newly trained apprentices, especially when they reach a point in their training when their skill level might begin to pay dividends to the factory. The fee minimally reimburses the factory for its efforts on the apprentice's behalf, while also guaranteeing a minimum level of commitment to learn.

Manager Wu has also had difficulty with labor turnover more generally, and has lost workers to Guangdong province where wages for skilled carvers are higher. While Wu is generally sympathetic to his workers' desires to better themselves, the investment of time and effort in the initial training of apprentices is significant enough to require that the latter pay a fee for the privilege.

Apprentices learn to care for their tools first and get their own set within the first three months or so. They get a living allowance *(shenghuo fei)* of ¥15/month for the first six months, and thereafter, wages of about ¥100/month. Highest wages in the factory are ¥300–400/month, but most workers are quite young and do not expect to earn such high wages until they have had a good deal more experience. Indeed, during our visits, apart from a small number of carvers in their thirties or forties, there was hardly a *lao shifu* (old master) in sight.

One *lao shifu* we did encounter is the general instructor for all apprentices at the Heng Dian Arts and Crafts Factory, Master Lu Jinlan, seventy years old in 1988, of Hu Tou Lu village, Heng Dian township. Lu was apprenticed to his *tang* uncle, Master Lu Runyi, in Shanghai at the age of sixteen. He worked for his master for fourteen hours a day, cooking, carrying water, and earning ¥3/month plus meals. At nineteen, he took a boat to Hong Kong, stopping at Swatow along the way. He worked in many small factories in Hong Kong, of which Da Wah Co. was the largest—originally owned by a Cantonese, eventually sold out to a Dongyang native.

He slept at his workbench at night, and ate the boss' rice, the cost of which was deducted from his salary. Between 1938 and 1942 he went back to Dongyang, but during this period of the Sino-Japanese War, the countryside was in chaos. He recalls seeing bodies floating in the water, streets filthy, debris everywhere. In 1946, Lu returned to Hong Kong where he worked for some seven years before leaving to return to Guangzhou in 1953, where he stayed until 1954. Acquainted with Guo Youxing in Hong Kong, he met up with Guo again in Guangzhou where both worked at the Xin Zhong Hua furniture factory. In 1955, he returned to Dongyang and went to work in the Lou Dian cooperative as a rough carver together with Du Yunsong, Lou Shuiming and the others. He worked in the newly organized Dongyang Woodcarving Factory from 1958 until 1979, when he retired. Lu has two sons, the elder of whom is employed in Jiangxi, the younger having taken over Lu's position in a *ding ti* arrangement at the Dongyang Woodcarving Factory. His only daughter is married and raising a family in Qi Tou village.

Lu is paid ¥200/month for the instruction he provides apprentices at the Heng Dian Arts and Crafts Factory, which taken together with his retirement pay from the Dongyang Woodcarving Factory leaves him with more than enough to get by (fieldnotes, 6/1/88, Heng Dian Arts and Crafts Factory).

The young work force works in small groups segregated by sex—boys' groups on one side, rough carving with one or two exceptions, girls' groups on the other side fine carving—with girls outnumbering boys. There is always lots of chatter in the factory as the workers converse freely in the course of work, although this does not stop the occasional worker from a brief catnap at the workbench. At about 2:45, the ice-cream man comes in, and many take a break from work to buy ice sticks (red bean during our visit). Master Lu acts as a general supervisor/chaperon of the young labor force, making sure that discipline is maintained.

The young workers earn production credits when they bring their completed panels to a production supervisor, who also works as a carver. He pencils in areas that need more work, or allots a slip certifying completion, and what it is worth in wages, noting this on his register. The present production supervisor was himself apprenticed under factory manager Wu Chuwei.

In 1988, there were 12 outworking shops (*jia gong dian*) with more than 100 workers performing work for the factory off the premises. In 1989, that number had increased to 20 shops, with some 400 workers. These *jia gong dian* increase Manager Wu's APV, reduce his administrative work, and make for greater flexibility in operations.

In 1989, there were 300 workers in the Heng Dian Woodcarving Arts and Crafts Factory itself, and another 300+ workers in an associated Classical Construction Company (Gudian Jianzhu Gongsi), with branches in Nanchang and Jing De Zhen in Jiangxi province, and the Zhejiang provincial capital, Hangzhou. Almost all the skilled workers in these branch enterprises are Dongyang folk, with other unskilled workers recruited locally.

Within the factory there are six workshops—raw materials acquisition, rough carving, fine carving, color painting of carved duck decoys, painting/varnishing of natural woodcarvings in relief, and carpentry. Women constitute 50 percent of the labor force.

Since 1987, the factory has been *cheng bao*ed to Wu by the Heng Dian Industrial Co., which, until its recent reorganization as a state-level unit, acted under authority from the Rural Industrial Bureau of the county. Whereas in 1987, Wu's contractual obligations to the Industrial Co. varied according to performance, his contract for the year 1989 called for a flat payment of ¥30,000/year to the company with no further obligations. With an expected APV of ¥4 million in carving and construction work for the year, the factory can expect to do very well indeed.

While much of his product is exported, generally through Hong Kong to Taiwan, Australia, Canada, and the United States, Wu's enterprise was not yet export autonomous. He still dealt through the state foreign trade companies *(waimao gongsi)* in Hangzhou and Shanghai, whose cut diminished the foreign exchange his enterprise might otherwise earn.

Manager Wu Chuwei lives with his wife, son, and daughter in a section of a beautiful old classical style house just northeast of the factory. Unfortunately, termites have taken their toll of this fine specimen of traditional "thirteen room" architecture (see Appendix 5) over the years, and the family will be moving as soon as their new ¥50,000–60,000 multistory brick and concrete home on the main street of Heng Dian town, just north of the factory, is completed (fieldnotes, 7/30/86, 5/31/88, 6/4/88, and 3/28/89).

Among Wu's workers in the Heng Dian factory was Mr. Ma Yangchun, son-in-law of Guo Youxing, who together with his wife has since moved on to establish the Heng Dian No. 2 Carving Factory.

Yangchun began carving at the age of fourteen in his native village of Ma Zhai. His master, also from Ma Zhai, was Ma Fenglou, a retired master of the Dongyang Woodcarving Factory, now deceased. Two years after graduating middle school, at the age of eighteen, Yangchun went to work in the brigade-run woodcarving enterprise in Heng Dian town that would become Wu Chuwei's township enterprise in subsequent years. Ma worked there for more than ten years, and there he met his future wife, Guo Youxing's daughter, Guo Shifang. They both left the factory in 1982, and traveled to Anhui to help organize a factory and train apprentices.

In the following year, they traveled to Jing Gang Shan in Jiangxi to work under similar terms for a factory there. They were among quite a number of woodworkers from Dongyang now in Jiangxi, either working in or running their own woodcarving establishments. They have been encouraged in this activity by local authorities in Jiangxi, anxious to take advantage of relatively abundant supplies of wood by having Dongyang workers educate a new generation of local young people in the skills and techniques of woodcarving.

After a year in Jiangxi, the couple returned to Heng Dian and took on a *cheng bao* contract from Wu Chuwei's factory to handle a portion of one of its classical construction projects, a ¥5,000 contract that took three months to complete.

The couple then traveled to Guangdong, where they stayed for a year, taking advantage of the connections *(guanxi)* of Shifang's father and brother in Guangdong to locate suitable employment, returning to Heng Dian in 1988. Through their work in Anhui, Jiangxi, and Guangdong, where their skills commanded a substantially higher wage than they do in Dongyang, the couple was able to accumulate the savings with which to begin their present enterprise—Heng Dian No. 2 Carving Factory.

No. 2 Factory was begun as a processing shop *(jia gong dian)*, but since its inception, the enterprise has expanded and Yangchun and Shifang now buy their own raw materials. However, they retain an outwork relationship with the Shanghai No. 1 Woodcarving Factory from which Shifang's father retired. They purchase wood for side panels of cremation urn boxes for ¥1 per piece, and receive a processing fee *(jia gong fei)* of ¥11 for each finished panel supplied to the Shanghai factory. They can turn out about 10,000 panels per year.

The enterprise is *cheng bao*ed to Ma by the Heng Dian village Communist Party committee on a year-by-year basis, and employs thirty workers. Originally, the village contributed the factory premises, but in 1989 the factory moved to a larger rented industrial flat in Heng Dian town for which they pay a rent of ¥1,500/year. The factory is still formally village run *(cun ban),* and while the couple had the option of buying out the enterprise to go private *(siying)* at the end of their contract in 1989, they planned to retain their *cheng bao* contract for a couple of years.

In 1988, the factory produced an APV of ¥100,000, of which some ¥60,000 was paid out in wages. The most skilled of their workers earn ¥300/month, while the average wage is about ¥200/month. The factory netted a profit in 1988 of about ¥17,000, some ¥10,000 of which (60 percent) was divided among the thirty-odd workers, with larger shares for the manager couple, the outside salesperson, and the shop foreman. The other 40 percent of profits was reinvested in the enterprise. The couple has two processing shops taking outwork from them, one in Ma's native village, Ma Zhai, another in the town of Nan Shang Hu to the northeast (fieldnotes, 3/29/89).

A number of elderly retired master carvers still reside in Heng Dian; among them is Manager Wu Chuwei's former master, Ge Zhangde, of Nan Jiang subdistrict, Xiao Yun village, seventy-six years old at the time of our interview. Ge Zhangde was himself trained under Master Ge Douliang, who took him to work in his perambulations around neighboring Sheng county. Zhangde worked there for 8 years altogether, after which he got a job in Shao Xing working at the Cao Wo temple for 3 years. Leaving Shao Xing, he traveled to Shanghai, where he worked in Lou Shuiming's workshop for 6 months, with six or seven of his Dongyang compatriots. He left Shanghai for Hangzhou, where he worked in the factory of Ma Yaozhang for 7 or 8 years, and returned to Dongyang. He managed to evade conscription in the Guomindang army for 5 years, working on an itinerant basis in a remote district of the county. When the Japanese were defeated, Ge went back to Shanghai where he worked for 3 years. He returned to Dongyang where he worked in Hu Qi township in the workshop of Zhang Shunhuo making antique furniture reproductions for 2 years. He left Hu Qi and went to work in the villages of Pan An for 3 to 4 years. After liberation, he worked in a cooperative carving team *(xiaodui)* in Xi Dui village in Nan Jiang *xiang* for 2 years, until his team was amalgamated together with others from Lou Dian, Heng Dian, Hu Qin and other towns, and moved to Xia Qi Tan village in Nan Shang Hu. Two years later, when the cooperative moved to Lu Zhai to become the Dongyang Woodcarving Factory, Ge became a team leader of twenty-six workers.

He found himself working until all hours of the night for a mere 31 *jin* of grain per month. Feeling he could do better as a farmer, Ge went back to the village in the early 1960s with three apprentices, among whom was Wu Chuwei. He worked with his apprentices as itinerants in Pan An county over five years, after which, remaining in Pan An county, Ge took on five more apprentices during the next six years. Since then, Ge has worked on his own in the villages. He receives a living allowance *(shenghuo fei)* of ¥23/month for his years at the Dongyang Woodcarving Factory, plus ¥6/day for the time he puts in teaching apprentices in the Heng Dian Arts and Crafts factory (fieldnotes, 3/28/89, interview with Ge Zhangde).

Among Ge's neighbors in Heng Dian was Master Ge Guangjin (1916–1988). Seventy-three years old at the time of our interview in 1988, Guangjin passed away in December of the same year. He began studying carving at 13, and apprenticed for 4 years with Master Huang Zijin. Huang had come to Heng Dian to work on items in a substantial dowry, and Ge got up the nerve to go and see him. Master Huang thought he looked bright and took him on.

After 4 years with Huang Zijin, Ge went to Shanghai, where he worked in many different factories, a few months at a time where there was work. After 2 years, he went to Hong Kong in the early 1930s, where he remained until the Japanese invasion, when he fled back to Dongyang by way of Shanghai. In 1988 Ge still spoke good Cantonese.

Back in Dongyang in the early 1940s, he worked at carving in his home, and opened a restaurant in Heng Dian town. In 1950, he went back to Shanghai and worked there as a carver until 1952, when he went to Guangzhou and worked side by side with Guo Youxing and Lu

Jinlan at the Xin Zhong Hua furniture factory. In 1960, during the "three bad years," Ge was sent back *(xia fang)* to his home in Heng Dian town. For three years he worked out of his home as a worker–farmer *(yigong yinong)*, performing labor-added tasks *(jia gong)* on subcontract for the Dongyang Woodcarving Factory. In 1971, Heng Dian production brigade *(da dui)* began a brigade factory, which in its heyday employed more than forty workers. Ge remained at the brigade factory till it closed down.

Ge has taken some forty apprentices in his time, most of them local kids from Heng Dian town. Some have continued to work in Heng Dian, and several still work at Wu Chuwei's factory, but more than ten are now in Guangzhou where their skills command higher wages.

In 1980, Ge was still in Heng Dian town when the Guangzhou factory where he had previously worked implemented a policy under which he became entitled to a modest retirement benefit despite his having been released in the early 1960s. His one daughter also works as a carver, and one granddaughter is in Guangzhou carving wood. A second granddaughter tested into the highly competitive branch school of the Dongyang Woodcarving Factory (fieldnotes, 6/4/88, 2/28/89, 3/27/89, interviews with Ge Guangjin and family).

While Heng Dian remains a significant center where Dongyang's traditions of woodcarving have been adapted to the new opportunities provided by economic reform, the town's recent history also shows the degree to which the craft has been superseded in its centrality to the local economy as a whole. Heng Dian's efforts in the development of its collective enterprise sector have made it the pride of Dongyang county's rural industrialization project. Much of its success can be attributed to the active role played by the Township Industrial Office, which has applied revenues from initial investments in innovative and creative ways to promote the further development of its rural industrial base.

Located in the shadow of Eight Face Mountain, some 18 km to the southeast of the county seat, Heng Dian township has an area of 39.7 square km, and a population of 24,300 people who inhabit some 40 villages and farm 12,300 *mu* of arable land in the town's hinterland (Heng Dian Industrial Co. 1988). Up to 1976, Heng Dian was exclusively an agricultural community, producing some silk and livestock (mainly pigs) in addition to food grains. Annual per capita income at the time was less than ¥75.

The 1950s had witnessed the creation of some cooperative woodcarving and construction contracting establishments associated with the production brigades of the agricultural communes, paying wages in work points (shares of the brigade's agricultural harvest for the year). Beginning in 1976, the Heng Dian commune authorities opened a silk-reeling factory, and within a few years the town's silk industry diversified further into the production of finished cloth.

Profits earned from these early enterprises generated new opportunities, and cotton knitting and undergarment factories were added in 1981 and 1982. In 1983, township industrial APV had grown to ¥10,000,000.

The Heng Dian Undergarment Factory (Neiyi Chang) was begun with a loan of ¥4,000,000 from the Township Industrial Office. For its first several years, the enterprise was permitted to reinvest 75 percent of its profits in production, and by 1985 was producing an APV of ¥7,000,000. Two years later APV was ¥8,600,000, with profits of ¥800,000. The original labor force of 160 workers had expanded by the late 1980s to 440 workers with an additional 50 casual workers hired from time to time to meet large orders. Regular workers earn average wages of ¥2,000/year of which about a third is made up of bonuses, awarded quarterly.

Their products are cotton, acrylic, and blended knit garments. On the premises, thread is reeled on spools, knit into cloth, and brushed on huge rollers. It is then cut into patterns, sewn into garments, silkscreened with lettering, washed, dried, and packaged. During our visit, jogging suits were being packaged for export to France (60 percent cotton, 40 percent acrylic).

In 1985, the dyeing workshop of the undergarment factory budded off as an independent enterprise with 110 of its own workers and an APV of ¥3,700,000 to become the Dongyang Dyeing Factory (Yin Liang Chang). In 1988, its labor force had expanded to 283 workers and its two managers held a *cheng bao* contract from the Heng Dian Industrial Company to operate the enterprise with a projected APV of more than ¥6,000,000 and profits of ¥650,000.

The factory processes white cloth—acrylics, cotton, and silk. Its most important customers are local Heng Dian firms, but the enterprise also does business with collectively managed knit clothing factories in Jinhua and Lanqi, and private enterprises in Yi Wu, Pu Jiang, and Yong Kang counties. Thirty percent of their business is with private enterprises.

Of the more than 200 different kinds of dyes employed, most are purchased in Shanghai, Wuxi, Changzhou, Jilin, and Tianjin, although some are also imported from abroad.

The enterprise is heavily dependent on operating loans from the state-run agricultural bank with the Industrial Company serving as guarantor. Fifty-five percent of after-tax profits go back into enterprise, most of which have generally been invested in new buildings. Twenty percent of profits go to bonuses to workers, while 25 percent is paid to the Industrial Office in *cheng bao* fees.

In 1984, the Township Industrial Office was reorganized into the Heng Dian Industrial Company *(gongye gongsi)* and became the focus of further expansion, managing the allocation of its share of enterprise profits into new investments. Significantly, it received no assistance or subsidies from the central government. By 1984, APV of the township's industrial enterprises had reached ¥19,000,000, and expansion continued unabated.

In 1985 APV doubled to reach ¥38,000,000; it nearly doubled again in 1986 to reach ¥60,000,000; and in 1987 it jumped to ¥110,000,000, nearly 90 percent of the town's combined agricultural, industrial, and sideline APV. In the same year there were 9,486 employees (5,976 in township-managed enterprises and 3,510 in village-run enterprises) who represented 74.6 percent of the total rural labor force of the township *(zhen)*. For the majority of Heng Dian residents, industry had supplanted agriculture as the primary source of income (Heng Dian Industrial Co. 1988).

The township industrial company oversaw 28 enterprises whose overall management and responsibility for policy, personnel and investment decisions were subcontracted *(cheng bao)* to factory heads directly in 1988. Of the 28 township enterprises, there were 7 in silk production, 8 in knitting and weaving, 7 in chemical production, 5 in electrical equipment, and 3 in craft and construction work. Fourteen of the twenty-eight possessed established export markets in Canada, and Eastern and Western Europe, and 4 of these each produced over ¥10,000,000 in APV. Nineteen of the township-managed enterprises produced over ¥1,000,000 in APV. Total foreign trade exports of the township in 1987 were ¥15,000,000, reached ¥25,000,000 in 1988, and by 1992 had jumped to ¥100,000,000.

Among the more successful of Heng Dian's second wave of more capital-intensive enterprises is the Dongyang No. 2 Magnetic Products and Materials Factory. The factory produces magnets for loudspeakers and other electrical appliances. Production is organized in several stages—materials are mixed in huge vats; stamped in large presses; and impressed with magnetism electrically; then baked in huge kilns. The factory works three consecutive eight-hour shifts, and remains in operation continuously. However, during our visit, a power outage meant that workers were dismissed for the day.

The enterprise was begun in 1985 with 240 workers and start-up capital of ¥1,750,000, most of which was provided by the Township Industrial Company. But like the knit goods factory of Guo Zhai, the factory also sold shares to its workers, each of whom was required to purchase ¥1,000 worth of shares to gain a spot in the labor force. In return each gets a 10 percent dividend on the investment each year in addition to wages and bonuses. The practice has continued as the labor force has expanded. In 1988, new workers were required to purchase shares of ¥300 for the privilege of employment.

In 1987, with a labor force of 420 workers, the factory produced an APV of ¥6,810,000 and earned after-tax profits of ¥680,000. In 1988, the enterprise had expanded its labor force to more than 650 workers, and was subcontracted *(cheng bao)* to its manager on the basis of competitive bidding. The manager earns a bonus of ¥10,000 for fulfilling production targets. His production manager and sales manager earn ¥7,000 in bonuses, and each worker may earn as much as ¥600 in annual bonuses.

For every ¥100 of profit earned, ¥55 goes to the state. Of the remaining ¥45, ¥15 goes to bonuses, while the *zhen* government in the guise of the Industrial Company gets ¥30. Surpassing production targets means still larger percentages in bonuses.

Through its suboffice for village-managed enterprises, the Township Industrial Company oversaw another 34 village-run enterprises (of which 4 had APV surpassing ¥1,000,000), and 346 joint household and privately run factories.

Among these latter is the Electrical Repair Shop (Dian Ji Xiuli Bu) run by Mr. Chen Tianhong. Mr. Chen's family was rather well-off at the time of the communist victory and was classified as a landlord household during land reform. Although he was able to finish upper middle school, Chen's "bad class background" caught up with him when he shot his mouth off during the Cultural Revolution. As a result, he spent more than eight years in labor reform *(lao gai),* during which time his wife divorced him. In 1979, his verdict was reversed, and he was released. He snagged a job near Hangzhou, but on account of his "criminal record," was not well received. In 1980, he returned to Heng Dian, married again, and opened the electrical repair shop, with no capital to speak of, "just a workbench."

He now employs seven workers, each of whom earns ¥100/month, and Chen has turned the little shop into a cash cow that nets him ¥50,000/year. Most of his business is with local factories, private and cooperative *(cheng bao)*. He attributes his success to the discrete and skillful manipulation of *guanxi,* the networks of obligation and reciprocity that he maintains with his customers and copper wire suppliers.* Chen takes no money from schools or hospitals for repairs that he makes on their behalf with dispatch. Doctors for whom he has performed such services treat him and his family members promptly, and with care and good humor.

But Chen is also very careful about his acquaintances, does not flaunt his new-found wealth, and is modest in his attire. He conceals his well-being, fearing future changes in government policies under which his success might be cause for reprisal.

Chen has built a modest three-story house on Heng Dian's main street for ¥45,000, largely as a hedge against inflation. The same house, if begun in 1989, would have cost him twice that. Chen measures inflation by looking at the rise in the cost of beef, ¥1.20/*jin* in the late 1970s, more than ¥8/*jin* in the late 1980s.

In early 1988, the Heng Dian Township Industrial Company had established branch factories and trading companies in the Zhu Hai Special Economic Zone in Guangdong province and in the city of Shanghai, in an effort to further project itself into the international market, and township APV in 1988 peaked at ¥125 million (Heng Dian Industrial Co. 1988). This effort appears to have been extremely successful as APV for the township grew to ¥180 million in 1990 during the first year of the eighth five-year plan, and increased again to ¥305 million in 1991, and ¥600 million in 1992. Exports expanded to ¥100 million in 1992 and annual per capita income surpassed ¥2,000 (Jiang n.d.k).

---

* Guanxi in modern business remains every bit as diffuse in its social, economic, political, and ritual manifestations as it was traditionally, although the distinctively political functions with which its cultivation was associated during the Cultural Revolution era have diminished in comparison with its significance in economic or commercial matters.

In 1993, with the approval of the State Council in Beijing, the Heng Dian Industrial Company took another innovative step and transformed itself into the Heng Dian Industrial Enterprise Group *(qiye jituan)*, a state-level management unit *(guoying danwei)*, the first of its kind in the nation. With direct management authority over 21 industrial group companies and factories, an additional 90 core member enterprises, 600 production member enterprises, 5 business offices outside the township, and 2 technical research institutes, its mission is to improve organization and management, and to coordinate the development of rural industrial enterprise in the township.

Under the Group's leadership, several new arrangements have been introduced in the issuing of stock and subscription of capital, and in 1993 the group invested ¥300 million in the township's enterprises. By the end of the eighth five-year plan (1995), township APV was projected to rise to ¥2 billion, with annual per capita income rising to ¥8,000.

Since the late 1980s, Heng Dian has been the leader in enterprise development in Jinhua prefecture. Its success owes much to the flexibility of the local township government in creating innovative institutional structures conducive to industrial diversification. As in our three previous communities but even more so, rural industry in Heng Dian has supplanted agriculture as the principal source of household income. Heng Dian finds itself increasingly linked to international markets for its increasingly diverse products, and its overall success seems sure to guarantee it a leading position in Zhejiang province on into the next century.

Chapter 7

The Dongyang Woodcarving Factory and Economic Reform

The Second Transition of Tradition

In the previous chapter, the experience of Heng Dian demonstrated the degree to which the woodcarving industry had been superseded in its importance to Dongyang county's economy by the development of the modern light and moderately heavy industrial sectors. Nevertheless, the artisanal sector of the rural economy has also witnessed significant development in its own right under the reforms of the Third Plenum of the Eleventh Central Committee (TPECC), both nationally and in Zhejiang province.

The new directions charted under the economic reforms of the TPECC had a decided impact on the fortunes of the woodcarving industry of Dongyang county, and inaugurated what might be called a "second transition of tradition." The Dongyang Woodcarving Factory, since its inception in the amalgamation of the Lou Dian and Weishan cooperatives in the 1950s, remains the largest factory in the line, and no discussion of artisan production in Dongyang would be complete without an examination of its experience of economic reform.

As we have discussed, the practice of subcontracting *(cheng bao)* had become pervasive in China by early 1989, giving a very entrepreneurial feel to many larger collective and even state-run enterprises of the county. In the case of the Dongyang Woodcarving Factory, which was for many years a large collective enterprise administered by county authorities, *cheng bao* meant first "factory manager responsibility," and since 1988, responsibility in a collective board of management whose nine members, mainly employees of the factory's design studio and "research institute," share collective responsibility for the enterprise's performance. What this means in practice is that they share in the bonuses for exceeding *cheng bao* contracted sales, and share in the penalties (thus far not relevant) of failing to fulfill them. In their first year of operation they exceeded their *cheng bao* contract by ¥3,000,000 in APV (see Table 7.1, page 165).

There is one overall factory manager, Mr. Lu Guanzheng (former apprentice of master Lou Shuiming), and five assistant managers responsible for production, technique, raw materials, support staff, and outside construction, respectively.

There are 8 workshops: carving #1 and #2, carpentry #1 and #2, painting, machine repair, metal work, and Japanese products, each with two administrators—one foreman *(zhuren)* and one quality control person—and 16 administrative staff.

There are 10 offices employing 40+ people—the factory central office, and one each for production, technique, quality, accounts, sales, raw materials, support staff *houqin,* union, security. There is also one office each for the Yi Hai Guest House and Yi Hai Garden (discussed below) (5/2/89, interview with Feng Wentu).

Under the *cheng bao* system the call went out for all cadres and workers to adopt a "master's attitude" when engaged in production and work, to strictly fulfill obligations and responsibilities with respect to value, quality, and time, and to respect all the rules and regulations. Simultaneous implementation of the *cheng bao* system "in every unit and office in our enterprise" was called for to "produce still greater economic results" (Ma Zhongyun 1988: 4).

In general, the *cheng bao* system has meant increased demands for labor discipline on the part of the work force, and indeed in May 1987 a form of piecework remuneration with bonuses and penalties cashed in at the end of the year was implemented "to make the responsibility system function completely and in good fashion." The wage system consisted of "two tracks," one a base wage for which minimum output was required, and a bonus track under which workers received bonuses of varying percentages for exceeding quotas (DYMDBAO 2: 4: May 25, 1987, untitled).

After a year in operation, several areas of concern were noted under the *cheng bao* arrangements. First, there appeared to be a tendency to emphasize quantity at the expense of quality. Second, sporadic displays of unwillingness to accept responsibility for work were noted. And third, a recalcitrant attitude was noted in some quarters with respect to changing old habits, or "sticking to the old way of doing things no matter what." These "strange tendencies," especially the neglect of quality, were seen to need attention as the factory changed from an individual to a shared managerial responsibility system (Feng 1988: 1–2).

Of the 1,200 workers in the Dongyang Woodcarving Factory in 1989, 400 were registered with urban household registrations *(hukou),* the rest with agricultural *hukou.* Wages were the same for each category of worker, and all workers enjoyed the privilege of lifetime employment, one of the unusual perks the Dongyang Woodcarving Factory offers as a former locally run state enterprise *(difang guoying qiye).* However, workers with urban registration "eat the state's rice," which is to say they have access to coupons to purchase grain at state-subsidized prices, while those with agricultural registration must rely on the grain produced by their own rural households. In addition, those with agricultural registration enjoy no provision for retirement pensions or health insurance.

The privilege of lifetime employment in the Dongyang Woodcarving Factory has made management somewhat averse to female workers. The labor force of the Dongyang Woodcarving Factory is only 30 percent female, whereas women, especially younger women, are more strongly represented in the labor force of private and collective enterprises in the woodcarving line which do not guarantee employment, offer no maternity leave or pay, and pay only for days worked (5/2/89, interview with Feng Wentu).

By early 1989, it was apparent that under the new management system, workers in the Dongyang Woodcarving Factory, while working with greater intensity and discipline, were in fact earning a great deal more than ever before. In 1980 wages in the industry averaged ¥80/month, whereas by 1988 the average base wage had climbed to ¥150/month, with bonuses in some cases bringing wages as high as ¥300–400/month. Nevertheless, in the export processing zones of Guangdong province and the lumber rich counties of Jiangxi province, a relatively inexperienced woodcarver with two years' experience could make ¥500–600/month, and an experienced master as much as ¥1,200 (fieldnotes, 3/14/89, interview with Lou Zhengzhi, Rural Industrial Bureau).

Many younger workers throughout the county, including Guo Youxing's younger son, daughter and son-in-law, have set out to these areas of the country to seek their fortunes under economic reform policies allowing greater geographic mobility, and done quite well in the process. Management at the Dongyang Woodcarving Factory denies the effect of the magnet of Guangdong's export zones on its labor force, emphasizing that workers in their factory have too much to lose in the way of security and benefits. They are free to go of course, but not to return (5/2/89, interview with Feng Wentu).

However, an item in the factory newsletter expressed concern about those workers who want to go off to Guangdong or Jiangxi "to earn a lot of money," "upsetting the work of our factory." It would seem that despite their protestations to the contrary, the management of the Dongyang Woodcarving Factory has not been immune to such influences (DYMDBAO 7: 1: September 25, 1987, "Dongyang Woodcarving Factory Party Committee...").

In any event, management of the Dongyang Woodcarving Factory has taken advantage of the opportunities afforded by the reforms to begin a variety of innovative projects. These represent both a return to and an elaboration of the traditions so assiduously restored through the efforts of the craft's older masters in the early post-liberation period. Among these innovations was the establishment in 1984 of a decorative construction shop whose primary charge was and continues to be to apply the skills of woodcarving to architectural restoration and modern construction work. In 1986, a specialized arts and crafts school was created to train future generations of workers. In 1987, a Japanese religious articles workshop and an imitation rosewood furniture line were added, and several branch factories in other parts of the country were established. In 1988, in an effort to both showcase its products and skills in construction design, and diversify its moneymaking ventures, factory management undertook construction of a hotel and pleasure garden.

More recently, the factory has participated in a series of provincial exams to assign prestige rankings to workers in its labor force, has gained export autonomy, and has attained unprecedented levels of annual production and profit.

The Return to Construction

For a long period beginning in the early twentieth century, the woodcarvers of Dongyang in a departure from their traditional association with decorative construction in architecture had devoted themselves primarily to the hand manufacture of carved wood curio furniture for the foreign market in colonial treaty port factories (see Chapter 2). For most of the post-liberation period, understandings about production organization established in the treaty ports provided the baseline model for reestablishing the woodcarving craft in the new socialist context, notwithstanding the specialization of design functions in a separate studio in the larger enterprises of the county (Lu 1988: 3).

However, woodcarvers from Dongyang never completely abandoned their association with construction, and were involved in several major projects from the 1950s to the 1970s, among which were the construction of the Chinese embassy in the USSR, restoration work at the Beijing Palace Museum, interior decoration at the West Lake Hotel in Hangzhou, construction of a memorial pavilion at Jing Gang Shan in Jiangxi province, and decoration of the Zhejiang Provincial Exhibition Hall in Hangzhou (DYMDBAO 1: 1, 3: April 25, 1987, untitled).

Beginning in the 1980s, however, the development of foreign tourism and trade, the construction of new large hotels and restaurants, parks, pavilions, and gardens, as well as the construction of Chinese restaurants and hotels overseas, led to an unprecedented demand for skills in decorative construction both in terms of processing work *(jia gong)* on materials and plans brought to the factory *(lai liao, lai yang)*, as well as on-site construction in all corners of the country and the globe (Lu 1988: 3). Restoration of traditional dwellings, temples, and monuments destroyed or vandalized during the Cultural Revolution also contributed to the demand for the skills of Dongyang woodcarvers in refurbishing these symbols of traditional Chinese culture. These factors combined to prompt a self-conscious "return to construction" in the line, and a reemphasis on the application of its workers' distinctive skills to architectural decoration in the modern period (DYMDBAO 1: 1, 3: April 25, 1987, untitled; and Xu 1987b: 3).

The "return to construction" as a strategy was galvanized in 1980, in the early period of economic reforms, as workers at the Dongyang Woodcarving Factory began the design and execution of a massive carved mural for the Dong Palace Hotel in Singapore. Under the direction of Master Lou Shuiming, the factory created 24 large panels, each 12 meters high and 1.2 meters wide, to decorate the lobby of the hotel. The subjects of each panel, in accord with the demands of the hotel's management, were chosen from among the stories and characters of China's ancient myths, folk tales, legends, classical literature, and opera. Among these were: Zheng He descends to the Western Sea, Tang Taizong unifies China, Mu Guiying assumes command, Cowherd and Weaving Girl reunited, Chang E ascends to the moon, and Eight Immortals Cross the Sea. The mural is never omitted from descriptions of the factory's achievements over the years, and at the time confirmed the factory leadership in its identification of a potentially lucrative market for its skills *(Zhejiang Gongyi Meishu* 1983: 2: 46).

The "return to construction" was given institutional expression in May of 1984, when the Dongyang County People's Government approved the establishment of the Dongyang Woodcarving Decorative Construction Co. The company coexists with the Dongyang Woodcarving General Factory as a "single organized unit with two signboards" (Pan 1988: 3).

In October 1984, a scholarly conference was organized by the newly established decorative construction company in the Dongcheng Hotel in the county town of Wu Ning, to which more than thirty experts, scholars, professors, and engineers were invited from institutes of higher education and architectural study societies in Beijing, Shanghai, Nanjing, and Hangzhou. At the meeting, the Dongyang Woodcarving Factory announced its newly formulated strategy to carry forward its two traditional strengths—woodcarving and construction—emphasizing that "Dongyang woodcarving having begun in decorative construction, now returns to a new level of carved wood construction and decoration." The conference would initiate what would become an ongoing inquiry and discussion by the factory leadership and relevant design personnel into the ways traditional decorative techniques could be applied to modern construction (DYMDBAO 1: 1, 3: April 25, 1987, untitled; see also Lu 1988: 3).

Between 1984, when the specialized company was formally inaugurated, and 1987, the Decorative Construction Company participated in more than 100 projects with a production value of more than ¥12,000,000, and the business has come to occupy an important place in the expanding ventures of the factory (DYMDBAO 10: 2: December 5, 1987, untitled). Planned decorative construction business for 1989 was ¥5 million, of which ¥3 million had already been commissioned by the end of the previous year (DYMDBAO 16: 1: January 10, 1989, "Unite in Struggle . . .").

Early on in the drive to construct new hotels with accommodations up to international standards, the Wang Hu (Lakeview) Guest House was built at the northeast corner of West Lake in Hangzhou, and for several years during the mid-1980s was the newest and arguably the best hotel in town. Within a few years, it was eclipsed by a flurry of new hotels constructed in the city, offering more luxurious accommodations and services, but the Wang Hu is nevertheless still a comfortable if no longer upscale haven.

The lobby of the Wang Hu was decorated with a massive carved wood mural more than three meters high and seven meters wide produced by craftsmen at the Decorative Construction Co. of the Dongyang Woodcarving Factory. The mural depicted a scene from a West Lake folk tale, the White Snake Chronicle *(Bai Se Zhuan),* appropriate to the setting, designed by the present factory head, Master Lu Guangzheng. The huge relief carving was elaborate in its detail and truly commanded the attention of anyone passing through the lobby *(People's Daily Overseas Edition* May 29, 1987: 7–8). The carving, however, suffered water damage due to leaking pipes and has been removed altogether in a recent remodeling and redecoration of the lobby.

The Decorative Construction Co. of the Dongyang Woodcarving Factory has had an enduring relationship with Bei Dai He park in Beijing. Their first work at Bei Dai He was begun in February of 1986, in a garden covering more than 12 hectares (nearly 5 acres), within which renovation work was carried out on classical Qing dynasty style hilltop rests, lakeside pavilions, hexagonal pagodas, a "nine curve" bridge, a "frolicking dragon" wall, a variety of rockeries, and buildings of various dimensions (Pan 1988: 3).

After completing this initial work in August, the factory was awarded a contract with the Bei Dai He city construction company to refurbish the Bi Luo (Jade Snail) Pagoda. The Pagoda is spiral in shape, like a snail, and some seven stories in height. It occupies some 2,000 square meters, required ¥4 million in funds to restore, and kept the workers of the Decorative Construction Co. busy through July of 1989 (DYMDBAO 8: 2: October 25, 1987, "Our factory . . .").

A contract with the Tianjin Television Broadcast studio brought with it a whole host of technical and functional requirements that made its design especially complex and difficult. But with the cooperation of acoustics experts from the Beijing Design Institute and the Central Television and Movie Design Institute, the work was successfully completed, and the Dongyang Decorative Construction Co. was awarded an additional contract to decorate the Beijing Number Four Recording Studio as a result of their success (Pan 1988: 3).

In October 1986, the Decorative Construction Co. of the factory was awarded the job of restoring the "Kui 'Reaching for the Clouds' Pavilion" in Fenghua county of Zhejiang province. The pavilion was originally part of the estate of Generalissimo Chiang Kaishek, located in the town of Qikou, on the peak of Wu Ling mountain, overlooking Yanqi. It had been one of Qikou's ten scenic spots, but was subjected to bombing attacks by Japanese airplanes in 1939, and only the vaguest outline of its foundation remained. With the cooperation of the factory's design studio, the Decorative Construction Co. of the Dongyang Woodcarving Factory successfully recreated the historically significant pavilion, and received a special commendation for the excellent quality of its work from the local offices concerned (DYMDBAO 2: 1: May 25, 1987, untitled).

In May of 1987, the Decorative Construction Co. contracted with officials of Zhuzhou city in Hunan province to restore and reconstruct the Main Hall of the Tomb of Yan Di, a figure of Chinese mythology sometimes identified with Shen Nong, the inventor of agriculture. The tomb, constructed in his honor in A.D. 967 during the Northern Song dynasty, was declared a structure of national historic significance in 1950, but its main hall was gutted by fire in 1954, and the monument suffered further vandalism during the Cultural Revolution. In June of 1986, with the approval of the Hunan Provincial People's Government, the decision was made to completely restore it, and the project was completed by the Decorative Construction Co. on time and up to standard (DYMDBAO 3: 1: June 25, 1987, "Restoration project...").

In May of 1987, a delegation under the leadership of Assistant Factory Head Xu Tulong went to Hangzhou to attend a meeting of the provincial Buddhist Association *(Fojiao xiehui)*, to discuss their requirements for restoration work on the great Buddhist figures in the Tian Zhu pagoda *(Tian Zhu Si)*, damaged during the Cultural Revolution. The factory reached agreement with the Buddhist Association to produce nineteen large figures of Buddha, the largest 3.5 meters high and 1.7 meters wide, the rest 1.8 meters high. Designs were completed and approved in June, and the figures were executed in fragrant camphorwood trimmed with gold leaf (DYMDBAO 2: 4: May 25, 1987, untitled).

During the first ten days of September 1987, the Decorative Construction Co. contracted with the Kaifeng museum in Anhui province to produce a large-scale carved mural, measuring 15.5 by 1.80 meters, on the theme "Qing Ming on the river." Modeled after a famous painted scroll of the Song dynasty artist Zhang Zeduan, it would decorate the "welcoming" wall *(ying mian)* of the main hall of the newly opened Kaifeng City Museum.

Design work was begun in October and completed in little more than a month's time, after which more than fifty skilled carvers executed the job during the next four months. As a result, it was possible to install the grand mural in the former capital of the Northern Song dynasty in time for Qing Ming festival of 1988, to the delight of the museum's management and staff (Feng and Ge 1988: 3).

In 1988, carpentry master Li Chengye traveled to Taizhou in Jiangsu province to work on a pavilion commemorating opera star Mei Lanfang. The pavilion measured 24 square meters, in a pentagonal single eave structure, decorated with plum flower motifs (the character for plum *[mei]* is the same as Mei Lanfang's surname). It was the first such traditional pavilion for which Master Li had taken full responsibility, and it was finished a month ahead of schedule. Li had also participated in the work at Bei Dai He, where he had charge of a group of young carpenters who received instruction under his guidance in the course of completing that project (Pan 1988: 3).

In June of 1988, design workers and assistants were summoned to Hangzhou by factory head Lu Guangzheng. Lu was there to carry out interior design work for restaurants on the three top floors of the newly completed high-rise office building and hotel, Hangzhou Mansions (Hangzhou daxia), the tallest building in the city. Because the demands of the work were great and time pressing, there was no way to complete the work without assistance from the additional design personnel. The newly arrived design workers were briefed by the building's general manager, who emphasized the importance of completing the projects before the end of September. The team toured the entire building, and began taking measurements and drawing up plans and charts for the restaurants on the three different floors.

After more than ten days of "spirited" design work, a decoration scheme in accord with the requirements of the management of the office building emerged. The design of the 25th floor required the division of space into separate small dining areas, each to be subcontracted *(cheng bao)* under separate management. The 26th floor was a banquet hall, able to accommodate 18 large round tables with 10 guests at each, the design for which adopted Shang dynasty motifs. The 27th floor was a Western style restaurant and coffee shop using natural wood finishes. The designs were completed in August, were adopted forthwith, and were completed and installed on schedule (Ma 1988: 2). In 1994, the restaurants on the 25th and 26th floors had gone out of business, the decorations nowhere to be seen, and the two floors converted to hotel rooms.

Since the inauguration of the Decorative Construction Co., its contract work has also brought it to the attention of international customers (DYMDBAO 10: 1: December 5, 1987, "Dongyang Woodcarving Factory moves forward . . ."). In recent years, the Company has participated in the construction and decoration of an International Meeting Center in Cairo, Egypt, and more than ten Chinese restaurants in West Germany, most recently three in Hamburg of which the Peking Duck restaurant in that city is the most elaborate *(People's Daily Overseas Edition,* May 29, 1987: 7–8).

In 1988, in order to expand its already existing international contacts, promote exports, promulgate more broadly its capabilities in the decorative construction area, and celebrate approval of its application for independent export autonomy by the Zhejiang Provincial Office of Economics and Trade (Jing Mao Ting), the Dongyang Woodcarving Factory hosted a joint "Study Meeting on the Application of Traditional Arts in Construction" and "First Export Commodity Trade Fair."

The study meeting was jointly organized by the China Construction Study Association (Jianzhu Xuehui), the China Arts and Crafts Study Association (Gongyi Meishu Xuehui), and the Dongyang Woodcarving General Factory. It involved discussions and exchanges of experiences on various subjects including the continuity and development of traditional Chinese crafts, the use of traditional craft skills in modern construction, and ways of improving the level of China's interior design and decoration work. More than 150 Chinese and foreign architecture specialists, arts and crafts specialists, and guests participated.

At the export commodities fair, more than 100 commercial and professional representatives from China's large hotels, friendship stores, arts and crafts sales offices *(fu wu bu),* and notables from the cultural and arts fields were in attendance. Guests from more than twenty countries including Japan, Hong Kong, Singapore, West Germany, Canada, and Australia participated. The affair was hailed as a crucial first step in realizing the factory's newly implemented self-managed export trade status, representing a broadening and deepening of its outward orientation, made possible by the economic reform policies of openness and livelihood. In addition to their academic and commercial activities, participants in both events were entertained by musical performance troupes from Hangzhou, Guangzhou and

Dongyang (DYMDBAO 15: 1: October 25, 1988, "Study meeting . . ."; and DYMDBAO 14: 1: August 30, 1988, "Adapting to reforms . . .").

By the end of the year, the Dongyang Woodcarving Factory had opened its own import–export office to compile information, and do reception and public relations work in Hangzhou Mansions, the new office building in the provincial capital whose three restaurants its artisans designed and decorated (DYMDBAO 16: 1: January 10, 1989, "Unite in Struggle . . ."). In January 1989, the import–export office saw its first consignment of self-managed export commodities valued at US$12,246.65, ordered at the commodities fair, loaded onto a ship in Shanghai bound for Hong Kong. In March, a second consignment of such goods was sent off to Australia. With self-managed export in place, foreign exchange earnings were projected to climb from 12.5 percent to 50 percent of the factory's receipts (DYMDBAO 17: 1: March 30, 1989, "General Factory first consignment . . .").

While not all of its exports over the next few years were self-managed, in 1990 the factory's export production value totaled ¥8,345,100 (US$1,700,000); in 1991 exports increased to ¥9,241,300; and in 1992, increased again to ¥12,243,700.

Export of Japanese Buddhist Images

Having enjoyed some success in 1986 using mainly scrap materials to produce small carved religious articles for Japanese Buddhist altars, valued at more than ¥250,000, the Dongyang Woodcarving Factory redoubled its efforts in that direction by establishing an independent specialized workshop. At the end of 1987, the factory allocated 1,000 square meters, 100 carvers, and a "backbone" group of 20 technical workers, to a workshop devoted exclusively to the production of Japanese religious articles (DYMDBAO 16: 1: January 10, 1989, "Adopting enthusiastic measures . . .").

Study teams were subsequently sent to Japan, and the workshop advanced from the production of partial products in the line to the production of complete Buddhist altars, greatly enhancing its ability to earn foreign exchange. The workshop's production value for 1987 was ¥600,000; in 1988 it jumped to ¥1,300,000 (DYMDBAO 10: 2: December 5, 1987, untitled).

Under present organizational arrangements, the workshop is subcontracted *(cheng bao)* from the general factory office to the workshop head who has full responsibility for orders, production, remuneration, and sales. Within the workshop, he has complete right of refusal to remunerate shoddy workmanship, as the Japanese customers whom the workshop serves are exceedingly exacting in their demands. The general factory lays down guidelines for processing fees, procures raw materials on behalf of the workshop, and insists on promptness and quality in fulfillment of contracts and targets, but the workshop has many of the characteristics of an independent factory.

In 1989, the workshop had more than 100 workers, most of whom were in their early twenties, or apprentices in their teens. It was explained that these younger workers perform the unfamiliar designs and patterns of the Japanese religious articles more effectively and with less resistance than the older masters (fieldnotes, 5/5/89, visit to the Japanese products workshop). Begun as an endeavor to make use of waste materials that would otherwise have been discarded, the Japanese religious articles workshop has become a major component of the operations of the Dongyang Woodcarving Factory, and in 1989 planned to produce commodities valued at ¥2.5 million.

While the Dongyang Woodcarving Factory has been expanding its overseas contract work in recent years, provincial-level export corporations and construction companies based in Hangzhou have also been busy cultivating the overseas market under the economic reforms encouraging outward orientation.

Members of the staff of the Zhejiang Province Arts and Crafts Import Export Corporation traveled to the United States and toured Los Angeles, New York, and Washington, D.C., during 1987 in a group studying market conditions and drying techniques for wood. Some members of the delegation attended classes at a school in North Carolina offering a crash course in precision techniques for measuring the degree of moisture in a variety of woods, while other members attended courses in modern furniture design in Houston (fieldnotes, 5/5/88, Hangzhou).

Taking advantage of China's most abundant resource, labor, provincial-level construction companies have also begun to enter the international construction market as labor contractors, and many Dongyang county residents have thereby had the opportunity for overseas travel.

Indeed, as we saw in Chapter 5, Guo Youxing's eldest son, Guo Wuliang, was sent to Iraq in 1982 for two years as an employee of the Zhejiang Province No. 4 Construction Co. in Hangzhou, to build and decorate mansions of the ruling elite, and spent another two years working on a similar project in Kuwait.

International Commodities Exhibitions

With the international market beckoning, the Dongyang Woodcarving Factory has also sent its representatives to a variety of international commodities exhibitions. In April 1986, in response to an invitation from the head of the Canadian Overseas Chinese General Chamber of Commerce, and in company with responsible comrades from the Provincial International Economic and Technical Cooperation Co., the Dongyang Woodcarving Factory sent a delegation to the 1986 World Exposition in Vancouver, Canada, for six months to demonstrate craft skills in the China Exhibition Hall. After fulfilling their responsibilities in technical performance, the delegation members returned home in October considerably chastened by the experience (Ma 1987a: 1).

One member of the group, an assistant factory manager and design worker, had the following thoughts:

> Although we speak in flowery terms of Dongyang woodcarving as having a "long history" and being "known all over the world," in the Euro-American market there is very little Dongyang woodcarving. Those engaged in decorative construction [internationally] are mainly from Taiwan, Hong Kong and South Korea. Because of this, we must organize on the basis of our strengths and expand the market in Europe and America for Dongyang carved wood decoration.
>
> In production, structure and form, Dongyang woodcarving still doesn't measure up to many other craft commodities of China, nor to those of the rest of the world. Thus, we cannot be completely content with the world as it is. We must continually adopt what we can of the strengths of our sister crafts, and take Dongyang woodcarving to new levels.
>
> We should recognize and study our shortcomings with respect to the decorative carving arts, especially those influenced by classical Greece. We must also overcome parochialism and pay attention to the strengths of the western arts to improve Dongyang woodcarving. The spirit and wisdom of a people does not lie in stubborn adherence to tradition, but in revamping while preserving tradition. We must continuously and seriously engage in self-examination and self-criticism, and on this basis carry out self-revitalization and renewal. (Ma 1987b: 1)

International exposure was a humbling experience. This craftsman gained an appreciation of how small and insignificant his place of work, indeed the entire tradition in which he worked, was in the greater world market. He went on to suggest that the tradition needed new ideas and directions, and he called on design personnel to "liberate their thinking," to "let a hundred flowers bloom," to improve their artistic talents and literary training. Based on his observations of trade at the fair, he went on to encourage development of the design and production of imitation rosewood *(hong mu)* furniture and household articles, especially dynastic reproductions. Finally, he encouraged the production of modern "abstract" or "symbolic" craft pieces and patterned decorations (Ma 1987b: 1).

Interestingly, within a short time of the publication of these recommendations, the Dongyang Woodcarving Factory imported a set of world-class carpentry machines from Italy and Japan to begin the production of undecorated furniture. At the same time, it acquired from domestic suppliers a furniture production assembly line for imitation rosewood furniture—altogether a capital investment of ¥2.6 million. After experiments in production in November, production began on January 1 (DYMDBAO 10: 2: December 5, 1987, untitled), and after two years of operation the two new product lines netted a profit of more than ¥1 million (DYMDBAO 16: 1: January 10, 1989, "Unite in Struggle...").

With increasing numbers of workers and personnel going abroad, security concerns of local county authorities were clearly aroused. Symptomatic of this arousal was a discussion meeting held on June 3, 1987, called by the County Communist Party discipline committee. Those personnel who had traveled abroad, among whom was Dongyang Woodcarving Factory head Lu Guangzheng, together with five other "comrades"—separately discussed the things they had seen and heard in Hong Kong, Japan, West Germany, Canada, and other countries. The summation of experiences for public consumption was predictable enough and, published in the factory newsletter, concluded in the following terms:

> Modern western scientific technique and enterprise management are worthy of study, but capitalist society is no heaven *(tiantang)*. In comparing the two social systems, it is clear that the socialist system is superior. (DYMDBAO 3: 1: June 26, 1987, "Leaders from the County party...")

Of course, foreign trade is also conducted closer to home. From October 14 to 20, 1987, Factory Head Lu Guangzheng, and Assistant Factory Head Xu Tulong traveled to Guangzhou to participate in the 62nd International Fall Trade Fair. Foreign trade personnel from the Zhejiang Provincial and Shanghai City Foreign Trade Companies *(wai mao gongsi)* reported that orders for Dongyang carved wood products were greater than in past years, placing a real strain on the labor force and raw materials supplies of the factory (Xu 1987a: 2).

At such times, the factory subcontracts its orders to its many off-premises processing shops *(jia gong dian)*. It maintains relations with some seventy or so of these shops of varying sizes. About one-third of them have fixed contractual arrangements with the Dongyang Woodcarving Factory. The others are only called upon when there is an overabundance of orders. The quality of the goods delivered is inspected, assessed, and awarded a processing fee *(jia gong fei)* on a piece-by-piece basis. If the items delivered require further work to pass inspection, it is performed by the *dian*'s workers either on the premises of Dongyang Woodcarving Factory or back at the *jia gong dian* (fieldnotes, 5/2/89, interview with Feng Wentu).

Rural Prosperity and the Expansion of the Domestic Market

While efforts were under way to expand exports and earn foreign exchange, the Chinese domestic market was also expanding. The implementation of the economic reforms has had a decidedly positive impact on the standard of living of rural folk, and domestic sales of art craft products have also increased. Many factories in the province that originally produced only export products began to establish specialized workshops to produce goods for the domestic market, creating products for tourists as well as new products for the domestic market and domestic consumption. In 1984, at a national exhibition of tourist and domestically marketed goods in Beijing, Zhejiang province was represented by 2,227 new products, took orders for ¥25,940,000, had 21.9 percent of total receipts for the exhibition, and was first among all provinces represented. In 1985, orders in the tourist and domestic market of Zhejiang province were already ¥339 million for the year; 13 times the figure for 1978 (DDZGZJ 1989: 385).

The carved furniture products of the Dongyang Woodcarving Factory, as well as the many individually and collectively managed factories in the line, literally jam the streets of the rural market fairs *(hui chang)* of Dongyang county (see Appendix 3). Furniture for bridal trousseaus, beds, cabinets, tables, and the like, are always on display, and in the late 1980s were selling well.

The Dongyang Woodcarving Factory has also been a participant in activities designed to cultivate this domestic market. In October 1987, the factory participated in the Second Joint Commodities Exhibition and Sales Fair of nine cities in the four provinces of Fujian, Zhejiang, Jiangxi, and Anhui. The fair was held in the Workers' Cultural Palace of Jinhua city. Dongyang county had its own exhibition room on the fourth floor of the Cultural Palace, at the main door of which stood a six-panel carved screen decorated with scenes from the classic novel *Dream of the Red Chamber*. A wide range of the products of the Dongyang Woodcarving Factory were also on display inside (DYMDBAO 8: 2: October 25, 1987, "Dongyang Woodcarving Factory participates in a commodities exhibition . . .").

In early 1988, the Dongyang Woodcarving Factory opened its own retail "Friendship" Store on Wu Ning East Street in the county town, in an effort to absorb some of the domestic demand for carved wood products. The ribbon-cutting ceremony was attended by the head of the County Communist Party Committee and Government Office Mr. Jin Desheng, the head of the County Commercial Bureau Mr. Chen Huisheng, the head of the County Foreign Trade Bureau Mr. Wu Chengrong, and five leaders from the Dongyang Woodcarving Factory. Thirteen traditional carved hexagonal palace lanterns, produced for the occasion, contributed to the festive atmosphere as a noisy crowd bustled about both inside and outside the store. In addition to carved wood products, the store stocks a variety of consumer durables from table lamps to motorcycles. This is a new direction for the Dongyang Woodcarving Factory, a diversification into retail sales under the reform policies of openness and securing livelihood (DYMDBAO 11: 2: March 5, 1988, untitled).

Domestically, the Dongyang Woodcarving Factory also markets large numbers of cremation urn boxes, produced on a putting-out basis by its many *jia gong dian*.

Branch Factories of the Dongyang Woodcarving Factory

As discussed in Chapter 1, one of the consequences of the economic reforms has been the increased autonomy rural enterprises have been allowed in managing their labor force and procuring raw materials. What this has meant in practice for the Dongyang Woodcarving Factory is that it has been thrown back on its own resources in acquiring necessary supplies of wood for its much expanded activities.

During the three years from 1984 to 1987, efforts were made to expand the factory's horizontal economic linkages, and to solve the problem of material supply shortages. In 1987, joint management enterprises were established with Chong Yi county in Jiangxi province, and Lin Jiang county in Jilin province, both centers of lumber production. These projects were begun to afford some security to the factory in obtaining its yearly requirements for more than 8,000 cubic meters of wood (DYMDBAO 10: 1: December 5, 1987, "Dongyang Woodcarving Factory moves forward...").

In February 1987, the Dongyang Woodcarving Factory formally signed "technical cooperation documents" with representatives of the Chong Yi County Wood Products General Processing Factory of Jiangxi province. At the beginning of April, the Dongyang factory sent six skilled workers (carpenters, carvers, and painters) to carry out technical instruction of apprentices at the newly established joint enterprise, imparting to them the basic skills necessary for independent production of carved wood articles (DYMDBAO 1: 2: April 25, 1987, "We carry out technical cooperation..."; and DYMDBAO 4: 2: July 25, 1987, "The exotic flower...").

Products of the new enterprise included moderately priced furniture for the domestic market, as well as export quality screens, table ornaments, and so forth. By the end of the year the new factory had established a forestry products store in Jiangxi, and the first batch of experimental products of the Dongyang Woodcarving Factory's technical team and its apprentices went on sale. The store opened on December 9, amid crowds of spectators and explosions of fireworks (DYMDBAO 11: 2: March 5, 1988, "Chong Yi carved wood products enter the Jiangxi market").

In September 1988, the Chong Yi branch factory participated in a five-day "Min Nan Golden Triangle Foreign Investment and Trade Conference" in Xiamen's Fushan exhibition hall. A group of carved wood articles was selected for exhibition—camphorwood chests, walking sticks, lamps and table plaques—as the branch factory geared up to enter the international market (DYMDBAO 15: 1: October 25, 1988, "Chong Yi carved wood products exhibited in Xiamen").

In June of 1987, the Dongyang Woodcarving Factory began a similar arrangement with authorities in the Bureau of Forestry of Lin Jiang county in Jilin province (Manchuria). As in the case of the Chong Yi enterprise, technical instruction in the skills of woodcarving was carried out by Dongyang factory personnel at the No. 3 Wood Materials Factory in Lin Jiang, and the Lin Jiang forestry bureau agreed to serve as a source of raw materials for the Dongyang factory (DYMDBAO 15: 1: October 25, 1988, "Fifth Board of Directors . . .").

The establishment of the Lin Jiang branch factory was hailed as an event of great significance in that it further diversified the Dongyang Woodcarving Factory's sources of raw materials, and enhanced the ability of the factory to earn foreign exchange through expanded exports (DYMDBAO 4: 1: July 25, 1987, "Lin Jiang branch factory . . .").

The link to Lin Jiang opened up at least one additional economic contact of interest in Jilin. In the middle of March 1988, the Dongyang Woodcarving Factory signed a contract with Xihan subdistrict of Nanfeng county in Jilin to cooperate in establishing a mushroom farm. The Dongyang factory agreed to supply the enterprise with wood chips, which apart from being the major component of the waste material of woodcarving, make a good bed for mushroom growing. In exchange for the chips, the Dongyang Woodcarving Factory enjoys a share of the produce of the mushroom farm (DYMDBAO 11: 1: March 5, 1988, "New plan . . .").

The establishment of these joint enterprises by the Dongyang Woodcarving Factory also increased the flow of personnel between the respective areas, as board of directors meetings were held in alternate years in Dongyang and the branch factories.

Labor Force Reproduction—The Arts and Crafts School of the Dongyang Woodcarving Factory

Throughout Dongyang county, labor force reproduction in the carved wood products industry is still achieved primarily through the completion of a three-year apprenticeship. In June 1988, along the road from the county town to the Dongyang Woodcarving Factory, two apprentices were at work in a room rented by their master as a site for their instruction. Their master was Zhao Yide, a graduate of the provincial Fine Arts Institute (Meishu Xueyuan) in Hangzhou, and an employee of the Dongyang Woodcarving Factory just down the road. The young apprentices worked on small pieces of scrap wood, copying ladies' faces, one after another. They were not complete pieces, just faces, repeated again and again till they began to approximate the model provided (fieldnotes, 6/6/88, Dongyang Woodcarving Factory).

Seldom were apprentices of the past trained so systematically, and this unusual example might be explained by the fact that the master involved had received formal higher education. In any event, in order to systematize its own labor force reproduction, the Dongyang Woodcarving Factory took steps in September 1986 to organize a middle-level specialized school *(zhong deng zhuan ye xuexiao)* to train the next generation of talent for the factory and its affiliated decorative construction company.

The school was begun with the support of the Ministry of Light Industry, which contributed ¥50,000 to the original school endowment, the Dongyang General Arts and Crafts Co., and the Zhejiang province, Jinhua city, and Dongyang County governments (Jin 1987: 1).

Back in 1958, two specialized lower middle schools had been established to train young woodcarvers, one each in the towns of Weishan and Nan Shang Hu where the early craft cooperatives were organized. At those early schools students studied for one and a half years in a curriculum of fine arts and culture to graduate, and only then *began* their apprenticeships in the cooperative. It is said that the skill level of that group was very high, and of the original class of 100 apprentices, some 30 are still working at the Dongyang Woodcarving Factory. Two more classes were brought along in 1960 and 1962 on the premises of the factory itself, but apparently it was difficult to maintain the school during the "three bad years" following the Great Leap Forward, and it was discontinued until the present school was started up in 1986. In the intervening years, labor force reproduction was carried out exclusively by in-factory apprenticeships assigned by the county Labor and Personnel Office (fieldnotes, 5/2/89, interview with Feng Wentu).

The present school, located on the grounds of the Dongyang Woodcarving Factory, employs four full-time teachers of whom Master Zhao Yide, mentioned above, is one. The apprentices observed in the rented room were not students in the school, but rather Master Zhao's privately contracted trainees. At the school, beyond instruction in upper middle school liberal arts subjects, students are also taught by members of the Dongyang Woodcarving Factory's design studio, who rotate in and out, teaching a few weeks at a time, and specialized art teachers sent by the Provincial Level Arts and Crafts Research Institute in Hangzhou (Jin 1987: 1).

In 1989 there were 90 students in the school, in two classes of 45 each. A new class enters every three years, recruited exclusively from among Dongyang youngsters. Four students from the branch factory in Jilin are supported by their unit at a cost of ¥1,000 for three years, and the Dongyang Woodcarving Factory assumes no responsibility for their expenses.

Those who desire admission must fill out an application, submit it to the factory leadership, take the unified City Upper Middle and Lower Middle Specialized School Recruitment Exam, and a supplementary exam in fine arts. Students with both agricultural and urban population registrations *(hukou)* are eligible (Dongyang Woodcarving Factory 1989).

Some 3,600 students take the test when it is offered once every three years. Ninety students were accepted in 1986, but in line with factory needs, the class of 1989 was limited to forty students. Students pay ¥50/semester to buy books. The factory pays ¥15/month in living expenses *(shenghuofei)* in the first year, ¥20/month in the second year, and ¥30/month in the third year. All but the worst of the graduates are given jobs in the Dongyang Woodcarving Factory.

Upon entering the school, each new student must post a bond *(jiajin)* of ¥800. The bond is returned after ten years—three years in school and seven years of work in the factory. If a student should discontinue study or fail to fulfill the obligatory seven years of work, apart from relinquishing his bond, he must also pay back the equivalent in fees incurred by the factory on his behalf for specialized technical school instruction.

In their first year of instruction, students take one-third of their classes in specialized subjects (Introduction to Art; Craft Technique; Literary and Artistic Theory; Modeling and Design; etc.), and two-thirds of their classes in general subjects (Politics; Language; Mathematics; History, etc.). In the second year, they take one-half specialized classes, and one-half general classes. In the third year, they take two-thirds specialized classes, and one-third general classes (fieldnotes, 5/2/89, interview with Feng Wentu).

Beginning with the graduating class of 1989, every student was required to design and execute a "masterpiece" for graduation, and the plan was to hold an exhibition of the student projects in the factory in the autumn following the graduation of each subsequent class (fieldnotes, 5/2/89, interview with Feng Wentu).

Upon completion of their studies with passing grades, the students are issued a certificate of graduation, and upon further approval of the County Labor and Personnel Office, the new graduates are assigned to work in the Dongyang Woodcarving Factory with the perks and privileges of a middle-level skilled worker.

Each year the factory allocates ¥30,000 to the school to send the student cohort on tours of China's major cities and historic landmarks to investigate the diversity of Chinese arts and crafts, broaden the students' cultural horizons, and raise their artistic level.

In December of 1986, the students and teachers at the school took part in the annual meeting of the Industrial Arts and Crafts Study Association of Jinhua city, held in Dongyang, and visited the exhibition held in conjunction. In the beginning of April 1987, the school sponsored an excursion to Hangzhou to visit the Zhejiang Provincial Arts and Crafts Select Products Exhibition, and to view the landmarks in the provincial capital. From January to April of 1987 the school mounted an exhibition of Chinese calligraphy *(shu hua)* in the factory, including a great variety of styles (Jin 1987: 1).

Within the school, the promotion of good citizenship is an important part of the curriculum. In August 1987, the Communist Youth League branch of the A class of the school held a contest on knowledge of the contents of the documents *(wen jian)* of the 13th Party Congress, but extracurricular activities of a more informal kind are also held. In November 1987, the class committee of the B class of the school organized a cookout, including a mountain climbing contest and a variety of competitive games (DYMDBAO 10: 4: December 5, 1987, untitled).

Honorific Titles

The process of labor force reproduction has also been systematized by the promulgation in 1988 of a series of provincial-level examinations through which workers may merit the conferral of a variety of honorific titles.

To achieve the title "craft master" *(gongyi shi),* one must have 5 to 8 years work experience, and pass an exam on the history of craft development and design. In addition, one must submit a portfolio of photographs of one's work, and have had an original essay published on one aspect or another of craft design or development. A second level of achievement is marked by the provincial title "high class craft master" *(gaoji gongyi shi)* (fieldnotes, 3/14/89, interview with Lou Zhengzhi, Rural Industrial Bureau).

A still higher honor is conferred at the national level, "China arts and crafts great master craftsman" *(Zhongguo gongyi meishu da shi)*. This exclusive title was created as a result of a document issued in January of 1988 by the National Science Committee and the Ministry of Light Industry in Beijing entitled "A trial method of titles of excellence in the arts and crafts professions." The document's regulations stated that once every three years the nation would bestow the honorific title "China arts and crafts great master craftsman," and compile a "Directory of Chinese arts and crafts great master craftsmen" (DYMDBAO 12: 1: 6/5/88, "Arts and Crafts Notables . . .").

The four criteria for the award of the title "China arts and crafts great master" were published in the newsletter of the Dongyang Woodcarving Factory in advance of the 1989 exams. A prospective candidate:

1. Must be experienced and creative in the production of articles of individual style and distinctiveness and/or innovative articles which achieve excellent economic results or desirable social benefits.
2. Must have a certain specialized theoretical knowledge, relatively high artistic education, and some accomplishment in the exploration of artistic form.
3. Must have won an award in a professional industrywide *(quan hangye)* or provincial-level competition, and have had an original article published in a journal or magazine at the provincial level or above.
4. Must have a long record of contribution to the promotion of the arts and crafts professions, have a reputation and influence locally and provincially (DYMDBAO 17:2: March 30, 1989, "Provincial Arts and Crafts Professions . . .").

The factory manager of the Dongyang Woodcarving Factory, Lu Guangzheng, has attained the national title of "China arts and crafts great master," two assistant factory managers the provincial title of "high class craft master," and thirteen design and factory workers the title of "craft master." More than 40 of the factory's workers presently occupy positions as "first level specialized technical personnel" (DYMDBAO 16: 1: January 10, 1989, "Unite in Struggle . . .").

Manager Lu's title was conferred at the Third National Arts and Crafts Congress, held in Beijing from April 25 to 28, 1988. At the same congress, High Class Master Craftsman and Assistant Factory Manager Feng Wentu was awarded a certificate and documents as a national "specialist practitioner of excellence in arts and crafts" *(you xiu gongyi meishu zhuan ye ren yuan)*.

Participating in the national arts and crafts congress were more than 600 people, 33 of whom were from Zhejiang province, 3 from Dongyang county. The congress designated 62 "China arts and crafts great master craftsmen" *(gongyi da shi),* and 150 "practitioners of excellence in arts and crafts" nationwide. On the afternoon of April 27, the conferees were received by Prime Minister of the State Council Li Peng, Assistant Prime Ministers Yao Yilin and Tian Jiyun, and photos were taken (DYMDBAO 12: 1: June 5, 1988, "Arts and Crafts Notables . . .").

Achieving such designations is for the most part a matter of prestige, but may also result in material benefits such as promotion to jobs in design, wage increases, and greater opportunities for horizontal labor mobility. Moreover, the titles also help to create a consciousness of and pride in the craft professions, and encourage craft workers to aspire to higher levels of creativity in their performance.

Further Diversification—The Yi Hai Hotel and Gardens

Spurred on by its numerous successes, the Dongyang Woodcarving Factory in 1988 embarked on what at the time seemed a somewhat questionable venture when it undertook to construct the Yi Hai Hotel and Pleasure Garden, a short walk from the factory. The project, at once a gallery to exhibit the works of the factory and a public park accessible for a small fee, also contains a luxury guest house for visitors to the factory or to the county. Guesthouse rooms are lavishly decorated in a variety of styles and woods, all of which demonstrate something of the skill of Dongyang woodcarvers. Its prices, however, were substantially higher than the refurbished Dongcheng Hotel (that relic of the Maoist period), or even the more newly established Nan Yang Hotel on South Street. In 1989 one could well have imagined the 18 rooms and 4 luxury suites of the Yi Hai guest house remaining vacant most of the time. Whether the traffic of returned expatriates and international businessmen coming through town would meet the ambitious expectations of those who conceived the project was anybody's guess.

Early indications were that the factory had overextended itself. Total costs were estimated at between ¥5 and 6 million, of which the factory contributed between ¥1 and 2 millions and borrowed about ¥4 million from the Bank of China branches in Jinhua city and Dongyang (fieldnotes, 5/2/89, interview with Feng Wentu). In 1989, with the guesthouse still incomplete, the word about town was that the factory was having trouble meeting the payments on its debt (who isn't?). The Bank of China in Hangzhou was unwilling to lend to them, and the factory leadership had to go to Beijing to secure further credit (fieldnotes, 4/28/89, interview with Lü Yunlei).

At the time it was conceivable that the profits from the factory's other endeavors might see its management through this difficult period, but it seemed more likely that before long, the factory would be forced to sell off the property at a loss to a local or expatriate entrepreneur to run with less profitable expectations.

But beginning in 1990, there was a great change in the fortunes of the guesthouse as its reputation grew, and guests began to appear. Overseas merchants and visitors began to request bookings in larger numbers, and the factory responded by adding nearly 100 rooms. According to the hotel manager, most of these are filled most of the time, and beginning in 1991, several provincial-level conferences were held there. The attached gardens have become a genuine tourist attraction, a must stop for all visitors to the county. With its performance and profitability increasing each year, the whole enterprise is now referred to in the county as the "money tree" of Dongyang Woodcarving Factory (Jiang n.d.e).

Professional Esprit de Corps

Workers at the Dongyang Woodcarving Factory are something of an aristocracy in the woodcarving labor force, enjoying as they do the perks and high status of employment at the largest woodcarving enterprise in the county. Although there may be entrepreneurs and workers in the myriad other woodcarving establishments of the county who earn more in cash amounts per month, the workers at the Dongyang Woodcarving Factory remain something of an elite group.

In general, esprit de corps at the Dongyang Woodcarving Factory is high, and is manifest in both professional and extracurricular activities sponsored by the factory leadership on behalf of its labor force. The factory newsletter serves not only as a conduit for information about national and provincial policy developments affecting the factory and the profession, but also as an outlet for expressions of worker identity and professional consciousness and pride. In one issue, a wistful poem appears, recounting the thoughts and reactions of a Dongyang worker in the Jiangxi province Chong Yi county branch factory upon receiving his copy of the factory newsletter in the mail (DYMDBAO 3: 4: June 25, 1987, untitled).

In another issue, a worker published the words and music to a song of his own composition called "Mudiao Dawang" (Big King of Woodcarving) (DYMDBAO 10: 4: December 5, 1987, untitled), and poems and songs extolling the virtues of the profession and its practitioners are a regular feature of the publication. Pictures of model workers who maintained high levels of quality in production appeared in one issue (DYMDBAO 12: 2: June 6, 1988, untitled).

The results of factory-sponsored competitions in both design and execution of craft products also appear in the newsletter. In 1988, the quality inspection office and leaders of the carving workshop organized a contest in which thirty participants turned out with their creations. Judging was based on excellence in execution of both rough carving and finishing. The articles of "comrades" Li Hongchun, Jiang Yaofang, Zhang Fansheng, and Lu Huifan placed first and were awarded cash prizes (DYMDBAO 14: 4: August 30, 1988, "Carving workshop holds a labor contest . . .").

In January 1989, the results of a factory-sponsored furniture design contest were published. From a total of 27 entries, 2 first prizes of ¥150, 4 second prizes of ¥80, and 9 third prizes of ¥40 were awarded. All other participants received consolation prizes of ¥10. First prizes went to Ma Lianghong and Lou Weidong (DYMDBAO 16: 2: January 10, 1989, "Announcement of the results . . .").

Extracurricular Activities

The factory's extracurricular activities are numerous and diverse, often organized by the factory union, youth league, or women's committee.

In June 1987 the factory union organized an "employee knowledge contest." Leaders of the factory Communist Party Committee served as the contest organizers. The contest questions were supplied by a committee consisting of Assistant Factory Managers Xu Tulong and Feng

Wentu, and union Vice Chairman Zhou Yantao. Questions were divided among technical professional knowledge, production management knowledge, contemporary political knowledge, legal knowledge, security and safety knowledge, and women workers' knowledge. There were six contestant teams competing. In the end, the *houqin* (support staff) team and the woodcarving team, both with a total of 78 points, tied for first place; the raw materials team, with 76 points, took third (DYMDBAO 4: 4: July 25, 1987, "Factory union . . .").

On an afternoon in October 1987 the youth league branch of the A class of the branch school, under the supervision of the factory youth league committee, hosted a Chinese chess tournament. There were twelve participants in the contest, which consisted of two days of elimination and round robin competition. Schoolmate Du Dongzheng took first prize (DYMDBAO 8: 4: October 25, 1987, untitled).

In November, the head of the marketing office of the factory, Mr. Chen Guiyun, went to Jinhua city to participate in a bridge tournament. In a "heroic struggle," he captured top honors, and returned to the factory in triumph (DYMDBAO 10: 1: December 5, 1987, "Delegate from our factory takes first place . . .").

To celebrate the two commendations that the factory attained for enterprise performance in 1987, and to welcome in the New Year of 1988, the factory union, youth league, and women's association held a jointly sponsored "Welcome the New Year Arts and Letters Evening." The evening featured factory workers performing music, song, dance, magic, martial arts, and so forth with prizes awarded for creativity and performance skill (DYMDBAO 7: 4: September 25, 1987, untitled).

In October 1988, the factory hosted a fishing contest. First prize for the largest fish went to Lu Youfa, whose catch weighed more than 6 catties *(jin)* (3 kg). Second prize for the most fish went to seventy-year-old Master Du Xuexian, son of the so-called Emperor of Dongyang Woodcarving, Master Du Yunsong (see Chapter 2). An account reads:

> How could there be any competition? At 8:10 A.M., this great *huang tai zi* (imperial prince) was anxious. He knit his eyebrows into the shape of the character for 8, as he tried to entice the fish. In the end, the fish jumped onto his hook continuously, and Master Du was able to achieve second place. Hale and hardy Master Du was heard to remark with a happy and bright face, "Thoroughly enjoyed myself . . . heh! heh! heh!"

as the laughter of all the onlookers engulfed him. (DYMDBAO 15: 4: October 14, 1988, "Report of the results of the fishing contest")

His achievement was characterized by those present with the following classical expression: *Shan chong shui jin yi wu lu, liu an hua ming you yi cun* (Mountain after mountain and river after river there seems no way to proceed; but beyond the shadows of the willows and amidst the flowers bright, there is a village), which is to say, Master Du was able to find a way despite apparently overwhelming obstacles.

The seventh annual factory winter basketball tournament began in December 1989. Six teams participated from support staff, branch school, materials shop, paint shop, woodcarving shop, and brass trimmings shop. First place was won by the branch school team, second by the woodcarving shop, third by the support staff team (DYMDBAO 16: 4: January 10, 1989, "General Factory presents . . .").

In August 1988, the factory arranged for workers to go in groups to the City People's Hospital for X-rays and other diagnostic tests. In the same month, the factory formally opened a new dining hall for workers. Divided into upper and lower stories, well lit, with lots of open space, it was hailed as a great improvement in the living conditions of the factory's labor force (DYMDBAO 14: 2: August 30, 1988, untitled).

All these activities reveal the Dongyang Woodcarving Factory as a dynamic and innovative force in county and national life. Under the recent economic reforms, the factory has expanded the social and economic horizons of the county, diversified its own activities both nationally and internationally in pursuit of expanded earnings, and greatly contributed to the earning power, well-being, and esprit de corps of its labor force.

Production Figures

Under the economic reforms, the Dongyang Woodcarving Factory's annual production and profit figures have risen consistently.

In May of 1987, the status of the Dongyang Woodcarving Factory was recognized with the addition of the character *zong* to its official title. It became the Dongyang Woodcarving General Factory, and in the process of accepting its new designation took note of the toils of

Table 7.1

Production Figures for the Dongyang Woodcarving Factory

	Annual Production Value	Profit
1978	¥2,500,700	¥455,000
1984	¥2,617,800	¥348,432
1986	¥6,952,880	¥613,240
	(325,000 religious articles)	
1987	¥10,000,000	¥1,000,000
	(600,000 religious articles)	
1988	¥11,002,900	¥1,072,100
	(1,300,000 religious articles)	
1989	¥13,579,100	¥1,107,700
	(5,000,000 in construction, 2,500,000 religious articles)	
1990	¥13,700,000	¥1,700,000
1991	¥15,023,200	¥692,600
		(due to rising production costs and payments on the Yi Hai garden and guest house)
1992	¥23,187,200	¥632,100

Sources: DYMDBAO 10:1, 12/5/87, "Dongyang woodcarving factory moves forward . . ."; DYMDBAO 10:2, 12/5/87, untitled; DYMDBAO 11:1, 3/5/88, "New plan for the year of the dragon . . ."; DYMDBAO 11:2, 3/5/88, "Celebrate Double One . . ."; Jiang n.d.e.

the elder generation of craftsmen that had prepared the basis for its success (DYMDBAO 2: 1: May 25, 1987, "Dongyang Woodcarving Factory's name changed . . ."). At the end of 1987, the factory achieved the milestone of ¥10 million in production value and ¥1 million in profits, and achieved designation as a "national second level enterprise" *(guo jia er ji qiye)* (DYMDBAO 4: 1: July 25, 1987, "Grasp the base, go up a level . . ."). To celebrate this "stirring event," the factory hosted an evening of performances on December 19 in the Dongyang Theater on South Street in the center of town. A group of local notables were in attendance, from the mayor of Jinhua City to the secretary of the County Communist Party Committee.

Special invitations to perform were accepted by well-known singers Jiang Dawei, Dong Wenhua, Zhang Peijun, famous banter artists Jiang Kun and Tang Jiezhong, and the Zhejiang province performance troupe *(ge wu tuan).* The morning of the following day, the performers toured the exhibition hall of the factory with factory head Lu

Guanzheng (DYMDBAO 11: 2: March 5, 1988, "Celebrate Double One . . .").

After Spring Festival, the yearly target of ¥15 million in APV was announced for 1988, more than twice the factory's contracted *cheng bao* amount, and while the contracted amount was overfulfilled, the ambitious yearly target was never reached (DYMDBAO 11: 1: March 5, 1988, "New plan for the year of the dragon . . ."). Annual APV for 1988 was ¥11,002,900, with profits of ¥1,072,100.

Later in the same year, after passing inspection, the Dongyang Woodcarving Factory received confirmation of designation as a Provincial Level Progressive Enterprise *(xianjin qiye)*. Also receiving the honor were the Dongyang Plaited Bamboo Products Factory, and the Weishan Metal and Electrical Products Factory. The Provincial People's Government presented plaques and documents commemorating the event (DYMDBAO 15: 1: October 25, 1988, untitled).

The factory was also cited at the national level as a Light Industry Export Earning Progressive Enterprise, and in August the factory gained membership in the China Light Industry Import–Export Commercial Association. In early 1989, the factory looked forward to producing goods valued at ¥20 million (DYMDBAO 16: 1: January 10, 1989, "Unite in Struggle . . ."), although its actual production value at year's end was ¥13,579,100, with profits of ¥1,107,700. The ¥20 million target was not reached until 1992 when the factory's APV was ¥23,187,200.

As the largest and most well-endowed woodcarving enterprise in the county at the start of the reforms, the Dongyang Woodcarving Factory clearly enjoyed something of a competitive advantage as regarded its access to resources, its pool of talented personnel, and its ability to invest in innovative projects. But notwithstanding these advantages, it is clear that the factory management has taken full advantage of the opportunities afforded by the reforms, and was not wooed into complacency by the commanding position the enterprise occupies in the industry. Rather, the factory has remained on the cutting edge of the industry in its efforts at diversification, innovation, and growth.

The proliferation of a great diversity of enterprises administered at a variety of bureaucratic levels within the woodcarving profession in Dongyang county represents an unprecedented level of competition for the Dongyang Woodcarving Factory, and have doubtless been a factor encouraging its efforts at innovation and diversification. Many of these factories began their existence processing products *(jia gong)* in subcontracting relations with the Dongyang Woodcarving Factory, but have now taken advantage of opportunities offered by the economic reforms to bud off in independent and semi-independent operation. Others have been started by former employees of the Dongyang Woodcarving Factory like Wu Pinju of Xia Qi Tan village, who left to start up their own enterprises under the economic reforms. The factory is, in this sense, the most significant fount of intra-county relations *(guanxi)* in the industry, although as we have seen, extra-county relationships have taken on greater significance since the implementation of the economic reforms.

While newly established enterprises compete for labor, raw materials, and markets with the Dongyang Woodcarving Factory, they have not really challenged its centrality in the industry. It is still a commanding economic presence in the line. Its masters are for the most part former apprentices of the most accomplished craftsmen of the previous generation, and its aesthetic influence in the field is unmatched. Finally, its leadership enjoys influence and prestige in the highest reaches of the national polity as representatives of the entire profession, giving the Dongyang Woodcarving Factory a prominence far beyond its fellow producers in the county.

Chapter 8

Conclusion

Flexible Production in Dongyang?

The previous chapters have documented the development and dynamism of the rural industrial and artisan sectors in several Dongyang communities under recent Chinese market-oriented reforms. The enterprises of such sectors have also figured prominently in recent theoretical discussions of economic development as models for industrial organization under contemporary world market conditions said to favor so-called flexible specialization (Piore and Sabel 1984), flexible production (Dirlik 1994), or flexible accumulation (Harvey 1990). In this chapter, we turn to examine Dongyang county's recent development experience in light of those discussions.

Piore and Sabel celebrate flexible specialization as "a strategy of permanent innovation: accommodation to ceaseless change, ... based on flexible multi-use equipment; skilled workers; and the creation ... of an industrial community that restricts the forms of competition to those favoring innovation" (1984: 17).

In Harvey's characterization,

> Flexible accumulation ... is marked by a direct confrontation with the rigidities of Fordism. It rests on flexibility with respect to labor processes, labor markets, products, and patterns of consumption. It is characterized by the emergence of entirely new sectors of production, new ways of providing financial services, new markets, and, above all, greatly intensified rates of commercial, technological, and organizational innovation. (Harvey 1990: 147)

Piore and Sabel see the historical triumph of Fordist mass production technology in the west as the result of contingent historical processes that might have led to a recognition of the positive characteristics of a so-called craft model, in which worker alienation deriving from detailed divisions of labor and the separation between conception and execution in production would be minimized.

For Piore and Sabel, "Technology is a refractory yet periodically malleable expression of the distribution of power in society" (1984: 21). Flexible specialization represents a revival of craft forms of production that were emarginated during the early stages of the industrial revolution. In Harvey's words, these forms were

> ... the missed opportunity of the mid-nineteenth century ... that had the potential to solve the problem of industrial organization along decentralized and democratically controlled lines.... With the new decentralized technologies of command and control, [such regimes] can successfully integrate with, and even subvert, the dominant and repressive forms of labor organization characteristic of corporate and multinational capital. (Harvey 1990: 189)

Piore and Sabel see the newly emergent industrial enterprises in and around Turin, Italy, as characteristic of such regimes. These firms consistently produce a wide range of products for highly differentiated regional markets at home and abroad, constantly altered in response to changing markets or tastes. They make flexible use of increasingly productive, widely applicable technology, and attempt to balance cooperation and competition among regionally affiliated firms (1984: 29). In Piore and Sabel's analysis,

> Four coincident factors were crucial to this innovative turn: the Italian extended family; the view of artisan work as a distinct type of economic activity; the existence of merchant traditions connecting the Italian provinces to world markets; and the willingness of municipal and regional governments (often allied to the labor movement) to help create the infrastructure that the firms required but could not themselves provide. (1984: 227)

The enterprises of Turin were family operations, in which members "put in long hours at low wages to meet deadlines and pay installments on the first pieces of machinery" (1984: 228). Technology was flexible "in both a narrow and a broad sense," permitting "quick, inexpensive shifts from one product to another within a family of goods," as well as diversification in the range of materials worked and operations performed, "to facilitate the transition from one whole family of products to another" (1984: 30). Municipal and regional governments contributed by constructing industrial parks for the small producers, improving roads, establishing vocational schools, and operating regional research centers (1984: 228).

In Piore and Sabel's formulation, flexible specialization is based on an artisan-like community in which workers and managers recognize that they must deal with one another over the long term. Thus not only are efforts made to stabilize relations among federated firms, but also to secure labor's place in the community. For such reasons, "prices of the goods and services exchanged reflect not momentary market circumstances but a mutually agreed upon rate of fair return" (Piore and Sabel 1984: 272).

Piore and Sabel rediscover Polanyi's "substantive economics" and Mauss's "total social phenomenon" in flexible production where

> it is hard to tell where society (in the form of the family and school ties or community celebrations of ethnic and political identity) ends, and where economic organization begins. Among the ironies of the resurgence of craft production is that its deployment of modern technology depends on its reinvigoration of affiliations that are associated with the preindustrial past. (1984: 275)

Blim (n.d. and 1992) has examined Piore and Sabel's central Italy paradigm case of flexible specialization, and takes the authors to task for ignoring a long period of "extensive proto-industrial development" that "not only provided postwar entrepreneurs with models for petty production and accumulation, but had trained a whole generation of urban workers and former sharecroppers in the methods of production, marketing, and entrepreneurial risk-taking" (n.d.: 9).

Furthermore, Blim is doubtful that any form of industrial organization would have made development possible in central Italy, absent the necessary condition of unprecedented post–World War II economic boom (1992: 94). Blim also notes that the flexibly organized central Italian shoe enterprises he studied soon encountered serious problems competing with emergent shoe industries in Taiwan, South Korea, and Brazil (1992: 97), and became "engaged in a painful and uncertain process of re-dimensioning their industry to meet the new challenge of a rapidly changing, and cheaper world market" (n.d.: 10).

Notwithstanding these reservations, Blim credits Piore and Sabel with reinforcing the notion that "regional development achieved by gaining access to a changing world market is an adaptive process in which producers can ... find a suitable niche for their efforts"; and with recognizing that

> small-scale industrialization, if executed on a regional basis by a broad-based, popular entrepreneurial stratum, may provide participating regions with greater possibilities for generating recoverable wealth. Less surplus is siphoned off by brokers and transnational firms. And because the wealth created is both modest in amount and widely dispersed ... more of it is likely to be consumed through the local purchase of goods and services" (n.d.: 12)

At a broader level, Harvey (1990) is critical of what he takes to be Piore and Sabel's rhapsodic descriptions of flexible production. Harvey is uncertain about whether flexible production, or as he prefers to call it, flexible accumulation, is really anything new, or just a jazzed-up version of capitalism (1990: 188), with a distinctive mix of accumulation strategies combining extraction of absolute surplus value (through extension of the workday coupled with an overall reduction in the standard of living of the work force), and relative surplus value (through organizational and technological change set in motion to gain temporary profits for innovative firms and more generalized profits as costs of goods that define the standard of living of labor are reduced) (1990: 186).

Harvey sees "much that is regressive and repressive" about such production regimes (1990: 189), not least of which is the difficulty that the labor force finds in articulating its class interests in small, family-run enterprises (1990: 153).

> Geographical mobility and decentralization are used against a union power which traditionally concentrated in the factories of mass production. Capital flight, deindustrialization of some regions, and industrialization of others, the destruction of traditional working class communities as power bases of class struggle, become leitmotifs of spatial transformation under more flexible conditions of accumulation. (Harvey 1990: 294)

Harvey notes that flexible accumulation has also fostered an increasing reliance on part-time, temporary, or subcontracted work arrangements (1990: 150). While he acknowledges that flexibility in scheduling can sometimes be mutually beneficial to both employer and worker, and subcontracting may be instrumental in creating opportunities for small business formation, both are also often associated with efforts to undermine labor's ability to organize, and with reliance on sweated labor under appalling conditions (1990: 152).

Harvey also notes that subcontracting has been a long-established pattern in Japan where, "even under Fordism, small business sub-contracting acted as a buffer to protect large corporations from the cost of market fluctuations" (1990: 151).

Neither Harvey nor Piore and Sabel expect that flexible production will replace Fordist mass production everywhere, and both authorities recognize that even in its heyday Fordism was never universal practice. Harvey sees the current world economy as

> characterized by a mix of highly efficient Fordist production . . . in some sectors and regions . . . and more traditional production systems . . . resting on artisanal, paternalistic or patriarchal labor relations, embodying quite different mechanisms of labor control [in others]. (Harvey 1990: 191)

Piore and Sabel interpret this mix in terms of a version of economic "dualism" deriving from the very nature of mass production machinery which enables the production of goods of a general nature using specialized resources—the more general the goods, the broader the market, allowing large investment in specialized machinery to be recouped by economies of scale.

But the special-purpose machinery required for mass production cannot itself be mass produced and

> must, in fact, be built according to a logic that is the mirror image of mass production: the production of specialized goods through general resources. Because the product is a specialty, with a limited market, production must be continually reorganized; and workers must have the range of skills and general understanding of the process that are classically attributed to preindustrial artisans. . . .
> At the fringe of almost every industry, therefore, small firms survive by supplying a changing variety of oddments or responding to surges in demand. In exceptional cases—for example, women's garments—most of an industry consists of such firms. (Piore and Sabel 1984: 27)

Gates has pointed out that flexible production was actually inspired by, and often adopted in direct imitation of, East Asian systems.

> The West did not borrow petty-capitalist organizational mechanisms until east Asia began to outcompete Fordist production. For east Asians, "domestic, familial, and paternalistic labour systems" were not "revived" in the mid-twentieth century; they are an autochthonous east Asian mode of labor regulation. (1996: 223)

Thus the petty capitalist institutions of China's emergent private sector "facilitate the embrace with [global] capitalism while making that intercourse less like rape" (Gates 1996: 226). In the right political-economic environment, petty capitalists have proved themselves capable

> of competition with foreign firms, of production of both simple and complex goods, of effective import–export activity, of creating flexible financial institutions, and of accumulating capital in a pattern in which very large numbers of families can participate. (Gates 1996: 226)

Whether authocthonous or not, there is much in the landscape of Dongyang county's rural industrial sector under current economic reforms that evokes the elements said to characterize such flexible industrial regimes, although the evidence is by no means unequivocal.

For example, Piore and Sabel's critical analysis of the triumph of the Fordist mass production regime in Western industrial organization echoes in many of its particulars the rhetoric of the Chinese Cultural Revolution. If "[T]echnology is a refractory yet periodically malleable expression of the distribution of power in society" (1984: 21), then the ways in which it is deployed would surely reflect the alignment of class forces in society, and the resources that capital and labor can bring to bear on the issue. Chairman Mao might well agree.

Indeed, Piore and Sabel (1984: 15) come close to adducing a position similar to that of Mao's "On Practice," which was used during the Cultural Revolution to argue that there is no class-neutral organization of production, that an enterprise expresses in its organization of production a distinct class perspective with respect to relations between laborer and employer.

While this perspective has scholarly adherents in the West (see, e.g., Edwards 1979), in the eyes of most Chinese who lived through the

Cultural Revolution, such analyses evoke memories of the politicization of the workplace and work life that characterized the period and a great deal of unpleasantness that went with it. The alternate organization of technology, vertical and horizontal job enlargement, attempts to create all-around generalist workers and eliminate the distinction in the division of labor between those who labor with their minds and those who labor with their hands—all of which Piore and Sabel tout as characteristic of the craft model of industrial organization (1984: 244)—were widely discussed during the Cultural Revolution in China and given token institutional expression in most enterprises by the creation of new management boards, the so-called revolutionary committees, on which ordinary workers were represented, along with the party and the army.

Nevertheless, we have seen that the Dongyang Woodcarving Factory continued to operate throughout the Cultural Revolution period with apparently little notice of the separation between conception and execution manifest in its design studio, let alone any attempt to reorganize production and eliminate this manifestation of capitalist alienation. This might be interpreted as a sign of superficiality in theoretical understanding, or even duplicity in the revolutionary rhetoric of the rebel faction, perhaps a measure of both.

In any case, the "revolutionary committees" have long since been dismantled, and former attempts to address issues of worker alienation arising from the organization of production and division of labor have now been repudiated in China as inefficient idealist deviations. There is thus a tendency in Dongyang, as well as other areas of China, for conceptions of efficiency to run essentially along Fordist lines. Detailed divisions of labor and the separation of conception and execution are accepted as the inevitable consequences of industrialization, as the "most efficient" solution.

The adoption of organizational forms characteristic of flexible production systems—artisan communities of labor, organized in patriarchal and paternalistic relations with petty capital—seem to coexist in Dongyang with a Fordist mentality regarding the technical division of labor and organization of production. Critical perspectives on Fordist mass production, again, evoke the horrors or folly of "class struggle" in the workplace associated with the Cultural Revolution, and are usually dismissed out of hand.

In many other respects, however, the development of Dongyang's rural industrial sector bears a striking resemblance to Piore and Sabel's account of the experience of Turin. In Dongyang, the "county of 100 skills," development was reflective of the county's own local endowments, and was shaped by traditions of artisan skill, high levels of education, and traditions of expatriation. Early efforts in industrialization under economic reform were based on such skills, and underwrote diversification, both within the woodcarving line and more broadly. The role of local government, most prominently the local township industrial offices *(gongye bangongshi)*, but also the county government, in providing infrastructure and financing for that diversification is similarly prominent in Dongyang's experience.

Within the woodcarving line, traditional skills proved flexible and adaptable in the self-conscious "return" to decorative construction, symbolized most dramatically in the grand screen of Singapore's Dong Palace Hotel, and the subsequent creation of specialized decorative construction companies among Dongyang county's rural enterprises. In this latter context, the return to construction also entailed a breaking out of the local and regional nexus into the arena of the international market.

The private enterprise of Zhang Wanlong, the Christian carver of Hu Qi town, adapted the traditional skills of carving to the production of decorative Christian art objects, creating a new market niche for carved wood products with export potential. The enterprise itself represents at once a "departure" with respect to Chinese traditions of representation in wood, and a "revival" of a later inflected, commoditized, missionized, colonial tradition of the early-twentieth-century Chinese treaty ports.

The market for cremation urn boxes provides one further instance of how Dongyang woodcarvers adapted flexibly to new conditions, creating a product in response to a need brought about by government regulations regarding the disposal of the dead in urban areas.

The Dongyang Woodcarving Factory's relatively strong capital position within the industry and the county allowed it to sponsor a vocational middle school, branch out into mass-produced "imitation rosewood" furniture, and even into hotel management, while extending the market for its traditional ware, exporting Buddhist altars and their appurtenances to new Japanese consumers.

But more significantly with respect to broader development goals, the woodcarving industry in Dongyang provided a base from which diversification into a variety of industrial lines was carried out, and the overall significance of woodcarving to the county economy superseded.

Where Dongyang's pre-reform woodcarving enterprises were for the most part cooperatives run by commune and production brigade authorities, once the reforms had taken hold, the familiar patriarchal patterns of Chinese family organization very quickly reemerged in the expanding private sector as the armature of organization and financing of rural enterprise.

The economic reforms of the 1980s gave residents of Dongyang new opportunities to build on their traditions of expatriation as well. Social networks *(guanxi)* deriving from the perambulations of past generations of craftsmen became instrumental under the economic reforms in finding employment outside the county, which in turn provided the basis on which to build savings for investment in private rural enterprise. Often such networks also helped in the discovery of new markets for already functioning enterprises. The reestablishment of links to Hong Kong and Taiwan expatriates may yet provide a basis for attracting foreign investment to the county, an area where Dongyang still lags behind its more well-placed coastal provincial sister cities of Ningbo, Shaoxing, and Wenzhou. The creation of the Dongyang Economic Development Zone is clearly designed to enhance Dongyang's competitive position relative to these other centers, and seems poised to achieve a measure of success.

Cultivation of *guanxi* at the local, national, and increasingly international level remains a central feature in social life, but the economic reforms have given it a somewhat revised significance. Traditionally, one's "network of relations" *(guanxiwang)* manifested a diffuseness of social, economic, ritual, and political function, the Maussian "total social phenomenon" par excellence, if you will. In the Maoist period, while no less "total" in its diffuseness, the emphasis in *guanxi* cultivation was very much on the political, since it was in relation to the political structure of society that rewards and benefits were allocated. Getting in the "back door" was achieved through political connections. While political connections still count for something in Dongyang, one of the refreshing things about the economic reforms has been the delinking of social life from considerations of political influence and connection. The cultivation of *guanxi,* still no less important and still no less diffuse, has shifted decidedly in its emphasis in the direction of the economic. The dominant feature of its rationale has shifted (see, e.g., Yang 1994: 159).

CONCLUSION—FLEXIBLE PRODUCTION IN DONGYANG? 177

Perhaps the most distinctive characteristic of Dongyang's flexibility is the diversity of ownership form encouraged in its rural industrial policy, and the trend toward privatization, implemented by the Communist Party that had on several previous occasions trampled on the private sector. Policy pronouncements from the Zhejiang provincial authorities during the late 1980s acknowledged that state-run, local collectively run, and private enterprises all had something to contribute to the development of the productive forces of society, and were supportive of a multilinear development strategy characterized by many patterns, many paths, and dependent on local regional endowments and skills.

Huang (1990) places such pronouncements in a national context, noting that economic policies of the central government adopted in the late 1980s came to reflect an appreciation of the significance of "differential optimums."

> Different kinds of production are optimal at different scales under different technological conditions. There need be no dogmatic attachment to either small-scale or large-scale production, the inclinations of the classical views of Smith and Marx notwithstanding. At this point, official [Chinese] thinking seems to be tending more and more toward flexibly conceived "appropriate scale economies" that vary with different conditions of production. (Huang 1990: 321)

The intent of such policies is even given metaphorical expression by Communist planners in Zhejiang who invoke the Eight Immortals of Daoist folklore (DDZGZJ: 1989: 1: 281), each of whom contributed their distinctive capabilities *(Ge Xian qi neng)* to the common goal of locomoting across the sea *(Ba Xian guo hai),* and defeating the Sea Dragon King (see Appendix 6). So too, should the many patterns, many paths, many forms of enterprise ownership have a chance to demonstrate their capabilities in advancing the development of the productive forces of society and establishing the material basis for a "socialism with Chinese characteristics."

The phrase "socialism with Chinese characteristics," which became current in the 1980s, expresses the flexibility of a socialist system in which the private sector is allowed considerable scope for accumulation, and foreign investment is welcomed in special economic zones, and more broadly, to encourage exports, earn foreign exchange, and stimulate economic growth by engaging the global world market. As we have noted, in China this strategy is also linked to preparing for the absorption of Hong Kong and reunification with Taiwan under the banner of "one country, two systems." In short, socialist China is willing to place itself on the pathways of transnational capital (Dirlik 1994: 88) to advance its political and development goals, while allowing an unprecedented accumulation of private wealth among its own citizens as well.

Dirlik has gone so far as to characterize "socialism with Chinese characteristics" as the "socialism of the period of flexible production" (1994: 55). For Dirlik, in its early years, Chinese socialism (following the Soviet example) "mimicked First World capitalist development" in its Fordist phase. In its market-oriented economic reforms, China now mimics the export development strategies of the newly industrialized countries in which subcontracting for multinationals plays a major part, and similar arrangements already tie China to the global economy (Dirlik 1994: 55).

Subcontracting, while present in Dongyang's local economy, is somewhat different from the phenomenon Dirlik and Harvey see as characteristic of flexible accumulation. Although Dongyang folk have been participants in labor contracts undertaken in transnational contexts, subcontracting from multinationals has not been a major factor in Dongyang's development as yet (much to the chagrin of county officials). But subcontracting in the form of *cheng bao* contracts between state and collective units and their managers, division heads, sales managers, and workshop foremen was pervasive in county life in the late 1980s and early 1990s, as were simple putting-out arrangements in woodcarving, wallcovering manufacture, and other product lines as well.

Cheng bao contracts were begun initially as a way of introducing more direct manager responsibility for enterprise performance in the context of state or collective control. As the practice caught on and spread, such contracts became stepping stones on the career path to private enterprise, either through experience gained or outright purchase. Thus, while subcontracting is ubiquitous in county life, it is a lower level variety than that involving multinational corporations. The disparities between partners to *cheng bao* subcontracts in Dongyang are far smaller than those in the pattern of subcontracts that Dirlik and Harvey have in mind.

Nevertheless, Dongyang is anxious to have more of the latter as well, and the county government has done what it can to woo more multinationals to the county. Like the Turin described by Piore and Sabel, Dongyang's county government has taken measures to improve local infrastructure, creating industrial development zones, widening roads, establishing vocational schools, building new housing blocks, constructing accommodations for visitors, and offering incentives to foreign investors.

The flexibility, if such there be, in Chinese economic reforms as they have been implemented in Dongyang is manifest most prominently with respect to forms of enterprise ownership—state, collective, and private. The distinctive configuration that the array of these forms has taken in Dongyang is representative of a broader regional flexibility in which toleration of many patterns and many paths to development allows local and regional skills and endowments to be given expression.

The encouragement of private accumulation and investment certainly manifest a degree of flexibility in contrast to the former policies of the socialist state under which collective farming and centralized planning had prevailed for 30 to 40 years, and private profit was considered a capitalist crime. In addition to considerably extending the meaning of flexibility implied in the term *flexible production,* this distinctive historical context also means that daily life in the increasingly privatized rural industrial sector is experienced as that much more exhilarating, fulfilling, and liberating.

Like the county town of Wu Ning, each of our field settings was experiencing dramatic and dynamic transformation. Industrial enterprise had come to replace agriculture as the principal source of household income, either in the form of wage labor or profit on capital invested. The standard of living was rising, savings were substantial, and material livelihood increasingly secure. Ties to expatriate kin in Hong Kong and Taiwan had been or increasingly were being reestablished. Opportunities for geographical and occupational mobility were also instrumental in enhancing earning power and savings of rural residents, making possible further investment in a variety of industrial fields. Prolonged absence in extra-community employment has left agriculture in the hands of the elderly, the "specialized households" of neighbors, or hired labor, providing new incentives for mechanization in some areas. The overall success of the reforms is marked most dramatically in improved housing, encouraged by a rather severe inflation of the local currency in the late 1980s to be sure, but still expressive of the economic vitality of all four communities.

Huang's conclusion with respect to the causes of increased prosperity of the Yangzi delta under the economic reforms would also seem to apply to Dongyang. Rather than any dramatic breakthrough in crop yields resulting from the supposedly superior incentive power of marketized family farming, it was the diversification of the rural economy and the diversion of underemployed labor power from farming into off-farm employment that was responsible (Huang 1990: 246). It was rural industry, by far the most dynamic and important source of off-farm employment, "more than anything else, that accounted for the increased rural prosperity of the 1980s" (Huang 1990: 284).

Dirlik has pointed to the paradox of China as an economy that has been incorporated into the global capitalist economy under the supervision of the Communist Party, and wonders whether the Communist Party can convert itself successfully into an overseer of such an economy (Dirlik 1994: 56–57).

An equally decisive question for the future would seem to be to what extent broad scope for economic democracy can be reconciled with continued Communist Party hegemony politically. In the short term, any challenge to that hegemony was headed off by the Tiananmen massacre in 1989, during the aftermath of which Dongyang's aspirations to become a university town suffered a major setback.

But the trend toward privatization as well as the amassing of considerable private fortunes in Dongyang continues, with increased efforts being made to attract foreign investment to achieve local development goals. The crackdown on political expression has not affected the expanded scope of economic rights implemented during the reforms of the 1980s. But the emergence of independent and increasingly large centers of economic power in the countryside remains for the party to reckon with.

Of course, the "four little dragons" of the Pacific—Taiwan, Hong Kong, Singapore, and South Korea (Jean Genet referred to them as the "four little whores")—have demonstrated to everyone's satisfaction that economic growth under conditions of flexible accumulation is not incompatible with an authoritarian political regime. China's southern provinces of Guangdong and Fujian, with their special economic zones and proximity to Hong Kong and Taiwan, are increasingly spoken of as a "fifth little dragon."

While Zhejiang province has experienced less spectacular growth than either Guangdong or Fujian, precisely for that reason I trust that our account of the development experience of Dongyang county, a relatively backward region of this relatively highly commercialized coastal province, has shed some light on the sources of economic dynamism presently reflected in the performance statistics of the Chinese economy as a whole (see, e.g., Overholt 1993: 27).

A good measure of that dynamism is surely attributable to patterns of development that theorists of "flexible production" would find familiar.

Appendix 1

Ham Production

Ham production has occupied rural households during the winter season throughout the Jinhua region since the Southern Song dynasty (A.D. 1127–1279), and merits detailed discussion. Among the more well known of Dongyang's native agricultural products, such Jinhua ham is produced from the distinctive local variety of pig, "two-headed crow" *(shuang tou wu)*, so named because its shoulders and haunches are typically black, and its midsection white.

The patron saint of ham making was a man called Zong Ze (A.D. 1059–1128), a native of Yi Wu county neighboring Dongyang to the west. A holder of the *jinshi* degree, he is said to have played a role in the Song dynasty wars against the invading armies of Jin, and even to have rescued the Song capital of Kaifeng from Jin forces.

According to one account, the patriotic people and militia from the area of Yi Wu and Dongyang who participated in the war effort on the side of the Song brought provisions to General Zong in Kaifeng. Among these was a "home county pork" *(jia xiang rou),* made of the best parts of the pig's legs, preserved with salt and dried to prevent its spoiling (Wang 1983: 14). In another account, Zong Ze is said to have commissioned the production of the salted meat to take along with him on his campaigns. In still another account, villagers brought the meat to the capital to commiserate with Zong Ze when he ran afoul of accusations against him originating with the peace faction at the Song court (Gong 1987: 5). In any event, Zong Ze has become associated with ham production, and his image is always hung in the shops that purvey Jinhua hams (Zhai 1981: 161).

It is said that "Jinhua ham comes from Dongyang, and Dongyang ham comes from Shang Jiang." Shang Jiang is a village of somewhat more than 100 households, 13 to 14 km due east of the county town of Wu Ning. Of its hams, the most prized is Xuefang Jiang tui, first produced in the Jiaqing reign period (1796–1820) of the Qing dynasty

APPENDIX 1: HAM PRODUCTION

A "two-headed crow" pig valued for the production of Dongyang hams.

by Mr. Jiang Xuefang, an extremely skillful master and manager of a ham curing workshop, whose products were of extraordinarily high quality (Zhai 1981: 163).

Every year he made several hundred hams for Mr. Hu Xueyan, the proprietor of Hu Qingyu Tang, a large Chinese herbal medicine shop in the provincial capital Hangzhou. The hams were taken to Beijing and presented as gifts to influential nobles, where they won approval and appreciation. When Jiang Xuefang died, his descendants continued his distinctive curing techniques under a variety of brands produced under separate management—Xue Fang Hou Ji, Xue Fang Zheng Ji, Xue Fang Sheng Ji, Xue Fang Shen Ji (Gong 1987: 20).

In 1915, Xuefang ham won a gold medal at the Panama Canal International Commodities Exhibition, and in 1929 it earned a medal for excellence at the Hangzhou, West Lake Commodities Exhibition (FSZ 1985: 35).

A fourth-generation descendant of Jiang Xuefang, Mr. Jiang Dingtu attributes the high quality of Shang Jiang hams to the strict care with which materials of standard weight, length, and girth are chosen; to the meticulousness with which fresh materials are processed according to schedule; and to adjustments made in processing to take account of weather conditions (Zhai 1981: 163).

In the 1930s, Dongyang farmers raised 170,000 pigs annually, about one-fourth of which were slaughtered locally to make fresh pork, another one-fourth of which were sent live to Hangzhou, Jiaxing, and other urban centers. One-half of the animals were processed locally into ham and bacon (Ministry of Industry 1935: 614).

Farmers typically bought suckling pigs weighing from 20 to 30 catties each from breeders, and fed them for six months, after which the pigs were full grown, weighing over 100 catties. Live pigs were sold through merchant associations *(hang)* in the cities, which charged a commission of 30 cents a head. The price paid for a pig depended on its weight, and an animal suitable for ham making, weighing 100 catties, was worth approximately ¥16.

The principal markets in Zhejiang for the hams and pork of Dongyang were Hangzhou, Ningbo, and Shaoxing, where supplies intended for Shanghai and foreign markets were first collected. For the wholesale trade, hams were packed in bamboo crates containing 40 to 50 pieces, weighing 180 catties (90 kilograms). The completion of the railway from Hangzhou to Jiangshan in the southwest of the province in the early 1930s facilitated the transport of hams from producing districts in Jinhua to Hangzhou, although commentators in 1935 noted that rail freight was slightly more expensive than traditional water transport (Ministry of Industry 1935: 616–617).

Prior to 1930, the Zhejiang provincial government imposed a tax on hams produced in the province which brought in ¥81,000 a year. This tax was farmed out to the Ham Manufacturer's Guild in Hangzhou, which sent agents to the producing districts to collect the tax at a rate of 9 *fen* per ham. This levy was discontinued when a business tax was imposed, and a wholesale merchant thereafter paid an annual tax of 5 percent on his capital, while a retailer paid 10 percent (Ministry of Industry 1935: 615).

Because the bulk of hams were produced in dispersed agricultural sideline activity in rural counties, statistics for production in the 1930s are less than totally reliable. Nevertheless, such statistics as are available show Dongyang county producing over a third of the hams in Zhejiang province in 1931 and 1932. The figures for Dongyang were more than 5,000 metric tons greater than for the county with the next largest production, Lanqi.

From the mid-1930s down to 1949, pig raising suffered a decline in the economic dislocation of the countryside. While in 1933 production

Table 1A

Ham and Bacon Production Figures (in metric tons)

	1931		1932	
	Hams	Bacon	Hams	Bacon
Dongyang	13,937	348.4	13,491	337.3
Zhejiang	40,959.9	1,017.8	34,607	865.2

	Value in Yuan			
	1931		1932	
	Hams	Bacon	Hams	Bacon
Dongyang	¥975,590	¥243,898	¥944,370	¥236,093
Zhejiang	2,849,693	712,506	2,422,495	605,525

of Jinhua hams had reached 837,130 pieces, in 1948 only 190,000 pieces were produced (Xu 1983: 2). Other sources put the production figure for "just prior to liberation" (presumably the year 1949) at 119,000 pieces (Zhai 1981: 162).

After liberation, ham production revived and developed. New processing plants were established all over the Jinhua region, reviving the traditional skills, and introducing some innovations (Xu 1983: 2–3). The highest production figure during the 1950s was 350,000 pieces; during the 1960s, 480,000 pieces; during the 1970s, 709,000 pieces. Figures for 1986 had already reached more than 1.3 million pieces (Gong 1987: 7).

In 1981, Jinhua ham was awarded a national gold medal for excellence and in recent years, exports of Jinhua ham have risen continuously. In 1975, 328 tons were exported; in 1982, 620 tons (Xu 1983: 3).

In Dongyang county ham production was also revived after 1949, under the unified management of the county Local Products Company (Tuchan Gongsi). By the early 1980s the county was producing 1,010,000 head of pigs, 475,300 of which were sold to the state (Pan 1984: 561ff.). In the early 1980s Dongyang was producing about 25 percent of all Jinhua hams. In 1982, the Xue Fang brand, still produced in Shang Jiang village, was designated a "national commodity of the highest quality," and assigned the new brand name, Tezhi Jinhua Jiang Tui. Of the total of 150,000 hams produced in Dongyang county in 1982, more than 5,000 were Te Zhi Jinhua Jiang Tui (Xu 1983: 5).

The folklore associated with ham is generally unsavory. In the old society, a gift of ham (song huo tui) was inevitably required when interceding on someone's behalf, seeking a favor, scheming for an official post, appearing before the magistrate, or in any sort of fraudulent or corrupt transaction. While commentators note that these customs were swept away for the most part in the first ten or so years after the establishment of the People's Republic, they also recognize that traditional Chinese ritual propriety, in which giving and receiving of gifts is considered appropriate in exchange for favors, still prevailed, and ham remained an important currency in such transactions (Wang 1983: 13).

Indeed, the Cultural Revolution was said to have brought gifts of ham back into more common practice as a means of "opening the back door." People say that each time the facts of a case were transferred up a level in the Communist bureaucracy during this period, two hams would do the trick. To get approval for expanding or building on to one's house, it is said that each bureau concerned had to eat its fill of ham. In general, ham is also given as a means of smoothing over humiliation or loss of face.

Production

The distinctive character of Jinhua hams is due primarily to the pigs from which they are made, the aforementioned *shuang tou wu* (two-headed crows). Their skin is thin, their bones are light, their back fat is thick, and the meat of their hind legs is soft and juicy (Zhai 1981: 163).

Most households in Dongyang raise at least one pig each year for consumption during New Year's. Considerable care is taken in choosing piglets, and differing colorations of black and white are distinguished. Traditionally, when one went to market to buy a pig one avoided piglets that were "white tails," "three leggers" (those with one white leg), or "white between the eyebrows" (those with white coloring on the neck) (FSZ 1985: 17). Nowadays, hybrid varieties are becoming more widespread, the most desirable of which are those bred of a female of the local "two-headed crow" variety and a male of a foreign breed, Yorkshire or Longwhite (FSZ 1985: 17).

Before taking a small pig to market for sale, one must first offer sacrifice to the pigpen spirit *(zhu lan shen)* using incense and paper money, and only then can the piglet be put in the pig basket. When a buyer decides on a small pig, the seller must send along a little rice straw from its pen, called *niang jia cao* (grass from its mother's family). If a male piglet has still not been neutered, the seller must make a concession in price for the neutering fee.

When a small pig changes hands, the buyer normally obtains a certificate endorsed by a guarantor on which the seller's name and address are written. If the pig is found to be sick, or dies within one market period (usually five days), it can be returned to the seller for a refund, or kept upon receipt of a refund of half the cost. Generally, the guarantor is a professional trader of the market, called a "tooth official" *(ya lang)* (FSZ 1985: 17–18).

When a pig is slaughtered it is said euphemistically to "come out of the pen" *(chu lan)*. Traditionally, before slaughtering the animal one first offered sacrifice to the pigpen spirit, requesting his permission, and only then could one enter the pen and get the pig. The service of slaughtering the pig was often performed by a specialist who received no money wage, only the pig's bristles and small intestines. But it was common for especially courteous families to invite the slaughterer to share in the first meal of pork from the pig in question. So the wages of the slaughterer were said to be "one bristle set, one complete intestine, one meal." Nowadays this habit has changed, and wages are paid in cash, more or less equivalent to the market value of these items (FSZ 1985: 18).

Jiang tui hams, the elite of Dongyang hams, use the hind legs of "two-headed crow" pigs of a gross weight of 120 to 140 market *jin* (60–70 kilos). The hind legs weigh about 9.5 to 12 market *jin* (5–6 kilos) each *(Jiang tui* n.d.; Xu 1983: 5). A dry atmosphere and even temperature are essential to the making of good hams, and consequently winter is the most active season for curing in Dongyang, though a small quantity of hams is also made in the spring. Curing activities usually begin on the first day of winter *(li dong)*, the nineteenth solar term, in early November, and continue till the onset of the twenty-fourth solar term *(da han)* in late January (Xu 1983: 6).

Carcasses are first divided into flanks, fore-quarters, and hind-quarters, the latter being made into hams, and the remainder used for salted pork and sausage (Ministry of Industry 1935: 615).

The actual production of ham consists of several stages. The first is removing the "embryo." In this stage the bones are chopped out of the center of the round-hind quarter, the fat separated, and the excess blood drained.

The second stage involves laying on the salt. Generally, every 10 *jin* (5 kilos) of meat requires 8 *liang* (about half a kilo) of salt—2 liang for the first salting, known as "out of the water" salt; 4 liang for the second salting, called "laying on the big salt," which must be performed on the following day; 1 liang for the third salting, called "near the bone salt," which must be spread in the joints four days after the "big salt"; and half a liang for the fourth salting, called "guard the bone salt," which must be performed six days later. During the intervals between salting, the hams must also be sprinkled with water at appropriate times.

The next stage, "washing and drying," commences after twenty-five days. First the hams are soaked overnight in clear water. On the next day, any mold that may have developed on the skin is trimmed away, and the hams are washed clean to remove any remaining blood, blemishes, or salt on the outer skin. They are then left to dry outside for four or five clear days, until oil begins to ooze from the outer skin, and thin cracks appear on the surface of the dry meat. They are then brought back inside and hung in a drafty corner, where they are left for half a year to ferment (FSZ 1985: 35).

During fermentation, the legs must be kept about seven centimeters apart and must not touch, to ensure proper ventilation. Before the hot season sets in, the hams must be taken from their frames, washed and dried again, and trimmed three times. Afterward, sesame oil is applied repeatedly to prevent harm from insects, and to give the hams a bright appearance. In the fall, the hams are taken down again, mold and fungus are removed, and oil applied for the last time *(Jiang tui* n.d.). Upon completion, each ham weighs between 5.5 and 7.5 *jin* (3 to 4 kilos), having lost 30 to 40 percent of its original weight in the process (Xu 1983: 6).

There are actually quite a number of varieties of ham produced in Dongyang which differ in their raw materials, seasons of processing, and curing processes. Ham cured in mid-winter *(long dong)* is known as *zheng dong tui*—"ham from the dead of winter." Ham cured at the start of winter *(chu dong)* is known as *zao dong tui* "early winter ham." Ham cured after the beginning of spring *(li chun)* is known as "spring ham." Ham that is formed in the shape of a crescent moon *(yue ya)* is known as "crescent moon ham." Ham that is made from the front legs of the pig, because its shape is rectangular, is called "square ham"—*fang tui.* Ham that is hung in the kitchen and receives the smoke of burning bamboo leaves, carries the aroma of the leaves and is called "bamboo leaf ham." Ham that is cured with white sugar is called "sugar ham." Ham that is made from dog's legs is called *xu tui*—"dog ham" (Gong 1987: 14–15).

The meat of dog ham is said to be especially tender and distinctive in flavor. Its method of production is the same as ordinary ham except for the meat employed. It is also produced between the onset of winter and the onset of spring, but is not fermented like regular ham. It is said to be high in minerals and low in fat, to relieve kidney ailments, aid the circulation of the blood, and be soothing to aches in the small of the back and knee joints (Xu 1983: 10–11; Zhai 1981: 162).

In recent years, still more varieties of Dongyang ham have been introduced, and Dongyang now markets "round ham," "frozen ham," "sweet sauce ham," "hot pepper ham," "banana ham," and "tangerine ham" (Zhai 1981: 162).

One of the more well-known innovators in the tradition of ham production is Mr. Sun Shichun, a native of Dongyang's Lu Zhai village, particularly skilled at making early winter and late spring hams. In 1954, the Dongyang native products corporation had a shortfall in winter hams, and did not fulfill its quota for the national plan. The corporation commissioned Mr. Sun to make an additional amount of "spring ham," more than 10,000 pieces. After undergoing inspection by the provincial food products corporation, the quality of his product was found to surpass that of traditional winter ham. As a result, a restriction against the sale of spring ham outside the county was lifted. The *Zhejiang Provincial Daily,* the *New People's Evening News,* and *Da Gong Bao* all carried items reporting this extraordinary event, and Mr. Sun became known as the Imperial Degree Candidate of ham production, the very best in his field (Zhai 1981: 165).

Appendix 2

Camphor Tree Mothers

In the 1930s, Wolfram Eberhard reported a number of "special customs" distinctive to Jinhua prefecture among which was the "cult of trees," usually large camphor trees. Eberhard thought it noteworthy that the trees were addressed as female deities, and characterized the practice as distinctive of southern Zhejiang province (Eberhard 1970: 19).

Nowadays in Dongyang, one can still find such camphor trees, with small red papers posted on the trunk, on which is written a saying like the following:

> The skies are blue, the [grain of the] earth is in flower, our family has a child [who cries in the night]—
> If someone walking by takes a look, the child will sleep till the morning light.
> *Tian cang cang, di mang man, wo jia you ge xiao er lang;*
> *Guo lu hang ren kan yi pian, yi shui jiao dao da tian liang.*

At the foot of the tree are the remains of burnt candles. This is a sign that in the vicinity there is a child who worships the tree as a "camphor tree mother" *(zhang shu niang niang)* (Ma n.d.e; fieldnotes, 4/20/89, on the road to Hong Qi *xiang,* Hu Tan village). The older the tree, the better; the more numerous its years, the greater its spiritual power to confer longevity and good fortune (JHFSZ 1984: 12, 150).

In the past if a baby was weak, of ill health, or difficult to care for, a camphor tree or even a large outcropping of stone was adopted as a "camphor tree mother" or "stone maiden," and worshipped in the hope that the child's health would improve or that it would be easier to care for (JHFSZ 1984: 87). But camphor tree mothers were also sought out to confer good fortune and longevity on completely healthy children as well (Ma n.d.e).

In acknowledging a "camphor tree mother," the head of the child's household used three cups of wine, a slice of pork, a bowl of rice, and a bowl of *doufu* to worship the "camphor tree mother" at the base of the tree. He would light incense and candles, burn yellow paper, and hang a little "three copper coin" red cloth bag on the tree trunk. The household head would hold the child out to the "camphor tree mother" and *bai* three times, asking that the *niang niang* accept the child. In this way, the child became the "godchild" *(gan nu er* or *gan er zi)* of the camphor tree mother. Once the child recognized the tree as its protector mother, he or she would prepare sacrifices and give gifts at every annual festival; at Duan Wu, he or she would offer *zong zi*; at New Year's, he or she would paste up "spring scrolls," and so forth (JHFSZ 1984: 12, 150).

When the child reached its tenth birthday, the family would make offerings to the camphor tree mother to thank her for her kindness, and the child was once again presented to its *niang niang* to seek good fortune and longevity.

Often the camphor tree mother was approached as a means to evade the misfortunes suggested by the results of divination. A fortune teller *(suan ming xian sheng)* might say, "this child clashes with its mother *(ke niang),"* or "in his fate, he is destined to have two mothers." The idea might be that the child was too much for his mother to handle, and a *hou niang* ("back[up] mother") was needed, or that its own mother would die, leaving it in the care of a stepmother.

There were several ways of saving a child from the fortune teller's prediction. One might have the child adopted by a *gan niang* ("god [stem] mother") in a neighboring village, have the child acknowledge a certain *pu sa* (Buddha) as a godmother, or have the child acknowledge a camphor tree as *niang niang* (Ma n.d.e).

After acknowledging the camphor tree mother, the child had already fulfilled the prophecy of having two mothers, so the danger of "getting a back mother *(hou niang* [stepmother]) as the result of the death of one's own mother" *(si qin niang, lai hou niang),* was thus forestalled, and the real mother's health and safety thereby guaranteed.

Since the establishment of the People's Republic, people's standard of living has gradually risen. Advances in medical treatment and hygiene, improved general health and well-being, and intensified propaganda against superstition during the Cultural Revolution all made the acknowledging of camphor tree mothers less common. Nevertheless in recent years, with the loosening of ideological controls in the countryside, the phenomenon of worshipping camphor trees has also increased in frequency.

According to a local primary school teacher of Huai Lu town, this may be associated with the fact that the institution of birth planning has made people more anxious about the health and fate of their fewer offspring. A sick child is brought to the hospital immediately, but as a kind of "double insurance" the camphor tree mother's protection is also sought out.

Nowadays the three copper red cloth sack is no longer hung on the tree, but a red paper with the supplicant's request is substituted. Some of these are also inscribed with the child's *ru ming,* or infant name, and the eight characters (year, month, date, and hour) of its birthdate on the red paper. However, the traditional acknowledgment ceremony remains more or less intact, after having made something of a comeback.

According to an article in *Qian River Evening News* (*Qian jiang wan bao* 6/19/89), a camphor tree in Yunho county is said to have more than 100 godchildren, and while the article ridiculed the superstition as "really funny," its author was forced to admit that the tree even attracted "supplicants from town," who presumably should have known better. In fact, given the lifespan of many of these old camphor-wood trees, each may have had thousands of godchildren over the course of its life.

One Dongyang villager confided that if one were to transform all the trees into people, the pines and cypress would be old strict fathers. Only the camphor tree in every respect could be a mother—the sturdiness of its trunk, the curve of its branches, all seem to be rich in feminine lines. Its leaves are plentiful, providing ample shade. In the summertime it protects people from the sun; in the wintertime it provides shelter from the wind. People enjoy resting under a camphor tree, like a child resting in its mother's arms. The camphor tree remains green during all four seasons, constantly fragrant and sweet smelling, just like a loving mother, fond of her own child.

Such trees, in their role as protectors of village children against misfortune, have thus been spared the axe, and continue to serve in their capacity as fixtures of village settlement down to the present day.

Appendix 3

The *Huichang* (Country Fair) Cycle

G. William Skinner (1964–65) has emphasized the importance of the rhythm of periodic standard markets in Chinese rural life as well as the significance of the standard market town and its associated standard market area as focal points of community life beyond the confines of the village. Skinner has shown how market periodicity was tied to a ten-day market week of which each lunar month had three, and how standard market schedules were coordinated locally to allow demand to accumulate, and itinerant peddlers and craftsmen to conveniently make the rounds between markets in a given region, purveying their wares and skills. The market schedules encountered in Xia Qi Tan and Li Tang villages, and Guo Zhai and Heng Dian towns, serve to confirm Skinner's understanding of that periodicity.

The history of such rural markets in Dongyang dates from the Tang dynasty (A.D. 618–907) when four markets were recorded in the landscape of the newly created county. By the Kang Xi reign period of the Qing dynasty (A.D. 1681) there were 18 such markets functioning in Dongyang, and by the Dao Guang reign period (1831) that number had expanded to 23. With the growing commercialization that ensued in the late Qing and early Republican period, Dongyang continued to add markets to the landscape and by 1932 there were 49 markets in operation, the most active of which were in the towns of Heng Dian and Qian Xiang (Jiang n.d.f).

Periodic rural markets in Dongyang suffered a decline in the early Communist period, especially after 1953, when unified sales and marketing cooperatives were created to take their place and private commodity trade was restricted. Markets continued to be held but there were very few goods on sale. Wu Ning "central" market in the county town was the busiest at the time, but drew only modest numbers of traders.

During the Great Leap Forward, many of the markets that remained were closed down completely as all commerce was placed under the control of the supply and marketing cooperatives of the newly organized communes. Distribution of goods was carried out through the use of more than thirty different kinds of coupons *(piao)* exchanged for grain, oil, cigarettes, wine, matches, and so forth. These were especially difficult for people with rural household registrations *(nongye hukou)* to obtain, and they were therefore unable to buy much at the cooperatives (Jiang n.d.f).

Beginning in 1961, as the state retreated from the ambitious goals of the Great Leap, private plots were reallocated to rural households, the private raising of poultry and pigs was legalized, and rural markets made something of a comeback in Dongyang. But the revival was shortlived. In 1967, when the Cultural Revolution began, private plots and family sidelines were eliminated, and markets were once again restricted to minimize the danger of a restoration of capitalism.

Since 1978, with the implementation of the economic reforms and the subsequent subcontracting *(cheng bao)* of responsibility in agriculture to the household, private trade has started up again. By 1988 there were thirty-eight markets throughout the county carrying on an annual volume of ¥126,680,000 in trade, nearly ten times the figure for 1978 (Jiang n.d.f). That the number of markets currently operating in the county is less than the figure for 1932 may be explained by the hiving off of two of Dongyang's districts into a separate Pan An county in 1985, and by advances in transport facility in recent years that have led to greater market accessibility to fewer markets on the part of the rural population (see Skinner 1964–65).

The pattern of rural market periodicity in Dongyang county accords well with Skinner's pioneering studies of the phenomenon. To be faithful to the market rhythms of rural life, however, some attention needs to be focused on an overlapping cycle of rural market fairs *(hui chang)*, or temple fairs *(miao hui)*, as they were known traditionally. Such fairs provided an opportunity for most rural folk to participate in a market for goods from a much broader region, and to regularly sample goods of greater variety and specialty than those available at the standard market town. In effect, the rural market fair brought the wares and services available at the intermediate or central market level to the peasant's doorstep in accord with an established if somewhat irregular annual rhythm.

Traditionally, such fairs were known as temple fairs *(miao hui)*, and each temple held its fair on one or two fixed days each year, usually on the birthdate of its god *(pu sa)* according to the lunar calendar. *Miao hui* have been a part of the rhythm of rural life in Zhejiang since the Tang dynasty, generally held during agricultural slack seasons—from the lunar first month (New Year's) to the fourth month, and from the seventh month to the ninth month. Their scope expanded during the Ming and Qing dynasties, especially so at the end of the Qing (He and Jin 1983: 5).

In Dongyang, there were many temple fairs in traditional times. In the southern subdistricts *(xiang),* they were held in Heng Dian town on lunar 6/14 and 8/13; in Hu Qi town on 6/4; in Qian Xiang town on 3/11, 6/11 and 9/11. In the northern subdistricts, temple fairs were held in Wei Shan town on 5/13; in Huai Lu town on 8/13; in Li Zhai town on 9/12; in Bai Tan town on 10/1; and in Wu Ning, the county town, on 3/28 and 8/13 (FSZ 1985: 117–18).

Among these, the most magnificent is reputed to have been the temple fair of Hu Gong, held in Hu Gong temples countywide, on the anniversary of his birth, lunar 8/13. Hu Gong (A.D. 963–1039) was something of a patron saint of Dongyang and neighboring Yong Kang counties, and his cult attracted large numbers of followers in traditional times. Named Hu Ze at birth, he was a native of Yong Kang county, bordering Dongyang on the south, and lived during the Northern Song dynasty (A.D. 960–1126). As an official, he enjoyed a reputation for honesty and righteousness. He understood and sympathized with the people's hardships, presenting memorials to the emperor during lean times, to excuse the local population from its tax obligations. The common people appreciated his virtue, and after his death they honored him with temples, and worshipped him as a protector of the people's security (see also Eberhhard 1970: 37ff.).

The following folk tale describes Hu Gong's marriage, and his intervention, assisted by his wife, on behalf of the local people of Zhejiang and Jiangsu provinces:

It is said that one day Hu Gong was on his way to town to take care of some business, and was passing a plot of irrigated land when suddenly he heard a woman calling: "Hu Gong save me, Hu Gong save me!" He stopped in his tracks, and looked all around, but saw no one. He felt this to be very unusual. Was there someone in the field? He took off his shoes and waded into the water for a closer look, but all he saw was a small white frog. Hu Gong thought the frog quite strange, but picked it up, put it in his pocket, and proceeded to town. After he had completed his business and returned home, it was already dark, and Hu Gong took the frog out of his pocket. Just as he held it up, the frog jumped out of Hu Gong's hand onto the floor with a thump. It gave a cry and changed into a beautiful girl, who focused her eyes on Hu Gong and smiled.

Hu Gong was delighted and took the girl to be his wife. Because she had been a *tian ji* ("field chicken," i.e., frog), she took the name Tian shi (woman of the Tian clan—Miss Tian). Actually, this girl was an immortal being from heaven. She adored Hu Gong, and had come to earth to help him become a Buddha. (According to the inscription written by the scholar Fan Zhongyan on Hu Ze's tomb, his wife was in reality surnamed Chen!) (Zhou 1987b: 193).

It is said that after Hu Gong and Miss Tian were married, their life together was quite happy. But at the time, the government taxes were quite unbearable, and the people's lives were miserable. Because of this, Hu Gong was very concerned, and begged his divine wife for assistance: "Oh my wife, you are skilled in the magical arts, isn't there anything we can do for the common people *(laobaixing)?"*

His wife responded, "If you can come up with a plan, I will help."

Hu Gong thought and thought, and finally had his wife plant a magic sapling in the doorway of the imperial palace on his birthday, lunar 8/13. When the emperor saw it growing in the doorway he found it quite repulsive, and ordered it cut down. But no matter who tried to cut it down, the tree just grew larger, till it was as tall as a pagoda. The emperor was frightened, and all his officials trembled. What sort of evil enchanted tree was this? Finally the emperor was at the end of his wits, and sent down a memorial, "Whoever can rid us of this tree will be given a high position and a grand horse to ride." When the memorial went out, monks, Daoists, and shamans of all kinds came to try to bring down the tree, but every one of them failed. And the tree? It was still standing, and growing taller!

At this time Hu Gong arrived on the scene. The emperor, on seeing this bookish man, shook his head, "Can such a one as you bring down this hellish tree?"

"I can," said Hu Gong, "but you must make me a promise."

"Just bring down this tree, never mind the conditions; 36,000 conditions I will grant you."

"Then I ask only that your highness give me the tax rolls for Jiangsu and Zhejiang."

These words pierced the emperor as a wound, but to rid himself of that devilish tree, he grit his teeth and handed the tax rolls over. Hu Gong took the tax rolls and burnt them to ashes. Then he took the ashes and rubbed them on the tree, and lo! the tree shrunk by half. He repeated his rubbing several times and when he was finished, the tree was as small as a white jade hairpin. Hu Gong picked it up lightly and put it in his pocket. The emperor, seeing that Hu Gong had brought down the devilish tree, asked him, "What sort of official position do you desire?"

Hu Gong responded, "I want no official position," and so saying, returned home.

Actually, that sapling was none other than Miss Tian's white jade hairpin. In this way, Hu Gong and Miss Tian were able to destroy the tax rolls of Jiangsu and Zhejiang, so that the common people were relieved of their tax burden. The people expressed their thanks to the couple by placing their images everywhere (Zhou 1987b: 194).

Indeed, Hu Gong temples are quite numerous throughout Dongyang, as well as Jinhua prefecture more broadly. The focus of the cult in traditional times, however, was the large Hu Gong temple in Fang Yan town in neighboring Yong Kang county (FSZ 1985: 116; JHFSZ 1984: 134, 137–38; Eberhard 1970: 37).

In pre-revolutionary times, during the days leading up to lunar 8/13, "good men and faithful women" all prepared incense and candles for the pilgrimage to the Hu Gong temple in Fang Yan to worship. On 8/12, 8/13, and 8/14, for three days, the road to Fang Yan was filled with "Fang Yan pilgrims" wearing brightly colored paper flowers in their hair, or with yellow colored incense bundles hanging from their belts (FSZ 1985: 113).

It was best to arrive in Fang Yan at sunrise, when the temple door was just open, and one could thereby join in the struggle to place the first incense. To do so was considered very lucky. So whereas normally one would expect the front of the temple to be rather empty so early in the morning, on the morning of 8/13 there were throngs of people jostling for position to be the first inside (Jiang n.d.b).

Supplicants would *bai* to Hu Gong requesting favors—success in the imperial exams, the birth of a son, a cure for illness or disease. Each would also want to drink a bowl of water from the small well on the temple grounds, or use the water to wash their eyes. It was said that this well water had the power to change one's luck from bad to good, improve one's sight, give sons to those who wanted them, and cure all kinds of disease (Jiang n.d.b; also see Eberhard for accounts of Hu Gong taken from schoolchildren in Jinhua in 1940).

Another local folk tale of Dongyang explains why it occurred that Hu Gong's cult ended up centered on Fang Yan rather than Dongyang:

After Hu Gong died he went up to heaven. The Jade emperor gave him a choice among the eight counties of Jinhua prefecture to place his image to receive offerings from the people. In order to select a spot, Hu Gong made a tour of the eight counties of Jinhua (Yong Kang, Dongyang, Yi Wu, Jin Hua, Wu Yi, Jin Yun, Lan Qi, Pu Jiang), and selected two areas— one was Dongyang's Third District *(san du)*; one was Fang Yan (in Yong Kang). He thought both spots were quite suitable. Third District's mountains, water, and caves were quite scenic, lacking only a heavenly gate *(tian men)*. Fang Yan had a heavenly gate, which could be reached in a hundred steps, but its caves were too small. In the end Hu Gong could not decide which spot was best, and could only return to heaven to report to the Jade emperor.

When the Jade emperor heard Hu Gong's report, he also felt it was a difficult decision. Finally, he came up with the following idea to help decide: he asked the mountain spirit of Dongyang's Third District to construct a heavenly gate, and asked the mountain spirit of Fang Yan to excavate a stone cave. The time period allotted was one evening, till the crow of the cock on the following morning. Whichever spirit finished the work first would have his spot chosen as the site.

Each mountain spirit wanted to be host to Hu Gong, but the mountain spirit of Fang Yan devised an evil scheme. He thought that to dig out a cave would be a waste of time and energy, and would be more time-consuming than the task set for the spirit of Third District. Thus he decided that rather than excavate a cave, it would be better to construct a statue of Hu Gong, who would then definitely come to Fang Yan. The mountain spirit of the Third District of Dongyang was honest, and piled up stone after stone, sparing no effort, working intensely.

When the cock crowed, the Fang Yan spirit had already finished the statue of Hu Gong, and the Third District spirit still lacked two pieces of stone to finish his heavenly gate. Hu Gong had no choice but to choose Fang Yan as his final residence. Because of this, until to today Fang Yan has been the center of Hu Gong's cult, and every year on 8/13 when Dongyang residents go to Fang Yan to present incense, and climb the mountain to the heavenly gate, they often tell this story of

Dongyang's ill fortune. But in order to give Hu Gong a place to live on his tours of inspection around the prefecture, Dongyang Third District also constructed a Hu Gong temple, and in imitation of Fang Yan, they also constructed a heaven's gate. Thus, on 8/13, there are also many pilgrims who go to the temple in the Third District (Zhou 1987b: 196).

In the northern *xiang* of Dongyang, the village lanes associated with various lineages "arranged tea" for the sacrifices on 8/13. In "arranging tea," molds were used, stuffed with glutinous rice, sesame, green beans, millet, and red beans, in the shape of lions, tigers, elephants, *qi lin,* deer, the five wild animals. The confections often attained grandiose proportions, pieced together in the form of screens depicting the Eight Immortals, "phoenix platforms," Hanging Flower pavilions, Four Star *(kui xing)* pavilions, commemorative arches *(pai fang),* and other elaborate designs, and were said to be a distinctive expression of the high level of craft technique in the "county of 100 skills" (FSZ 1985: 113).

In the southern *xiang,* rural households characteristically prepared "dark rice" and "sesame cakes" to eat and to exchange with relatives and friends. This custom was begun in commemoration of one Xu Honggang, who had been a secretary of state in the military ministry of the Ming dynasty, and was a native of Xu Zhai village of Gong Tang subdistrict of Dongyang county. In the 1620s he gave up his official career and returned home, where he performed many good works for the common people. According to legend, when Xu Honggang was a youth, he studied assiduously, often to the point of total absorption in his work. One year, on Hu Gong's birthday, lunar 8/13, his mother, as was customary, prepared sesame glutinous rice cakes to eat, and served him a bowl for lunch with a dish of powdered sugar. At this time Xu was in the midst of reading and was preoccupied. As he ate, he dipped one of the cakes into his inkstone instead of the dish of sugar, blackening his teeth without realizing. In later times, people commemorated the event, and it became the custom on 8/13 to eat dark rice and sesame glutinous rice cakes (FSZ 1985: 113). Xu is thus remembered along with Hu Gong in the southern part of the county on 8/13.

And then there is the fair itself. The Dongyang towns with temples to Hu Gong—Wu Ning, Xu Zhai, Heng Dian, Huai Lu, Ma Che Bu, Nan Ma, and of course Guo Zhai, whose "great candles" were traditionally placed in Hu Gong's temple—played host to markets of regional proportions on lunar 8/13. Martial arts aficionados, opera troupes, performers of all kinds, and food hawkers attracted great crowds all along the streets. All manner of performances and displays of skill were on view, and merchants and peddlers gathered in great swarms. Goods from north and south were displayed every which way, competing for space in the streets. "Mountains and seas of people," is how one account describes the multitudes (FSZ 1985: 117–18).

Apart from the inevitable operatic performances of local *wu ju* theatrical troupes on makeshift stages, several ceremonies were also performed during such fairs in Dongyang. Among these were welcoming the great flag, "turning over the nine stories [tower]" *(fan jiu lou)*, and welcoming the Buddha.

A 1910 middle-school text on the history of Dongyang describes welcoming the great flag as part of the celebrations carried out "in honor of Hu Gong. The flags were constructed of long bolts of silk, thirty to fifty feet long, bound to long poles, carried by participants who paraded out to She Mu temple, and returned to Wu Ning on the following day with drums and fifes leading the way and onlookers lining the road" (DYXXLJS 1910: 70).

In the southern *xiang* of Dongyang, it is reported (remarkably) that in greeting the flag, a single flag was stitched together of pieces of cloth to the size of 60 square *zhang* in area (1 sq. *zhang* = 11 sq. m!), and the flagpole was said to be 9 *zhang* tall (1 *zhang* = 3.3 m!). To carry the flag for the "greeting" was said to require more than forty strong men (Zhou 1987a: 4).

Fan jiu lou was performed by inserting two China fir trees firmly in the ground with the tops bent over touching the roots and tied up securely, to make supporting pillars. A "9–story platform" *(jiu lou tai)* was erected by piling more than 20 "Eight Immortals" tables one on top of another anchored against the supporting pillars and tied securely. A Daoist adept, together with several assistants, all with red cloth bound around their heads and cloth sashes strapped around their waists, wearing shoes made of straw, first kowtowed under the platform, chanting incantations. The adept would draw near the tables, perform a somersault, and climb. On the top of the platform he would perform martial arts movements, handstands, shadow boxing, dance the great ball, and so on. His movements were alarmingly dangerous and provoked oohs and ahhs from the onlookers. Finally, he would take some mantou or other objects carried aloft for the purpose, and fling them about in all directions, as the spectators vied to grab them as tokens of good luck *(li shi)*. At last, from top to bottom the tables were successively turned over, and the ceremony was concluded. Fan Jiu Lou was also celebrated at large religious festivals and the opening of temples (FSZ 1985: 59–60).

Welcoming the Buddha ceremonies were not limited to the Hu Gong temple fair, but were carried out in association with all such *miao hui* regardless of their sponsoring temple. Buddhism reached Dongyang in the Tang dynasty, and proliferated in the Yuan and Ming dynasties. By Republican times, the county had 87 temples with resident monks or nuns, and close to 1,000 smaller Buddhist halls used only on special occasions.

Welcoming the Buddha involved taking the images of Buddha out of the temples, or alternatively shaping small Buddhas and placing them in a ceremonial sedan chair. The images were carried around the streets on a tour of inspection, led along with incense and lanterns and a musical group clearing a path through the streets, followed by paper horses, images of the gods *(shen),* and a flag brigade.

People flocked behind the sedan chair carrying flowers of all kinds, beating flower drums, carrying images of the Eight Immortals, performing with the "horse king" whip, dancing the "copper cash" sword, walking on stilts, dancing the "big head" dance, escorted by honor guards with flags and weapons, with a lion dance troupe and a cohort of strong young men bringing up the rear. The multitude was said to be "vast and mighty," and exciting to watch. On the day of the temple fair, after the welcoming ceremony was over, "good men and faithful women" would burn incense and worship Buddha in the temple (FSZ 1985: 117–118).

In Chapter 1, it was mentioned that the Hu Gong temple fair figured in Communist Party organizing activities in Dongyang during the 1930s, first as the site of a planned insurrection, and later as a site from which to spread propaganda for the struggle against Japan. The party was thus familiar with the temple fair as an institution, and not surprisingly, after the establishment of the People's Republic, party members set about harnessing it to their purposes. In 1952, the Hu Gong temple fair of Wu Ning town was again put to use, this time to host a secular commodity exchange fair lasting three days, attended by 80,000 people, and more than 3,300 merchants from as far away as Jinhua and Hangzhou (DYSZ 1993: 472).

In subsequent years the practice continued, with the traditional Buddhist religious rituals suppressed. Indeed, in 1989 the old Hu Gong

Crowds attending the rural market fair in Hu Qi town.

temple in the village of Quan Fu just outside the town of Nan Ma was nothing but ruins, and evoked scenes from the mystery novels of Robert van Gulik. There was no telling what spirits dwelt in the deteriorating masonry and rotting timbers of the old temple after dark.

From the late 1950s onward, however, even the secularized fairs were alternately suppressed or rigorously controlled. During the Great Leap Forward, and again during the Cultural Revolution of the late 1960s, such commodity trade was denounced as encouraging capitalist tendencies. It was not until the period of economic reform begun in late 1978 that such fairs have resurfaced as a linchpin in a renaissance of rural regional trade. Since that time, when there were still 1,051 such rural fairs operating in Zhejiang province dealing mainly in agricultural sideline products, rural market fairs have been promoted as part of a "mutually interlinked multifunctional commercial network" extending in all directions, an important arena for commodity exchange in the "united socialist market." By 1985, the number of such fairs had more than doubled to 2,149, and they continue to proliferate in Zhejiang down to the present, extending from the coast, to the interior, to the mountain districts and the coastal islands (DDZGZJ 1989: 500).

The modern fairs, now called *hui chang* or *jiaoliu hui*, are managed by local market regulation offices, which take charge of public safety

Carved wood furniture for sale at the market fair in Hu Qi.

arrangements, licensing traders and their wares, and collecting taxes on goods sold. There is the characteristic feverish commercial and social activity of the traditional *miao hui* with all kinds of goods on sale, and traditional theatrical performances, movies, circuses, artistic exhibitions, displays of skill, athletic performances, and other recreational activities (FSZ 1985: 26, 117–18).

At the spring fair in Hu Qi town in 1988, goods rolling into town on carts and trucks were assessed a tax on the road, and received a registration stamp at the entrance to town, allowing them to be sold at the fair. The streets and alleys of the town were lined with furniture, carved cabinets, bed frames, clothes, agricultural equipment, tools, basketry, medicines, vegetables, sweet potato shoots for planting, and purveyors of prepared foods of all kinds.

A maker of wooden tubs displays his proceeds of the day at the market fair in Hu Qi.

A circus troupe, featuring performing dogs, a contortionist girl who could support two people on her stomach while twisted backward over herself, a boy who puffed smoke through a mouthful of sand, a snake handler, and a performing bear, entertained on the river bank.

At the middle school in town, a variety of games of chance were offered. Ten *fen* earned the spin of an electric wheel with a chance to win a small trinket, ring, whistle, or such, if the spinner landed on the chosen number. For ¥1, one could try to shoot five balloons with a rifle, and win a pack of cigarettes. A primitive marble pinball game won the player a small prize for so many points.

The market was replete with games of chance elsewhere as well. Draw five cards and the host pays on certain posted totals; the rest lose. Quite a number of such games were strung out along the footbridge over the river into town, where one could also have one's fortune read in one's facial features *(kan xiang)*.

An exhibition by a young *qi gong* master drew a substantial crowd. He put on quite a show, whooping and hollering, clapping hands and beating his breast, climaxing by smashing a brick on his head, where all the *qi* of his body was focused. At the end of his performance, he distributed envelopes of herbs to be steeped in wine and drunk to heal pains in the bones, requesting "donations" from those who accepted the envelopes.

The pig market and livestock market also did a roaring trade, and the best of the lot were sold quickly. By midday only a few undesirable unsold stragglers remained with most of the market depleted (fieldnotes, 6/14/88). For the rest of the market, transactions reach a climax between 2:00 and 3:00 in the afternoon, because customers want to survey the entire market, checking prices and quality of goods before making their choices. Prices tend to be higher earlier in the day and begin to drop around 4:00 or 5:00 P.M., so those who live in the vicinity and expect to make purchases generally take their time arriving on the scene. They may even wait until the morning after when there may still be sellers looking to unload the last of their wares at bargain prices (Jiang n.d.f).

As mentioned in the Introduction, our itinerary of 1989 coincided with a segment of the cycle of *hui chang* in the southern *xiang* of the county. As we proceeded from Heng Dian on lunar 2/23, to Nan Ma on 2/25, to Huang Tian Fan on 3/3, to Lou Xi Zhai on 3/11, to Wu Ning on 3/28, we encountered a *hui chang* in every town. Our itinerary also coincided with those of the many peddlers we encountered repeatedly at each successive venue. It was clear that they follow the cycle of fairs from town to town through the county during the *hui chang* season, much like their itinerant cousins who frequent the periodic standard markets of the regular market week.

In Huang Tian Fan on lunar 3/3, the whole length of newly reclaimed river bank was filled with agricultural equipment, winnowing machines, tools, furniture, and such. Lumber for sale was set up in great tepees, and lots of bamboo and woven reed products were on sale, as well as fishing nets, hemp raincoats, oodles of carved wood furniture, and dough figurines for the children. The streets were so literally jammed with people that just walking was a problem. Water buffalo were for sale on the other side of the bridge in a great open field on the river bank for ¥1,000+ per buffalo. A calf could be had for only ¥1,000 since, "not knowing the plough," it would have to be trained. Musk oxen, less desirable as draft animals, fetched ¥600–700.

One enterprising peddler was hawking rat poison at a table on which past victims of his wares were posed, dressed in little vests and hats, holding flags attesting to the potency of the poison.

Peddlers with relatively small stalls must pay about ¥200 in fees to participate in the *hui chang* at Huang Tian Fan, and such fees are similar for *hui chang* in the other towns of the county. In addition, the

THE *HUICHANG* CYCLE 207

A blind singer performs at the market fair in Huang Tian Fan.

peddlers must also meet expenses for room and board in town for a night or two, which puts some pressure on them to sell enough to make back their costs. But it was also clear that business was booming in the spring of 1989, and there was no shortage of such peddlers willing to take the risks involved.

In the present period, *hui chang* once again punctuate the rhythm of the annual agricultural cycle. The modern fairs in Dongyang county are held on exactly the same traditional lunar dates as the old temple fairs, of which there were many beside the one held on the birthday of Hu Gong. In the course of the economic reforms, Communist authorities have stepped into and revivified the traditional commercial milieu, while coopting it as a means of stimulating rural commodity trade. In doing so, the authorities have been self-conscious in their use of *miao hui* as a means to effect "changes in prevailing habits and customs; transformations of social traditions" *(yifeng yisu)*. The reemergence of this traditional arena of commodity trade as a positive force in the rural economy might well be said to be one of the modern transformed institutions that make for a "socialism with Chinese characteristics" (Dong 1981: 10–11; He and Jin 1983: 8).

In 1985, trade conducted at country fairs in Zhejiang province amounted to ¥4 billion (sixth in the nation), 4.1 times the trade volume of 1978. Of the total, ¥3.4 billion were sales of products of agricultural sidelines, and a whopping ¥1 billion were sales of industrial products, second in the nation. In Dongyang county in 1988 there were 43 sites at which 74 fairs were held, carrying on some ¥10,915,000 in trade (DYSZ 1993: 472).

Such fairs represent one of the important institutions of rural life not previously identified in studies of the Chinese economy, and serve as one of the sources of dynamism in the contemporary rural economy.

Appendix 4

Specimen *Cheng Bao* Contract

Dongyang County <u>Xiangzhen</u> Enterprise
Economic <u>Cheng bao</u> Agreement
(<u>Cheng bao</u> period, the____year)

    Enterprise name_____
    Legal representative_____
    Date of contract_____

APPENDIX 4: SPECIMEN *CHENG BAO* CONTRACT

Part 1. General Situation of the Enterprise

1. Present no. of employees___; no. of workers employed outside___

2. Fixed capital assets at the end of last year___yuan

3. Surplus of quota floating capital at the end of last year___yuan
     finished products___yuan
     materials___yuan
     in products___yuan

4. Surplus of non quota floating capital at the end of last year___yuan.
     commodities produced___yuan
     outstanding payments for goods___yuan

5. Enterprise accumulation, own floating capital___yuan
     depreciation___yuan
     special purpose fund___yuan

6. Outside capital
     bank loans___yuan
        portion for equipment___yuan
     office (<u>bumen</u>) loans
        (fund kept from financial turnover)___yuan
     collective loans___yuan
     employee capital contribution___yuan
     shareholder contribution___yuan

7. Amount owed at the end of last year___yuan
     portion owed in payment for goods___yuan
     advance payment for goods___yuan

Part 2. Economic <u>Cheng bao</u> Target

In order to implement the policies and regulations of the central government with respect to "positive support, appropriate planning, proper guidance, and strengthening administration" in developing rural enterprise, to actively fulfill the management <u>cheng bao</u> responsiblity system, improve the enterprises results and its social contribution, increase enterprise accumulation, enhance the vitality and stamina of the enterprise, make the enterprise move forward quickly and healthily, to stimulate the many contributions to Dongyang's economy, the <u>xiang</u> (<u>zhen</u>) <u>gongsi</u> (<u>gong ban</u>) or village party committee (<u>jia fang</u>) and_____factory (<u>yi fang</u>), having gone through full consultation, conclude the economic <u>cheng bao</u> contract for 1987 as follows:

   1. Assessment targets for the <u>cheng bao</u> period:
      1. production value_____0000 yuan
      2. profit_____0000 yuan
      3. proportion of products marketed___%
      4. quality of products
      5. security of production

APPENDIX 4: SPECIMEN *CHENG BAO* CONTRACT 211

General summary of various assessment quotas/targets:

Item \ Order	1	2	3	4	5	Total
reference assessment points	20	30	20	15	15	100
gong ban assessment points						100
shi de fen points realized						

2. Planned expense reserves (unabsorbed direct costs)

Order	Item	Recovery standard	Projected reserve	Actual yearend reserve
1	fixed capital depreciation	9%		
2	repair fund			
3	taxable wage amount	average ¥60-80/mo/worker		
4	employee welfare fund	11% of standard wage ¥60/worker		
5	employee educ. fund	1.5% of standard wage ¥60/worker		
6	guanlifei	0.5% of sales income		
7	union funds	2% of total wages paid		
8	technical development fund	1% of sales income		

Note: The above reserve standards may be changed by national tax policy during the period of the cheng bao contract; if so, the new standards will apply.

3. Profit disbursement (absolute amount, taking yearly final accounting as standard):
    a. Before paying income tax, in accord with policies and regulations, according to realized before tax profits, pay 10% to xiang zhen gong ban, for use in social expenses, projected amount____yuan.
    b. After reduction of various reserve funds, enterprise actual taxable profit____yuan.
    c. After tax profit disbursement should be in accord with Zhejiang provincial government (84)#44 document regulations:
        Within cheng bao base amount:
        ____% to remain in enterprise for reinvestment and expansion of production, ____0000 Yuan amount.
        ____% to pay to xiang (cun), ____0000 Yuan amount.
        ____% for use in enterprise bonuses or welfare,____0000 Yuan amount.

        Portion exceeding cheng bao base amount:
        ____% to remain in enterprise for reinvestment and expansion of production, ____0000 yuan amount
        ____% to pay to xiang (cun), ____0000 yuan amount
        ____% for use in enterprise bonuses or welfare,____0000 yuan amount.

(Note: Various tax reductions or benefits granted to the enterprise by the tax bureau must be reserved according to the various specialized funds. The general amount of surplus wages saved as a result cannot be put into profit disbursement; the [method of] disbursement of bonuses must be reported to the gong ban for examination and verification, and only after approval implemented. The granting of all bonuses and the proof of bonus tax must all be paid out of the reward fund; other capital cannot be used; the cheng bao person may not make a false report of profits, and may not pick the enterprise clean; otherwise it is required to investigate who is responsible, and recover the excess "bonus.")

    4. New increases in enterprise accumulation of capital____yuan:
        According to current policies and regulations, and according to the above reckoning:
For the year 1987, newly increased accumulation____yuan
        a. Amount for fixed capital depreciation and fund for large repairs (total amount)____yuan.
        b. Cash surplus from calculation of tax wages____yuan.
        c. State industrial and commercial tax reduction____yuan. Income tax____yuan.
        d. Total profit from commodities of the "three wastes" [gas, water, and industrial residues] left to the enterprise by the state____yuan.
        e. Amount from calculation of tax wages disbursed to welfare and education____yuan.
        f. Net after-taxes profits____yuan.

Part 3. Responsibilities, Rights and Benefits of the Factory manager
    The factory manager is responsible to the greatest extent for completing or exceeding the annual production plan of his enterprise. With respect to the production of his enterprise, he carries out unified leadership in management, has full responsibility; after the enterprise fulfills its various assessed targets, the factory manager's bonus is according to his excellence, and his yearly income may be ____times that of the average wage of enterprise employees.

APPENDIX 4: SPECIMEN *CHENG BAO* CONTRACT 213

Part 4. Contract Signature Page

Jia fang:

Representative: _____ _____
                      Signature   Official seal

                1986____month____day

Yi fang:

Representative: _____ _____
                      Signature   Official seal

                1986____month____day

Certifying unit _____ _____
               Xiang (Zhen) government Official seal

                1986____month____day

The contract is made in five copies; both partners to it retain one copy; report to Rural Industrial Bureau, the bank of account, and the tax bureau one copy each.

Several points of explanation regarding management cheng bao contracts:

    1. Concerning assessed quotas/targets:

        a. Five items that must be assessed/checked by each enterprise are already fixed; backbone enterprises should increase labor productivity of their workers, daily amount of floating capital turnover, the rate of equipment depreciation, and other assessments; in the event assessed/checked items increase, each assessment can be separately and voluntarily adjusted.

        b. The determination of assessment standards and quality targets may be decided according to [the characteristics of] different enterprises; if the product is determined to be below the fixed standard, the proportion of goods for which payment is returned for quality reasons should be stored in overstock, etc.

        c. Security of production quotas/targets: after any accident, [if] the direct economic losses do not exceed ¥200, with no serious injuries or death, [there will be no adjustments].

    2. Assessment target scoring and bonuses. Method of calculating welfare disbursements: the total amount that an enterprise can disperse in bonuses and welfare = the reserved enterprise annual bonus fund X % of assessment realized

        % of assessment realized = $\dfrac{\text{points achieved}}{\text{points that should be achieved}}$

3. Proportion of various expenses reserved:

   a. In calculating tax wages, ¥60-80 is the conventional figure within the scope of the whole province; standards in various places may vary, and can be decided according to local conditions.

   b. Fund for large-scale repairs: limited only to the four sectors of communication/transportation, construction materials, chemicals, refrigeration; specific standards for each occupation may vary; standards should be according to tax bureau regulations.

   c. Union funds refer to enterprises that have already established a union, and can be paid according to the standard.

Appendix 5

The Thirteen Room House

The old style rural "people's house" *(min fang)* of Dongyang county was a symmetrical brick and wood structure of two stories. Its archetype was the U-shaped "thirteen room head" *(shi san jian tou)*, the open end of which generally faced south. An enclosing *yi zi* wall (in the shape of the character for "one"—*yi zi*—a single horizontal line) was constructed at the open end of the U-shaped construction. In the middle of the enclosing wall was a large doorway, called the big terrace door *(da tai men)* or main door *(zheng men)*, which was usually locked, and only opened at "happy occasions" *(xi shi)*, or when an honored guest arrived (FSZ 1985: 41).

Outside the enclosing wall there was usually an open space "stair edge" *(jie yan)*, used to lay out and dry grain, or to hang clothes to dry. A mortar and grinding dish and other implements were usually placed there, and stools of stone and wood were commonly set out, making it a place for household members to sit and for itinerant peddlers to stop and rest. "Stair edges" of adjacent houses were usually connected to facilitate coming and going.

Eaves projecting over the inner walls of the U-shaped structure were divided into upper and lower levels, between which were windows that allowed ventilation in the upper story. All sorts of items, from newly harvested corn to just-washed clothing, were suspended from the lower eave to dry, or for later use (FSZ 1985: 40).

Three rooms, known as *zheng wu,* or "proper rooms," composed the cross piece of the U and faced south. Together they were considered to constitute a *ting*. Two rooms at the back half of the *ting,* each of which was called a *ting ta (ting* couch/bed), were marked off by wood board partitions. Generally, a *ting* staircase leading up to the second story was constructed in the western *ting ta.*

The main room of the *ting* was the *tang wu* ([lineage] hall room),

Figure 5A. Thirteen Room Head.

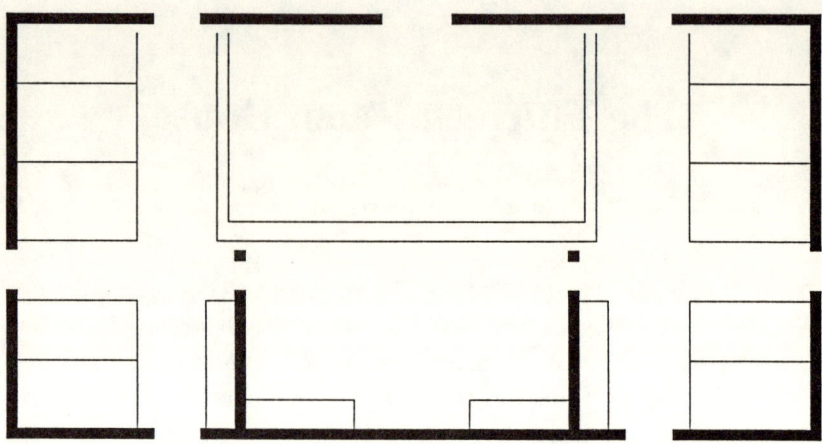

and was usually open to the central courtyard. The *tang wu* was shared by the various households of the joint family for storing firewood and miscellaneous large farm equipment (winnowers, hand- and foot-powered water pumps, etc.). On ceremonial occasions, each family removed what it had stored there. For funerals, it was used to rest the corpse, and as a mourning hall. After the corpse was taken out, a banquet was set in the *tang wu* to thank the guests. For marriages, the sedan chair that carried the bride, together with her quilt chests and other dowry items, were set down in the *tang wu* where the wedding feast was later held. During New Year's, large portraits of the ancestors were hung in the *tang wu* for descendants to look upon with reverence and worship. If the *tang wu* required major maintenance, all households contributed collectively (FSZ 1985: 42).

In a "thirteen room head," the two wings of the U, east and west, each had five rooms. Those on the east side were called the "east wing rooms" and faced west; those on the west side were called the "west wing rooms" and faced east (see Figure 5A). Each wing room was named; from front to back they were "little room" *(xiao fang)*, "little middle room" *(xiao zhong fang)*, "big room" *(da fang)*. Then, interrupted by a crossing corridor *(nong tang)* were in succession two "under the cave rooms" *(dong xia wu)* in each wing, so called because they were blocked from the open courtyard by the walls and eaves of the *ting*. The stairs to the upper story of the wing rooms were always in the first "under the cave room" against the wall of the crossing corridor *(nong tang)*. Pigpen and toilet were always in one of the "under the cave rooms" near one or another of the *bei tai men,* or north terrace doors.

Since the "under the cave rooms" were blocked by the *zheng wu,* their only light came from a small "light well" *(tian jing)* above the corridor separating the rooms from the *ting.* Because of this they were rather dim, but the other three "wing" rooms, because they front on the wide courtyard, were relatively well lit, and bright.

The "little middle room" *(xiao zhong fang)* was used to greet guests *(hui ke shi).* The "big and little rooms," *da fang* and *xiao fang,* were bedrooms. In Dongyang, the latter were commonly just called "rooms." If the family head had four sons, then they would divide the rooms as living quarters according to their rank in age—eldest in the east big room, next eldest in the west big room, east small room next, and west small room last.

The walls separating neighboring "wing" rooms were supported by five wooden pillars, together conceived of as a set. From front to rear of the wing rooms, the pillars were named front small step, front big step, ridge pillar, back big step, back little step. In construction, the units of length were the Luban foot, *chi* (3.6 *chi* = one meter), and *zhang* (1 *zhang* = 10 *chi).* The front and back big steps were each 8 Luban feet from the ridgepole. The distance between the big and little step pillars was 6 Luban feet.

Thus the depth of the wing sections of the house was usually Luban measure 2 *zhang,* 8 *chi* (2 × 8 *chi* + 2 × 6 *chi* = 28 *chi* = 2 *zhang,* 8 *chi).* Colloquially the arrangement was referred to a "two eights, two sixes" *(liang ba liang liu).* Each of the wing rooms was 1 *zhang,* 3 *chi* wide, and typically the three *zheng wu* that made up the *ting* were each 1 *zhang* 4 *chi* wide.

The space between each "front small step pillar" and "front big step pillar" was actually outside the wing rooms, supporting a walkway that ran the length of the wing, also called a *jie yan* ("stair edge"). The walkway that ran between the "under the cave rooms" and the "big room" was called a *nong tang* (alley/lane) (Ma n.d.a).

A thirteen room head has a total of 88 pillars in its structure. There are 18 sets of pillars, each set containing 5, so there should be 90. But because two of those sets in the middle of the *ting* main room have no ridge pillar, there are two short of 90, or 88 pillars altogether. That the specific numbers and spacing of parts in the construction of a house in

Dongyang should be subject to such systematization is not altogether surprising given Ruitenbeek's observation that carpenters typically knew the number of wooden parts needed for houses of various types by heart. Often the lists were framed in mnemonic rhymes (Ruitenbeek 1993: 62).

The rafters that run between the "big and small step pillars" immediately above the inner "stair edge," just outside the wing rooms in the courtyard, are commonly ornamented with various relief carvings of flowers, animals, and other scenes from folk stories. The so-called cow's shanks *(niu tui)* that jut forward and outward at the end of the rafters just below the eaves usually display people or animals carved in the round. Often seen are images of one or another of the Eight Immortals, Sakyamuni (Buddha), generals, and scholars *(xian, shi, jiang, shi)*. Elephants, tigers, and deer are also common motifs (FSZ 1985: 41).

Relief carvings decorate the walls of the wing rooms that face the courtyard, often interspersed with carved latticework designs. The carvings are generally portrayals of emperors, generals, and ministers, talented scholars or beautiful ladies of Chinese romances, accompanied by carts and horses, or depicted in pavilions, on small bridges, or beside streams. Occasionally these walls may also be decorated with landscape paintings. The inner face of the main front wall is often painted with musical instruments, flags, quotations, and pictures. Regarding house decoration, Knapp has noted that singly or in groups, no human figures are more common in the iconography of Chinese homes and temples than the Eight Immortals (Knapp 1989: 163–67).

Also common in house decoration are the characters Fu (luck), Lu (wealth), Shou (longevity), Xi (happiness), the four symbols of good fortune in China's popular folklore. The characters themselves may be used in decorative motifs, or in inscriptions like the following:

> The heavenly officials bestow **luck**—*Tian guan ci fu,*
> The star of **wealth** enjoys peaches—*Lu xing xi tao,*
> Magu bestows **longevity**—*Ma gu xian shou,*
> **Happy** sons fill up the hall—*Xi er man tang.*
> (DYMDBAO 10: 4: December 5, 1987, *"Fu Lu Shou Xi"*)

Altogether there are seven doors in a thirteen room head—three in the enclosing wall of the U, two in the wall of the crosspiece of the U, and one in each wing, between the "under the cave rooms" and the three front rooms. Above each door, four character expressions are often inscribed.

"Room of irises and orchids"—*zhi lan qi shi*
(i.e., a room of noble character and true friendship);
"Benefit from modesty and brightness"—*lian guang shou yi.*

There are still quite a number of extant examples of thirteen room architecture in Dongyang, but they are readily abandoned in favor of modern style brick and concrete structures equipped with running water and modern conveniences when residents are financially able.

Appendix 6

Eight Immortals Cross the Sea
(One Version of the Myth in Translation)

It is said that after the Eight Immortals gathered at Zhong Nan Mountain, they spent their days in self-cultivation and discussion of the Dao, until it was difficult to remain interested. A restive Lü Dongbin suggested, "Why don't we go to Peng Lai Immortal Island, and cheer ourselves up." The others all agreed. So they all rose up on clouds and arrived at Peng Lai Immortal Island on the edge of the Eastern Sea.

On the island, they walked East, looked West, and frolicked happily. One day they were all standing on Dan Yai Ting (Red Cliff Peak) looking at the seascape, when Lü Dongbin asked, "Aiya, what is that black speck out there?"

Han Zhongli replied, "Isn't that part of a group of islands; why don't we go have a look around?"

All agreed. But looking down to the seashore they could see no boats; what to do? Lü Dongbin said, "We are not mere mortals, we can go without boats. As I see it, we can use this opportunity to demonstrate our abilities."

The Immortals did as suggested. Li Tieguai, in accord with the suggestion, threw his iron crutch down from the cliff. When it hit the surface of the water, it made a nasty splash. He jumped down from the cliff saying, "I'm first." As the others watched, the iron crutch turned into a small wooden boat. Li Tieguai, obviously pleased, sat in the boat with a happy expression on his face. Han Zhongli followed. He patted his stomach saying, "Watch me!." As he said this, he opened his fan, blew a mouthful of Immortal breath, saying "change," and the fan instantly became more than one *zhang* long. Han Zhongli sat on the fan, and gleefully followed Li Tieguai. Close behind, Zhang Guolao cast down his paper mule, He Xiangu threw down her bamboo ladle,

---

Version translated and edited from Ouyang Jingyi, *Ba Xian Chuan Qi* (Dramas/Legends of the Eight Immortals), Taibei: Ke Shu Bookstore, 1990, pp. 88–95.

Lü Dongbin used his bamboo flute, Han Xiangzi placed down his flower basket, Lan Caihe used his castanets, Cao Guojiu his jade blocks. The Eight Immortals all landed on the surface of the sea, and with a great commotion displayed their supernatural powers on the journey to the islands.

Just as they set out, Lan Caihe fell behind, saying, "You all go on ahead, I want to see just how great the power of my castanets is."

The Dragon King of the eastern sea was holding council in his palace, and was distracted by a patch of brightness on the surface of the water, illuminating the clear roof tiles of his quartz palace. He thought this strange, and quickly sent Number Three Prince to the water's surface to investigate. Number Three Prince, upon receiving the orders, took a group of soldiers to the surface to look around, but saw only Lan Caihe with his castanets under foot, floating on the water passing by.

Number Three Prince thought to himself, "In my dragon palace there are many precious objects, but nothing like this beautiful, strange and rare thing. If I cannot snatch it, what kind of a son am I?"

Number Three Prince sent the dragon soldiers to attack, capturing Lan Caihe and his castanets back to the dragon palace. Back at the palace, he locked up Lan Caihe, and took the castanets to show to the Dragon King. When the Dragon King saw the jade clappers, he knew they were objects of rare value. Delighted by his good fate, he sent down orders to prepare a great feast in the dragon palace, to celebrate his acquisition of the precious objects.

Meanwhile, the other Immortals reached the shore, and missing Lan Caihe, waited for him for some time. After awhile, they began to get annoyed. How could Lan Caihe have disappeared without a trace?

Li Tieguai thought out loud, "This is a bad thing, definitely the work of the Dragon King of the eastern seas. We had better go to his palace to look for him."

Zhang Guolao disagreed, saying, "What you say may be true, but you are drunk. Maybe you shouldn't make trouble in such a state. As I see it, you had better not go."

Lü Dongbin suggested that they first look for Lan Caihe along the shore, but they looked and looked and could not find him. Lü Dongbin stood at the shore and shouted: "Sea Dragon King, listen to me; if you return Lan Caihe to me, everything is forgiven; if not I will set a fire and dry up your sea."

Number Three Prince's ears were sharp, and he heard Lü Dongbin's call. He raced to the surface and called back, "What person with the gall of a dog dares to be so disorderly and rude?"

Lü Dongbin recognized him and said, "Prince, I am the Immortal of the Eight Caves, Lü Shunyang. I have come back to look for my friend Lan Caihe who was lost while crossing the sea. I know he is locked up in your palace. Go back and report to your king. Make haste to return him to me."

Number Three Prince did not see Lü Dongbin clearly, but pointed at his nose and scolded him, "Old son, don't speak wildly; you had better be off lest you, too, will be locked up in the palace."

Lü Dongbin was really angry. He took out his precious sword and brandished it at Number Three Prince. Number Three Prince was no match for him, and escaped into the sea. Lü Dongbin followed him and put his fire gourd into the sea, blowing a mouthful of immortal breath onto it. All at once, hot air began to issue forth, heating the sea water as if in a wok.

The Dragon King in his palace got hotter and hotter, but there was no place to hide. As he felt the sea become so hot around him, he said to Number Three Prince, "We already have the precious objects, why do we need to keep the immortal here? Why not hurry up and free him, and save further trouble?"

Number Three Prince responded and dispatched his dragon soldiers to escort Lan Caihe back to the shore. Lü Dongbin, upon seeing Lan Caihe return, retrieved his gourd, and accompanied him back to the other Immortals.

When the others saw Lan Caihe return, they were very happy. But Lan Caihe was beside himself, "What's the use of my coming back, my precious jade castanets are still in their hands. In all my days as an Immortal, I have never imagined such humiliation as I suffered today. My fellows, you must help me avenge myself." Having said this, Lan Caihe began to wail and cry, shaking heaven and earth.

The others agreed that the Dragon King had gone too far, and began to discuss ways of retrieving the jade castanets.

Li Tieguai said, "The magic of these water clans is not great. That they dare to act in such a fashion is most unreasonable. We have many means at our disposal. We still haven't used my bottle gourd. We need only use it to boil the eastern sea to dryness. Do not grieve at not being able to retrieve your castanets."

When Zhang Guolao heard this, he lost his temper and scolded Li Tieguai, "Brother Iron Crutch, don't be anxious. Let Lü Dongbin go again and request them. If the Dragon King refuses again, we will still have plenty of time to boil him dry."

He Xiangu accompanied Lü Dongbin out on the sea. They shouted for a long time, arousing the demons who patrolled the seas, who in turn reported to Number Three Prince. When the prince heard that Lü Dongbin had come again, he jumped up and said, "Didn't we release the Immortal without a fight? What precious thing has he come for today? He has some gall. I will take a few soldiers and capture him."

When Lü Dongbin saw the dragon prince with shrimp soldiers and crab generals racing toward them, he took out his pair of swords to do battle. Number Three Prince was no match for Lü Dongbin, and after several encounters, left the battlefield defeated. His shrimp soldiers and crab generals followed him fleeing for their lives in all directions. No sooner had Number Three Prince begun to escape back to the dragon palace, then He Xiangu threw her ladle down on the spot, and Number Three Prince was trapped under a great bamboo canopy. Lü Dongbin laughed out loud, "You brute, where will you run to?" He held up his sword and brought it down on Number Three Prince, killing him. To the shrimp soldiers and crab generals also trapped under the canopy, Lü Dongbin issued a death warning, and with one great display of martial power, killed them all.

When the Dragon King heard that Number Three Prince had been killed, he was quite shaken, and quickly ordered Number Two Prince to take soldiers into battle. He Xiangu and Lü Dongbin mustered for battle, but Number Two Prince's martial abilities were quite strong, and he surrounded them with soldiers of the water clans of the dragon palace, so that they could not escape. Lü Dongbin looked around quickly and threw up his swords, chanting an incantation, and suddenly the two swords became thousands of flying blades, killing countless numbers of the water clan soldiers.

The two Immortals walked out triumphantly and came upon Number Two Prince. Lü Dongbin, with one swipe of his sword, cut off the Prince's right arm. Number Two Prince gave a great cry, jumped into the sea, and with the water clan soldiers beat a hasty retreat back to the dragon palace.

At this time, the Dragon King had just heard the news, and seeing Number Two Prince come back with his severed arm and most of his soldiers killed, he shouted out angrily, gnashing his teeth, "So, Lü Dongbin, you have killed one and hurt another of my princes. If I cannot avenge this, I am not the ruler of the eastern sea. I will never forgive you."

The Dragon King, bent on revenge, mustered 100,000 soldiers of the water clans. Donning his own full uniform, he led his troops to the battlefront, loudly abusing Lü Dongbin, declaring his intention to avenge the death of Number Three Prince.

Zhongli Quan saw the Dragon King coming, and took the lead coming out and across to meet the Dragon King's forces from the flank. The Dragon King was already waiting patiently, and when he saw Han Zhongli come out, the hatred was roused within him, and he set out to kill him with a spear. The two engaged more than fifty times, till heaven and earth reverberated with the sound. For days on end they battled, neither able to gain final victory. When the forces of the water clans saw that the Dragon King could not defeat Zhongli Quan, they all circled around to help. Zhang Guolao saw this, and realized that Zhongli was in trouble. He hoisted a signal flag summoning the others, who responded with great hue and cry, coming out to fight from all sides. The Dragon King was quite taken aback, and was unsure how many soldiers were attacking. The Eight Immortals battled ever more fiercely, killing untold numbers of the water clans soldiers. The Dragon King saw that he could not attain victory, and retreated.

When the Immortals saw the old Dragon King retreat, Li Tieguai and Lü Dongbin let loose the fire from their gourds, and after awhile they dried up the whole sea. The ghosts and demons of the sea let out great cries, clouds of smoke rose up, and the Dragon King could only take his wife and sons and flee to the southern sea.

His brother, the Dragon King of the southern sea, had meanwhile noticed the great cloud of steam rising from the eastern sea. When he inquired of its source, his patrols reported, "The Dragon King of the eastern sea has done battle with the Eight Immortals." Just as they were making their report, there was a great confusing noise from outside the palace, and the announcement was made, "Your brother, the Dragon King of the eastern sea and his wife have come to see you."

When the Dragon King of the southern sea heard this, he was frightened, and quickly rose to receive his brother into his palace. Hearing all of his kinsman's lamentations, the southern Dragon King could not sit still. "That the prince took the castanets of the Eight Immortals does not warrant their killing him. That the Eight Immortals should be living in your palace is too much to bear. Big brother, don't worry. Your younger brother will avenge you and get your palace back for you. How many soldiers do they have? Where are they stationed?"

When the Dragon King of the southern sea heard that there were only eight, and all still in the dragon palace, he thought up a poisonous plan, "Heh, heh, they dare to occupy a dragon palace? That will surely be their death. I will use the combined water of the three remaining seas to inundate the palace. How can eight beings, not to say 80,000, survive such a flood?"

The Dragon King of the eastern sea and his brother of the south set about implementing their plan of revenge. They sent urgent messages to the dragon kings of the western and northern seas, instructing them to wait for a signal (the sound of fireworks) on the following day at five o'clock sharp, and to release water together into the eastern sea to flood out the Eight Immortals.

Meanwhile, the Eight Immortals, having taken the dragon palace, were quite satisfied in victory. All around them lay strange and wonderful precious objects. When they inspected the back of the palace, they found the castanets, and Lan Caihe happily ran to retrieve them. By now the sky was already dark and the Eight Immortals decided to spend the night in the dragon palace, and resume their journey on the next day without further delay.

But at four o'clock heavenly time, Zhang Guolao was awakened by a clamor outside and woke the others. Li Tieguai's ears were sharp, and listening carefully to the noise outside, he said, "We had better get out of this swamp. The Dragon King will flood it, and I am not eager to become part of a fish soup."

Zhongli Quan agreed, and quickly called Lü Dongbin outside to have a look at what was happening. As soon as Lü Dongbin went out, he heard the sound of fireworks, and the sound of death from all sides—a great wave of water like a mountain rumbling down. Within a moment, water inundated the palace, and the Eight Immortals were soaked in the water.

Just as the Eight Immortals were about to panic, Cao Guojiu grabbed his water evading pouch, and a path through the water suddenly opened up. The others saw this, and ran to Cao Guojiu's side, managing to scramble up to shore at the very last minute.

The four Dragon Kings sat on the surface of the sea with their soldiers, hoping to capture the Eight Immortals in their confusion. They waited a long time without seeing a trace of the eight, and decided that they must have been drowned to death. Finally, the dragon kings called back their soldiers, and retired to the palace of the Dragon King of the eastern sea to celebrate their victory.

When the Immortals reached the shore, they were irritable to the depths of their stomachs. Lü Dongbin jumped up and said, "If these dragon kings can flood us with water, let us teach them a lesson and fill up the eastern sea by pushing Qin Mountain into it! Even if we don't crush the Dragon King to death, he will still be unable to muster soldiers to fight with us again. Wouldn't that be a victory for us?"

The others thought this a grand idea, and together they ascended Qin Mountain. They spread out in eight directions, and together lifted up Qin Mountain. With a great rumble and roar, Qin Mountain turned over into the eastern sea.

The Dragon Kings of the four seas were just in the midst of drinking and making merry when they felt heaven and earth open up with a loud crash and rocks suddenly began flying around. The Dragon King of the southern sea cried out, "Damn, the Eight Immortals have come to attack us again." No sooner had he spoken, than he saw the great mountain tumble into the sea, and most of the soldiers of the combined water clans crushed to death. Only the Dragon Kings of the four seas and several of their close soldiers escaped.

The Dragon King of the eastern sea turned and looked, and became so angry he could hardly control himself. The great span of eastern sea had become flat ground. The few remaining water clansmen and the dragon kings of the four seas could only escape to the southern sea.

When the Eight Immortals saw the results of their efforts, they laughed till they swayed back and forth, "Now we can surely relax." They looked toward the sea for a long time, and seeing no trace of any dragon soldiers, happily continued their journey. But from this time forward, the Dragon Kings and the Eight Immortals have kept up a deep animosity and hatred.

Glossary

anzhao guiding 按照规定

Ba Xian guo hai 八仙过海

bai 拜

bai shifu 拜师傅

Bai Qi 白溪

Bai Se Zhuan 白蛇转

Bai Tan 白坦

bai gong zhi xiang 百工之乡

GLOSSARY

banzuo 半作

bao gan dao hu 包干到户

bao gong bao fan 包工包饭

bao gong tou 包工头

bao huang pai 保皇派

chang tian 常田

chengbao 承包

cheng xiong dao di 称兄道弟

chi da guo fan 吃大锅饭

chu ba 初八
chu er 初二
chu liu 初六
chu jiu 初九
chu qi 初七
chu san 初三

chu si 初四
chu wu 初五
chu yi 初一

chu shi 出师

citang 祠堂

cun 村
cun ban 村办
cun weiyuanhui 村委员会
cun zhang 村长

da dui 大队

dahuitang 大会堂

da jiti 大集体

da zi bao 大字报

da zibenjia 大资本家

da qiao ren 搭桥人

dan 担

dan wei 单位

Daoshi wu kou 道士捂口

Deng Ta renmin gongshe 灯塔人民公社

di 地

dian xin 点心

difang guoying qiye 地方国营企业

Ding Feng Tang 鼎丰堂

ding ti 顶替

Dongyang liang tiao lan duchang,
sha ren bu yong qiang
东阳两条烂肚肠，杀人不用枪。

Dongyang Mudiaochang 东阳木雕厂

dou 斗

Duan Ai Tang 端霭糖

Duan Wu 端午

duo lao duo de 多劳多得

duo lu 多路

fan jiu lou 翻九楼

fanshen 翻身

fang 房

fang tui 方腿

Fang Yan 方岩

fen gan 粉干

feng shui 风水

Fojiao xiehui 佛教协会

fu lu shou (xi) 福录寿（喜）

Fu Shun Tang 服顺堂

Fu Xing Tang 福兴堂

fu ye 副业

gaige, kaifang, gaohuo 改革，开放，搞活

ganbu 干部

gan erzi 干儿子

gan niang 干娘

gan nuer 干女儿

gaoji gongyishi 高级工艺师

geti 个体

ge wu tuan 歌舞团

ge xian qi neng 各显其能

gong ban 工办

gong fan dian ri 供饭点日
gong fan bao gong 供饭包工

Gong Hou Di 公侯弟

gong ji jin 公积金

gong shang chu 工商处

gongye bangongshi 工业办公室

gongye gongsi 工业公司

gongyi da shi 工艺大师

Gongyi Meishu Gongsi 工艺美术公司

gongyi meishu shi 工艺美术师

Gongyi meishu xuehui 工艺美术学会

Gongyi Meishu Xuexiao 工艺美术学校

gongyishi 工艺师

Gudian Jianzhu Gongsi 古典建筑公司

guanli fei 管理费

guanli ju 管理局

guan ting yi ri, shuo xi yi nian
观厅一日，说戏一年

guanxi 关系

guojia erji qiye 国家二级企业

guojia shui 国家税

guojia gongyi meishu jia 国家工艺美术家

guo yin, guo yin 过瘾，过瘾

Guo Zhai 郭宅

Guo Dengshan 郭登山
Guo Zhenbao 郭珍保
Guo Zhiliang 郭志良

hangye 行业

Hangzhou Daxia 杭州大厦

He Hua Xin 荷花心

hezuoshe 合作社

Heng Dian 横店

hong mu 红木

hou niang 后娘

houqin 后勤

hu 户
  hukou 户口
  nong ye hukou 农业户口

Hu Gong 胡公

Hu Qi 湖溪

hua ting 花亭

Huailu 怀鲁

huang taizi 皇太子

hui chang 会场

huitang doufugan 回汤豆腐干

jia 家

jia gong 加工

jia gong dian 加工点

jia gong fei 加工费

jiating fuye 家庭副业

jia xiang rou 家鄉肉

Jiang tui 蒋腿

jiaoliu hui 交流会

jin 斤

Jin 金

Jinhua 金华

jingji weiyuanhui 经济委员会

jinshi 进士

jiudi qucai, jiudi jiagong, jiudi shao shou
就地取材，就地加工，就地销售

jiu lou tai 九楼台

ju min qu 居民区

juren 举人

kaifa qu 开发区

kaifang 开放

ke niang 克娘

kua hao jing fu 夸豪竞富

lai liao, jia gong 来料加工

lai liao, lai yang 来料来样

laobaixing 老百姓

lao gai 劳改

laonian xiehui 老年协会

lao touzi 老头子

Lei shen 雷神

li 里

li zi 李子

Liu Shi Kou 六石口

GLOSSARY

Lou Xi Zhai 楼西宅

Lu Zhai 卢宅

Luban Jing 鲁班经

man shi 满师

man shi jiu 满师酒

meihua 梅花

Meishu Xueyuan 美术学院

miao 庙

miaohui 庙会

min fang 民房

Minjian Yiren Yanjiusuo 民间艺人研究所

mu 亩

Mudiao Da Wang 木雕大王

Nan Shang Hu 南上湖

Nan Si Ta 南寺塔

nan xiang 南鄉

ni, mu, zhu, shi, tie 泥，木，竹，石，铁

ni gong 泥工

niu tui 牛腿

niu wang shen 牛王神

nong mang 农忙

paifang 牌坊

Pan An 磐安

pi Lin pi Kong 批林批孔

pojiu lixin 破旧立新

pusa 菩萨

qigong 气功

qian gong zhi chuang 千工之床

Qian Xiang 千祥

qingshui yamen 清水衙门

qu 区

rong yao ti mian 荣耀体面

ren 仁

renminbi 人民币

ru ming 孺名

san du 三都

san gang wu chang 三纲五常

san jiu di 三就地

san nian xuetu, si nian banzuo
三年学徒，四年半作

shan di 山地

shan chong shui jin yi wu lu, liu an hua ming you yi c
山重水尽疑无路，柳暗花明又一村

shangye ju 商业局

she dui qiye 社队企业

she zhang 社长

Shen De Tang 慎德堂

Shen Xiu Tang 慎修堂

sheng yuan 生员

shenghuo fei 生活费

shi 市

Shi Dong Shuyuan 石洞书院

shifu 师傅

shisan jian tou 十三间头

shougongye zuofang shengchan fangshi
手工业作坊生产方式

shuang tou wu 双头乌

Si qin niang, lai hou niang 死亲娘，来后娘

siying qiye 私营企业

Song He Tu 松鹤图

song huotui 送火腿

suanming xiansheng 算命先生

sucai 素菜

Su Yong Tang 肃雍堂

tang 堂

tang wu 堂屋

Tezhi Jinhua Jiang tui 特制金华蒋腿

tian 田

tian ji 田鸡

Tian shi 田氏

tian men 天门

tian tang 天堂

Tian Zhu Si 天竺寺

Tie Benji 铁畚箕

Tie Saoba 铁扫把

Tuo Tang 托塘

waijiao bu 外交部

GLOSSARY 245

waimao gongsi 外贸公司

waimao ju 外贸局

waipo jia 外婆家

Wei Shan 巍山

Wenhua gong 文化宫

wenwu dian 文物点

Wenwu Guanliju 文物管理局

Wu 吴

Wu Baichuan 吴柏川
Wu Leshan 吴乐善
Wu Leishan 吴雷山
Wu Qinshan 吴琴山
Wu Sanhuai 吴三槐
Wu Yiling 吴益陵
Wu Zhishan 吴芝山
Wu Ziyan 吴紫岩

Wu Ben Tang 务本堂

wu fan 乌饭

Wugui Shan 乌龟山

wu jin shangdian 五金商店

wu ju 婺剧

Wu Ning 吴宁

xia fang 下放

xia shan laoshu 下山老鼠

Xia Qi Tan 夏溪潭

xian 县

xian ban de 县办的

xian bing 宪兵

xian, shi, jiang, shi 仙，释，将，仕

xianjin qiye 先进企业

xiang 乡

xiang ban de 乡办的

xiangzhenqiye 乡镇企业

xiangzhenqiye ju 乡镇企业局

Xiang Hou 香后

xiaodui 小队

xiao zhong fang 小中房

Xin Huating 新花厅

Xu Honggang 许弘纲

xu tui 戌腿

Xu Zhai 许宅

Xuefang Hou Ji 雪舫厚记

Xuefang Jiang tui 雪舫蒋腿

Xuefang Sheng Ji 雪舫升记

Xuefang Shen Ji 雪舫慎记

Xuefang Zheng Ji 雪舫正记

Xun Zhi Tang 逊志堂

Xunzi 荀子

ya jin 押金

yanjiu zu 研究组

yifeng yisu 易风易俗

yigong yinong 亦工亦农

yi jia yi hu 一家一户

Yi Jing Tang 一经堂

Yi Wu 义乌

ying mian 迎面

Yong Kong 永康

yong tian quan 用田权

you xiu gongyimeishu zhuanye renyuan
优秀工艺美术专业人员

you Zhongguo tese de shehuizhuyi
有中国特色的社会主义

Yu Fo Si 玉佛寺

yuan hu 元胡

Yue 越

yue ju 越剧

zai xiang 宰相

zao dong tui 早冬腿

zao fan pai 造反派

Zeng Feng 增丰

zhai 斋

Zhang Cun 樟村

zhang shu niangniang 樟树娘娘

zhaoshang hui 招商会

zhen 镇

zheng dong tui 正冬腿

zheng wu 正屋

Zhi Ho Tang 致和堂

Zhongguo gongyimeishu da shi
中国工艺美术大师

Zhu Ji 诸暨

Zhu Xi 朱熹

zhuang yuan 状元

zhuanye hu 专业户

Zong Ze 宗泽

Bibliography

Blim, Michael. 1992. "Small-Scale Industrialization in a Rapidly Changing World Market." In F. Rothstein and M. Blim, eds. *Anthropology and the Global Factory: Studies of the New Industrialization in the Late Twentieth Century.* New York: Bergin and Garvey.
———. n.d. "A Second Look at Small Is Beautiful: Problems and Prospects for Small-Scale Industrialization in Central Italy and Beyond." Paper read at American Anthropological Association annual meetings, Washington, D.C., 1986.
Bourdieu, Pierre. 1977. *Outline of a Theory of Practice.* Cambridge: Cambridge University Press.
Braverman, Harry. 1974. *Monopoly Capital.* New York: Monthly Review Press.
Burgess, J.S. 1928. *The Guilds of Peking.* New York: Columbia University Press.
Chen Chongren. 1989. "A discussion of carvings of traditional operas." *DYMDBAO* 17: 3: 3/30/89.
Chen Feng. 1995. *Economic Transition and Political Legitimacy in Post Mao China: Ideology and Reform.* Albany: SUNY Press.
Chinese Economic Journal. 1927. "Labor Conditions in Chekiang." *Chinese Economic Journal* 1: 2: 216–25.
Ch'u, C.C., and T.C. Blaisdell. 1924. "Peking Rugs and Peking Boys." *Chinese Social and Political Science Review,* Special Supplement.
Comaroff, John, and Jean Comaroff. 1992. *Ethnography and the Historical Imagination.* Boulder: Westview Press.
Cook, Scott, and Leigh Binford. 1990. *Obliging Need: Rural Petty Industry in Mexican Capitalism.* Austin: University of Texas Press.
Cooper, Eugene. 1979. "The 'Liberation' of Hong Kong." *Asian Wall Street Journal* 3 (184): 4: May 22.
———. 1980a. *The Woodcarvers of Hong Kong: Craft Production in the World Capitalist Periphery.* Cambridge: Cambridge University Press.
———. 1980b. "Craft Development: Socialist and Capitalist." *China Quarterly* 83: 447–60.
———. 1994. "The Life and Times of Guo Youxing: Chinese Artisanry in the Twentieth Century." *Arts and Crafts Quarterly* 7: 2: 18–23.
Cooper, Eugene, and Xiong Pan. 1992. "Rural Industry and Socialism with Chinese Characteristics." In F. Rothstein and M. Blim, eds., *Anthropology, Industry and Labor: Studies of the New Industrialization of the Late Twentieth Century.* Westport, CT: Greenwood Press.
DDZGZJ. 1989. *Dang Dai Zhongguo de Zhejiang* (Contemporary China's

Zhejiang Province). 2 volumes. Shang Jingcai, ed. Beijing: China Social Science Publishers.

Dirlik, Arif. 1994. *After the Revolution: Waking to Global Capitalism.* Hanover: Wesleyan University Press.

Dong Tianze. 1981. *"Miao Hui Za Tan"* (Miscellaneous Notes on Temple Fairs). *Zhejiang Minsu* 4: November: 10–11.

DYMDBAO (Dongyang Mu Diao Bao—Dongyang Woodcarving News) 1: 1, 3: 4/25/87, untitled.

———. 1: 2: 4/25/87, "We carry out technical cooperation with Chong Yi county."

———. 2: 1, 4: 5/25/87, untitled.

———. 2: 1: 5/25/87, "Dongyang Woodcarving Factory name changed to Dongyang Woodcarving 'General' Factory."

———. 3: 1: 6/25/87, "Restoration project of the main hall of Tomb of Yan Di commences."

———. 3: 1: 6/25/87, "Leaders from the County party committee call a discussion meeting of those from Dongyang Woodcarving Factory who have traveled abroad."

———. 3: 4: 6/25/87, untitled.

———. 4: 1: 7/25/87, "Grasp the base, go up a level, raise the quality of enterprise management."

———. 4: 1: 7/25/87, "Lin Jiang branch factory satisfactorily concludes its third board of directors meeting."

———. 4: 2: 7/25/87, "The exotic flower of woodcarving opens up in the southern mountain districts of Jiangxi."

———. 4: 4: 7/25/87, "Factory union holds first employee knowledge contest."

———. 7: 1: 9/25/87, "Dongyang Woodcarving Factory Party Committee begins multifaceted work in propaganda and education."

———. 7: 1: 9/25/87, untitled.

———. 7: 2: 9/25/87, untitled.

———. 7: 4: 9/25/87, untitled.

———. 8: 2: 10/25/87, "Our factory signs a contract with the Beijing city construction committee to refurbish the Bi Luo Pagoda in Bei Dai Ho."

———. 8: 2: 10/25/87, "Dongyang Woodcarving Factory participates in a commodities exhibition of nine local cities in four provinces Fujian, Zhejiang, Jiangxi, Anhui."

———. 8: 4: 10/25/87, untitled.

———. 10: 1: 12/5/87, "Dongyang Woodcarving Factory moves forward under the economic reforms."

———. 10: 1: 12/5/87, "Delegate from our factory takes first place in the [Jinhua] city bridge contest."

———. 10: 2, 4: 12/5/87, untitled.

———. 10: 4: 12/5/87, *"Fu Lu Shou Xi."*

———. 11: 1: 3/5/88, "New plan for the year of the dragon; achieve production value of ¥15,000,000."

———. 11: 2: 3/5/88, "Celebrate Double One, welcome the year of the Dragon."

———. 11: 2: 3/5/88, "Chong Yi carved wood products enter the Jiangxi market."

———. 11: 2: 3/5/88, untitled.

———. 12: 1: 6/5/88, "Arts and Crafts Notables assemble in Beijing; the fame of

Woodcarving craftsmen spreads—Lu Guangzheng and Feng Wentu return from Beijing Arts Congress having received praise."
———. 12: 2: 6/5/88, untitled.
———. 14: 1: 8/30/88, "Adapting to reforms in the foreign trade system, broaden the road of export earnings."
———. 14: 1: 8/30/88, "China's Light Industrial Arts and Crafts Import Export Commercial Association is formed in Beijing—General Factory was accepted as member."
———. 14: 2: 8/30/88, untitled.
———. 14: 4: 8/30/88, "Carving workshop holds a labor contest—grasp quality, move forward."
———. 14: 4: 8/30/88, "Notice of the County Union chess, 'go' and bridge contests."
———. 15: 1: 10/25/88, "Study meeting of the Application of Traditional Arts in Construction and The First Commodity Trade Fair of the Dongyang Woodcarving Factory are a great success."
———. 15: 1: 10/25/88, "Chong Yi carved wood products exhibited in Xiamen."
———. 15: 1: 10/25/88, "Fifth Board of Directors Meeting of the Lin Jiang Branch factory held at the Dongyang Woodcarving Factory."
———. 15: 1: 10/25/88, untitled.
———. 15: 4: 10/14/88, "Report of the results of the fishing contest."
———. 16: 1: 1/10/89, "Unite in Struggle, share joys and hardships, work hard to bring the Dongyang Woodcarving Factory to a new plateau."
———. 16: 1: 1/10/89, "Adopting enthusiastic measures to change small pieces of wood into valuables—general factory's export of Buddhist articles reaches ¥1,300,000 in production value."
———. 16: 2: 1/10/89, "Announcement of the results of the General Factory Furniture design contest."
———. 16: 4: 1/10/89, "General Factory presents the Winter employees' basketball tournament."
———. 17: 1: 3/30/89, "General Factory first consignment of self-managed foreign trade items sets off for Hong Kong."
———. 17: 2: 3/30/89, "Provincial Arts and Crafts Professions Honorific Titles Examination Criteria."
DYSZ. 1993. *Dongyang Shi Zhi*. (Records of Dongyang City). Dongyang Shi Di Fang Zhi Editorial Committee. Shanghai: Hanyu Da Zidian Publishers.
Dongyang Tong Xiang Hui of Hong Kong. n.d. *Dongyang Jian Jie* (A Brief Introduction to Dongyang). Hong Kong: Dongyang Same Native Place Association.
Dongyang Woodcarving Factory. 1989. Advertisement soliciting students for Branch School, March 16.
DYWZX. 1985. *Dongyang Wenshi Ziliao Xuanji* (Selections of Dongyang Historical Materials). Volume 1. Dongyang: Historical Materials Committee.
DYXXLJS. 1910. *Dongyang Xian Xiangtu Lishi Jiaoke Shu* (Textbook of Dongyang County Local History). 4 parts. Dongyang: County Government.
DYXZ. 1978 (1829). *Dongyang Xian Zhi* (Dongyang County Gazetteer). 2 volumes. Taibei: Taibei City Dongyang Same Native Place Association.
Duara, Prasenjit. 1988. *Culture, Power, and the State: Rural North China 1900–1942*. Stanford: Stanford University Press.

Eberhard, Wolfram. 1970. *Studies in Chinese Folklore and Related Essays*. The Hague: Mouton.
———. 1983. *A Dictionary of Chinese Symbols*. London: Routledge.
Edwards, R. 1979. *Contested Terrain*. Cambridge: Harvard University Press.
Fei, Hsiao-tung. 1939. *Peasant Life in China*. London: Routledge.
Feng Wentu. 1988. "Strengthen consciousness of quality, grasp quality control" *DYMDBAO* 12: 1–2: 6/5/88.
Feng Wentu and Ge Feiyong. 1988. "Construction of large-scale woodcarved mural 'Qing Ming on the river' is completed" *DYMDBAO* 11: 3: 3/5/88.
FSZ. 1985. *Dongyang Fengsu Zhi* (Habits and Customs of Dongyang). Dongyang: Dongyang Cultural Palace.
Fieldnotes (1986)
———. 7/25/86, interview with Feng Wentu, Wu Ning.
———. 7/26/86, 4/28/89, interviews with Lü Yunlei, manager, Dongyang No. 2 Woodcarving Factory, Wu Ning town.
———. 7/29/86, Wu Ning town.
———. 7/29/86, 6/10/88, 3/13/89, & 4/9/89, interviews with Li Zhijiang, factory head, Dongyang Arts and Crafts Experimental Factory, Wu Ning town.
———. 7/30/86, 5/31/88, 6/4/88, & 3/28/89, interviews with Wu Chuwei, factory head, Heng Dian Woodcarving Arts and Crafts Factory, Heng Dian town.
———. 8/1/86, interview with Lu Xibing, Wu Ning town.
———. 8/2/86, 7/5/87, 5/15/88, & 3/15/89, interviews with Wu Pinju, factory head, San Xing Woodcarving Factory, Lu Zhai village, later Wu Ning town.
———. 8/10/86, interview with Yu Yaoming, Hangzhou.
Fieldnotes (1987)
———. 7/5/87, interview with Lu Xibing, Wu Ning town.
———. 7/9/87, Beijing.
Fieldnotes (1988)
———. 5/5/88, Hangzhou.
———. 5/14/88, Wu Ning.
———. 5/16/88, interview with Wu Guosheng, Xia Qi Tan.
———. 5/16/88, Xia Qi Tan.
———. 5/18/88, Xia Qi Tan.
———. 5/19/88, interview with Wu Fengde, Xia Qi Tan.
———. 5/19/88, interview with Wu Pinfang, Xia Qi Tan.
———. 5/20/88, interview with Wu Guosheng, Xia Qi Tan.
———. 5/21/88, Xia Qi Tan.
———. 5/21/88, interview with Wu Changsheng, Xia Qi Tan.
———. 5/21/88, interview with Wu Fengde.
———. 5/22/88, interview with Wu Changsheng.
———. 5/23/88, interview with Wu Changsheng.
———. 5/30/88, Wu Ning.
———. 6/1/88, Heng Dian Arts and Crafts Factory.
———. 6/4/88, 2/28/89, 3/27/89, interviews with Ge Guangjin and family.
———. 6/5/88, interview with Du Paiqing, Wu Ning city construction office.
———. 6/6/88, Dongyang Woodcarving Factory.
———. 6/14/88, Li Tang village.
———. 6/15/88, interview with Zhang Guimu, party secretary Li Tang.

———. 6/15/88, Li Tang.
———. 6/18/88, interview with Zhang Fude interview, Li Tang.
———. 6/20/88, Li Tang.
———. 6/20/88, interview with Zhang Songyao.
———. 6/21/88, Li Tang.
———. 6/23/88, Guo Zhai town.
———. 6/23/88, interview with Guo Youxing.
———. 6/25/88, interview with Xu Wenxin, proprietor, Xu Wenxin Jia Gong Dian (processing shop), Guo Zhai town.
———. 6/25/88, interview with Guo Zhigen and Wang Wenfa.
———. 6/27/88, Guo Zhai.
———. 7/4/88, interview with Lou Zhengzhi, County Rural Industrial Bureau, Wu Ning.
———. 7/5/88, interview with Zhang Xiaoyang, Wu Ning City construction office.
———. 7/30/88, interview with Wu Pinfang, Hong Kong.
Fieldnotes (1989)
———. 3/14/89, Wu Ning.
———. 3/14/89, visit to Rural Industrial Bureau with Li Zhijiang.
———. 3/14/89, interview with Lou Zhengzhi, Dongyang Rural Industrial Bureau.
———. 3/20/89, interview with *peitong* Mr. Lou.
———. 3/21/89, interview with Lü Weiqing, proprietor, Te Mei Woodcarving Factory *(si ying* enterprise), Nan Jiang subdistrict, Xi Tui village.
———. 3/22/89, interview with Zhang Zhengxi, Hu Qi town.
———. 3/22/89, interview with Zhang Wanlong, proprietor, Ai De Artcraft Products Factory, Hu Qi town.
———. 3/25/89, interview with Zhang Fude, Li Tang.
———. 3/27/89, interview with Ma Jinpin, 38, proprietor, Xin Sheng Woodcarving Factory, Nan Shang Hu town.
———. 3/28/89, interview with Ge Zhangde.
———. 3/29/89, interview with Lou Shunho, adopted son of Lou Shuiming.
———. 3/29/89, interview with Ma Yangchun, proprietor, Heng Dian No. 2 Carving Factory, Heng Dian town.
———. 4/2/89, interview with Zhou Fangchun, Fang Jun village.
———. 4/15/89, Lou Xi Zhai
———. 4/20/89, on the road to Hong Qi *xiang,* Hu Tan village.
———. 4/22/89, interview with Wu Guiyu, Xia Qi Tan.
———. 4/26/89, Wu Ning.
———. 4/28/89, interview with Lü Yunlei, Wu Ning.
———. 5/2/89, interview with Feng Wentu, Dongyang Woodcarving Factory, Lu Zhai village.
———. 5/3/89, interview with Lu Zhongxiao, factory head, Lu Zhai Woodcarving Arts and Crafts Factory, Lu Zhai village.
———. 5/3/89, interview with Hua Dehan (aka Xu Wen), Wu Ning.
———. 5/5/89, visit to the Japanese products workshop, Dongyang Woodcarving Factory.
———. 5/5/89, interview with Chen Jiayou, head, Design Research Institute, Dongyang Woodcarving Factory.

———. 5/8/89, Jinhua city.
———. 5/19/89, interview with Shen Fuxin, Hangzhou.
———. 5/20/89, 5/24/89, interviews with Hu Zhonghe, Hangzhou.
———. 5/22/89, interview with Shen Fuxin, Hangzhou.
———. 6/27/89, interview with Huang Lisan, Pasadena, CA.
Fong, H.D., and Y.T. Ku. 1934. "Shoemaking in a North China Port." *Chinese Social and Political Science Review* 18: 505–536.
Forster, Keith. 1990. *Rebellion and Factionalism in a Chinese Province, Zhejiang 1966–1976.* Armonk: M.E. Sharpe.
Friedman, Edward, Paul Pickowicz, and Mark Selden. 1991. *Chinese Village, Socialist State.* New Haven: Yale University Press.
Gates, Hill. 1996. *China's Motor: A Thousand Years of Petty Capitalism.* Ithaca: Cornell University Press.
Gong Runlong, ed. 1987. *Jinhua Huo Tui Jiagong Jishu* (The Processing Technique of Jinhua Ham). Jinhua: Scientific Universal Publishers.
Gudeman, Stephen, and Alberto Rivera. 1990. *Conversations in Colombia: The Domestic Economy in Life and Text.* Cambridge: Cambridge University Press.
Harvey, David. 1990. *The Condition of Postmodernity.* Cambridge: Blackwell.
He Huan, and Jin Tianshu. 1983. *"Miao Hui Fengsu yu Qunzhong Wenhua"* (The Habits and Customs of Temple Fairs and Mass Culture). *Zhejiang Minsu* 9: March: 2–9.
Heng Dian Industrial Company. 1988. Brief Introduction to Heng Dian Rural Enterprise, mimeo.
Hinton, William. 1966. *Fanshen.* New York: Monthly Review Press.
Hommel, Rudolph P. 1937. *China at Work.* New York: MIT Press.
Huang, Phillip C.C. 1990. *The Peasant Family and Rural Development in the Yangzi Delta, 1350–1988.* Stanford: Stanford University Press.
Jiang Yinhuo. n.d.a. *"Ba Xian Zai Dongyang Minsu Wenhua de Diwei he Yingxiang"* (The Place and Influence of the Eight Immortals in Folk Culture of Dongyang county). Unpublished notes.
———. n.d.b. *"Hu Gong Zai Dongyang Minsu Wenhua Zhong de Diwei he Yingxiang"* (Hu Gong's Place and Influence in the Folk Culture of Dongyang). Unpublished notes.
———. n.d.c. *"Dongyang Hun yin fengsu"* (Habits and Customs of Marriage in Dongyang). Unpublished notes.
———. n.d.d. *"Dongyang shi Shehui Jingji Zongshu"* (An Overview of the Society and Economy of Dongyang City). Unpublished notes.
———. n.d.e. *"Dongyang Mudiao Xilie Tan"* (A Series of Discussions of Dongyang Woodcarving). Unpublished notes.
———. n.d.f. *"Dongyang Cunzhuang, Shichang he Huichang* (Dongyang Villages, Markets and Fairs). Unpublished notes.
———. n.d.g. *"Dongyang Xiangzhen Qiye Fazhan de Chengjiu"* (The Accomplishments of Dongyang's Rural Industrial Development). Unpublished notes.
———. n.d.h. *"Dongyang Xiangzhen Qiye Fazhan Cunzai de Wenti"* (Some Existing Problems in the Development of Dongyang Rural Industrial Enterprise). Unpublished notes.
———. n.d.i. *"Dongyang Zhuzhai Jianzhu Moshi"* (The Pattern of Dongyang House Construction). Unpublished notes.

———. n.d.j. *"Dongyang Gu Jianzhu Mudiao Zhuangshi Ti"* (The Subjects of Woodcarving Decorative Motifs in Dongyang Classical Architecture). Unpublished notes.
———. n.d.k. *"Heng Dian Xiangzhen Qiye Moshi"* (The Heng Dian Model of Rural Enterprise). Unpublished notes.
Jiang tui (The Ham of [Shang] Jiang [village]). n.d. Anonymous ms.
Jin Shan. 1987. "Promising young people reaching a strong and healthy maturity." *DYMDBAO* 3: 1: 6/25/87.
JHFSZ. 1984. *Jinhua Difang Fengsu Zhi* (The Local Habits and Customs of Jinhua). Jinhua: Arts Palace of the Masses.
JHWSZL. 1987. *Jinhua Wenshi Ziliao* (Historical Materials of Jinhua). Jinhua: Zhejiang People's Publishers,
Knapp, Ronald G. 1989. *China's Vernacular Architecture.* Honolulu: University of Hawaii Press.
Liao, T.C. 1948. "The Apprentices in Ch'eng Tu During and After the War." *Yenching Journal of Social Studies* 4: 89–103.
Liu Feibai, ed. 1990. *Ba Xian Zhuanqi* (Legends of the Eight Immortals). Taibei: Xing Guang Publishers.
Lu Changsheng. 1987. "Carpentry construction and structure in Dongyang carved wood furniture." *DYMDBAO* 4: 3: 7/25/87.
Lu Guangzheng. 1988. "The practice and function of woodcarving decoration in modern construction." *DYMDBAO* 12: 3: 6/5/88.
Ma Liangyong. 1987a. "Eyewitness report of the International World Exhibition of 1986." *DYMDBAO* 2: 1: 5/25/87.
———. 1987b. "New directions in the development of Dongyang woodcarving." *DYMDBAO* 9: 1: 11/15/87.
———. 1988. "Trip to the city of Hangzhou." *DYMDBAO* 14: 2: 8/30/88.
Ma Yirui. n.d.a. *"Dongyang Nongcun Laoshi Minfang Shiyang Jianjie."* (Introduction to the Old Style Rural *Min Fang* House Type of Dongyang county). Unpublished ms.
———. n.d.b. *"Dongyang Hunyin Fengsu"* (Dongyang Marriage Customs). Unpublished ms.
———. n.d.c. *"Dongyang Nong Shi Li"* (The Agricultural Calendar of Dongyang). Unpublished ms.
———. n.d.d. *"Dongyang ren guo Chunjie de fengsu"* (The Habits and Customs of Passing New Year's in Dongyang). Unpublished ms.
———. n.d.e. *"Zhangshu Niangniang"* (Camphor Tree Mother). Unpublished ms.
Ma Zhangyun. 1988. "Strengthen work rules, guarantee the smooth functioning of our enterprise's *cheng bao* [subcontract]." *DYMDBAO* 11: 4: 3/5/88.
Marx, Karl. 1967. *Capital.* New York: International Publishers.
Ministry of Industry. 1935. *China Industrial Handbooks—Chekiang.* Shanghai: Ministry of Industry.
Morse, H.B. 1909. *The Gilds of China.* London: Longman, Green & Co.
NCNA. 1972. New China News Agency, Dispatch No. 5278: 19.
Nolan, Peter. 1989. "Petty Commodity Production in a Socialist Economy: Chinese Rural Development post-Mao." In Peter Nolan and Fureng Dong, eds., *Market Forces in China.* London: Zed Books.

Ouyang Jingyi, ed. 1990. *Ba Xian de Chuan Qi* (Dramas/Legends of the Eight Immortals). Taibei: Ke Shu Bookstore.
Overholt, William H. 1993. *The Rise of China: How Economic Reform Is Creating a New Superpower*. New York: Norton.
Pan Genrong. 1988. "A simple introduction to the Dongyang Woodcarving Decorative Construction Co.." *DYMDBAO* 14: 3: 8/30/88.
Pan Yiping, ed. 1984. *Zhejiang Fen Xian Jianzhi* (Brief Account of the Counties of Zhejiang Province). Hangzhou: People's Publishers.
People's Daily Overseas Edition. 1987. "Dongyang: County of a Hundred Skills." 5/29/87: 7–8.
Piore, Michael, and Charles Sabel. 1984. *The Second Industrial Divide: Possibilities for Prosperity*. New York: Basic Books.
Potter, Jack, and Sulamith Potter. 1990. *China's Peasants*. Cambridge: Cambridge University Press.
Qian jiang wan bao (Qian River Evening News). 1989. "Untitled." June 19.
Rankin, Mary Backus. 1986. *Elite Activism and Political Transformation in China: Zhejiang Province, 1865–1911*. Stanford: Stanford University Press.
Ruitenbeek, Klaas. 1986. "Craft and Ritual in Traditional Chinese Carpentry." *Chinese Science* 7: 1–23.
———. 1993. *Carpentry and Building in Late Imperial China: A Study of the Carpenter's Manual Luban Jing*. New York: E.J. Brill.
Sabel, C., and J. Zeitlin. l985. "Historical Alternatives to Mass Production: Politics, Markets and Technology in Nineteenth Century Industrialization." *Past and Present* 108 (August).
Schoppa, Keith. 1982. *Chinese Elites and Political Change: Zhejiang Province in the Early Twentieth Century*. Cambridge: Harvard University Press.
Siu, Helen F. 1989. *Agents and Victims in South China*. New Haven: Yale University Press.
Skinner, G.W. 1964–65. "Marketing and Social Structure in Rural China." *Journal of Asian Studies* 24: 3 & 4.
———. 1977. *The City in Late Imperial China*. Stanford: Stanford University Press.
Sowerby, Arthur de C. 1926. "A New Art-craft in Shanghai." *The China Journal of Science and the Arts* 8: 1.
Taussig, Michael. 1986. *Shamanism, Colonialism and the Wild Man: A Study in Terror and Healing*. Chicago: University of Chicago Press.
Tayler, J.B. 1930. "The Hopei Pottery Industry and the Problem of Modernization." *Chinese Social and Political Science Review* 14: 184–209.
Wang Xuancheng. 1983. *"Cong huo tui xiang dao Zhong ze"* (Thinking of Zhong Ze and Ham). In Wang Xuancheng, ed., *Liang Zhe Shanshui, Lishi, Renwu* (The Scenery, History and Noteable People of Zhejiang and Jiangsu). Hangzhou: Zhejiang People's Publishers.
Xu Tulong. 1987a. "Canton fall trade fair concludes, our factory does very well in orders." *DYMDBAO* 8: 2: 10/25/87.
———. 1987b. "A Brief Discussion of the Craft and Applications of Dongyang Woodcarving." *DYMDBAO* 4: 3: 7/25/87.
Xu Wen. 1986. *"Dongyang Mudiao Shihua"* (A Historical Discussion of Dongyang Woodcarving). In *Dongyang Jianzhu* (Dongyang Construction) 9: 5: 11–18.

Xu Wen, Lu Guangzheng, and Feng Wentu. 1994. *Dongyang Mudiao Yishu* (The Art of Dongyang Woodcarving). Shanghai: Shuhua Publishers.
Xu Zhenghua. 1983. *"Jinhua Huo Tui"* (Jinhua Ham). In Xu Zhenghua, ed. *Jinhua Diqu Quantong Ming Chan* (Traditional Famous Products of the Jinhua Region). Jinhua: Scientific and Technical Committee.
Yang, C.K. 1959. *Chinese Communist Society: The Family and the Village*. Cambridge: MIT Press.
Yang, Mayfair Mei-hui. 1994. *Gifts, Favors and Banquets: The Art of Social Relationships in China*. Ithaca: Cornell University Press.
Zhai, Xiangsong. 1981. *"Jin hua huo tui hua jin xi"* (The Past and Present of Jinhua Hams). In Zhu Guocai, ed., *Zhejiang Mingchan Qu Tan* (A Discussion of the Famous Products of Zhejiang). Beijing: China Travel Service.
Zhejiang Ribao (Zhejiang Daily News). 1986. "Untitled." July 30: 3.
———. 1989 "Lü Lianshui voluntarily pays adjusted individual income tax." April 9: 4.
Zhejiang Gongyi Meishu (Zhejiang Arts and Crafts). 1979. "The Imperial Degree Candidate of Woodcarving—Lou Shuiming." Experimental Volume (Jan): 16–18.
———. 1983 "Dongyang woodcarving grand screen attains acclaim in Singapore." 2: 46.
Zhejiang People's Publishing Company. 1985. *Zhejiang Fengwuzhi* (A Record of the Scenic Places of Zhejiang Province). Hangzhou: People's Publishing Co.
Zhejiang Provincial Government. 1985. *Dongyang Xian Di Ming Zhi* (A Record of Place Names of Dongyang County). Hangzhou: Zhejiang Provincial Government.
Zhejiang Rural Industrial Bureau. 1986. *"Dui Wai Kaifang Zhong de Zhejiang Xiangzhen Qiye."* (Zhejiang Rural Enterprise in [the Context of] Opening to the Outside World). Hangzhou: Provincial Rural Industrial Bureau.
ZJNCDC. 1932. *Zhejiang Sheng Nongcun Diaocha* (Rural Investigation of Zhejiang Province) esp. pp. 66–97, "Dongyang county." Hangzhou: Provincial Government Press.
ZSQGY. 1986. *Zhejiang Sheng Qing Gai Yao* (Outline of the Condition of Zhejiang Province) pp. 127–29, "Zhejiang Xiang Zhen Qi Ye." (Rural Enterprise in Zhejiang). Hangzhou: Zhejiang Province Economic Study Center.
Zhou Yaoming. 1987a. *"Dongyang Denghui Minsu de Diaocha he Yanjiu"* (An Investigation and Study of the Customs of the Dongyang Lantern Festival). *Zhejiang Minsu* 23: March: 1–12.
———, ed. 1987b. *Dongyang Xian Gushi Zhuan* (A collection of stories from Dongyang County). Hangzhou: Zhejiang Provincial Office of Popular Literature.

Index

A

Agriculture, 3, 5, 11
  cooperativization in, 13–14, 18–19, 76–77, 80–81, 97–98
  Great Leap Forward and, 77, 112
  Guo Zhai town, 112, 115, 120–21
  Heng Dian town, 132
  land reform, 76, 79, 96–97
  Li Tang village, 92, 94–99, 108
    cooperativization, 97–98
    land reform, 96–97
    subcontracting, 99
  subcontracting, 79–80, 99, 140
  Xia Qi Tan village, 72, 74
    cooperativization, 76–77, 80–81
    land reform, 76, 79
    subcontracting, 79–80
Ai De Artcraft Products Factory, 105–8
Apprenticeship, woodcarving, 50–51, 53, 155–58
Architecture
  Bei Dai He park, 144
  Bi Luo Pagoda, 144
  decorative construction, 141–48
  design specialization, 60–62, 64–65
  Dong Palace Hotel, 142–43
  Kui Pavilion, 144–45
  operatic themes, 43–46

Architecture *(continued)*
  religious images, 41–42, 46, 145, 148–49
  Shen De Tang, 44–45
  Shen Xiu Tang, 44–45
  Su Yong Tang, 9, 42–43
  Wang Hu Guest House, 143–44
  Yi Hai Hotel and Pleasure Garden, 160–61

B

Bei Dai He park, 144
Bi Luo Pagoda, 144
Bottle cap factory (Xia Qi Tan), 86
Bridal dowries, 46, 53

C

Camphorwood, 8
  ritual for, 191–93
Capitalism, 16–17
  flexible production and, 171, 173, 180
Carpentry shop (Li Tang), 104–5
Christianity, 105–8
Commune and Brigade Enterprise Management Bureau, 19
Communist Party
  establishment of, 11–13
  flexible production and, 177, 180
  Heng Dian town, 125, 130

263

Communist Party *(continued)*
  Li Tang village, 93, 96–97, 98–99
  woodcarving industry and, 53, 54
  Xia Qi Tan village, 75–78
Confucianism, 9
Construction, decorative, 141, 143–48
Construction contractors (Li Tang), 104
Construction industry (Guo Zhai), 115–17
Cooperativization
  in agriculture, 13–14, 18–19
    Li Tang village, 97–98
    Xia Qi Tan village, 76–77, 80–81
  decline of, 22
  Dongyang Wall Covering Factory, 100
  establishment of, 13–15, 18–19, 21
  Great Leap Forward and, 14–15, 63–64, 76, 98, 112, 194–95
  Guo Zhai town, 112, 117
  in woodcarving industry, 54–56, 61–63
Cultural Revolution (1966–1976), 15–19
  flexible production and, 173–74
  Li Tang village, 98
  woodcarving industry and, 18, 43, 46, 64–66, 142
  Xia Qi Tan village, 77–78

D

Decorative Construction Company, 141, 143–48
Design specialization, woodcarving, 60–62, 64–65
Dong Palace Hotel, 142–43

Dongyang County
  agriculture of, 3, 5, 11, 13–14, 18–19
  capitalism in, 16–17
  Confucianism in, 9
  cooperativization in, 13–15, 18–19, 21, 22
  Cultural Revolution and, 15–19, 43, 46
  economic development, 13–15
    expansion of, 26–30
    expatriation and, 29–30, 176
    exportation, 27
    foreign investment, 27, 30, 39
    privatization and, 25, 26–27, 39–40, 68
    reform of, 19–22
    subcontracting, 22–25
    woodcarving industry, 21, 26
  economic zones
    agriculture, 5
    camphorwood, 8
    ham production, 5
    lumber production, 5, 8
    silk production, 5, 92
    woodcarving, 5
  education in, 8, 29–30
  geographical division, 3, 5
  historical background, 3–13
    Communist Party establishment, 11–13
    Japanese occupation, 10, 12–13
    migration, 11, 12–13
  population, 3, 9
  socialism in, 15–19, 61–62
  Wu Ning town, 3, 5, 12
    development in, 30–36
    entertainment in, 36–39
    lineage in, 36

Dongyang Dyeing Factory Yin Liang Chang, 133–34
Dongyang No. 6 Knitting Factory, 117–18, 123
Dongyang No. 2 Magnetic Products and Materials Factory, 134–35
Dongyang Wall Covering Factory, 100–103
Dongyang Woodcarving Factory, 18, 58–60, 84–85
  apprenticeship school, 155–58
  competition and, 166–67
  decorative construction, 141–48
  Decorative Construction Company, 141, 143–48
  diversification of, 153–55, 160–61
  domestic market expansion, 152–53
  economic reform and, 138, 153–54, 166–67
  elitism status of, 161–62
  employee extracurricular activities, 161–64
  exportation and, 147–48, 149, 154, 166
  flexible production and, 175–76
  honorific titles, 158–60
  imitation rosewood furniture, 151–52
  innovations in, 141
  international exposure, 150–51
  management of, 139, 140–41
  organization of, 139
  production figures, 143, 148, 151, 152, 161, 164–66
  religious images, 145, 148–49
  subcontracting, 138–40, 148–49, 152
  wages, 139, 140
  women and, 140
  See also Woodcarving industry

Duan Ai Tang, 43
Du Yunsong, 48, 56–57
Dying materials company (Li Tang), 103

E

Economic reform
  capitalism and, 16–17
    flexible production, 171, 173, 180
  Dongyang County, 19–22
  Guo Zhai town, 114, 115, 123
  Heng Dian town, 126, 132
  land reform, 76, 79, 96–97
  Li Tang village, 96–97, 99, 108
  socialism and, 15–19, 61–62
    flexible production, 177–78
  woodcarving industry, 66–68
    Dongyang Woodcarving Factory, 138, 153–54, 166–67
  Xia Qi Tan village, 76, 79–80, 86–87
  See also Exportation; Flexible production; Subcontracting
Economic zones
  agriculture, 5
  camphorwood, 8
  ham production, 5
  lumber production, 5, 8
  silk production, 5, 92
  woodcarving, 5
Education, 8, 29–30
  Guo Zhai town, 111–12, 116–17
  Li Tang village, 99
  Stone Cave Academy, 8, 111–12
  Xia Qi Tan village, 86
Electrical Repair Shop (Heng Dian), 135–36
Expatriation, 29–30, 176

Exportation, 27
   Guo Zhai town, 117, 123
   Heng Dian town, 128, 134, 136, 137
   Li Tang village, 101, 107, 108
   woodcarving industry, 48, 64, 66–68
      Dongyang Woodcarving Factory, 147–48, 149, 154, 166

F

Fang Ru Xing, 14
Flexible production
   capitalism and, 171, 173, 180
   Communist Party and, 177, 180
   Cultural Revolution and, 173–74
   economic reform and, 176, 179–80
   expatriation and, 176
   flexible accumulation, 168–69, 171–72
   flexible specialization, 168–71
   privatization and, 177, 179–80
   socialism and, 177–78
   subcontracting and, 171–72, 178
   technology and, 168–69
   vs. mass production, 168–69, 172–73, 174
   wealth accumulation and, 179–80
Flower Pavilion, 18, 44
Foreign investment, 27, 30, 39
Four Cleanups campaign, 15
Furniture, 43, 46–49
   imitation rosewood, 151–52

G

Good Fortune Rising Hall, 44
Great Leap Forward, 115

Great Leap Forward *(continued)*
   agriculture and, 77, 112
   cooperativization, 14–15, 63–64, 76, 98, 112, 194–95
   lumber production and, 5
   woodcarving industry and, 58, 63–64
Guangzhou, 11
Guo Yi village, 112–13
Guo Youxing, 5, 13
Guo Zhai town, 5
   agriculture, 112, 115, 120–21
   construction industry, 115–17
   cooperativization, 112, 117
   Dongyang No. 6 Knitting Factory, 117–18, 123
   economic reform and, 114, 115, 123
   education, 111–12, 116–17
   exportation, 117, 123
   lineage of, 109–11, 116
   market days, 112
   Pan An Electric Lightbulb Factory, 118–19, 123
   photography, 121–22
   population, 112
   subcontracting, 118–19
   woodcarving industry, 113–14, 116, 122–23
   Xiang Shan Paper Products Factory, 119–20
   Xi Wu Orchards, 120–21

H

Ham production, 5
   development of, 183–87
   ham varieties, 189–90
   Jinhua ham, 183–84, 185–86

Ham production *(continued)*
  markets for, 185
  ritual in, 187–88
  stages of, 188–89
  taxation on, 185
Hangzhou, 8, 11
  woodcarving industry in, 46–49, 67
Heng Dian Industrial Company, 125, 128, 133, 134, 135, 136, 137
Heng Dian Industrial Enterprise Group, 137
Heng Dian No. 2 Woodcarving Factory, 129–30
Heng Dian town, 5
  agriculture, 132
  Communist Party and, 125, 130
  Dongyang Dyeing Factory Yin Liang Chang, 133–34
  Dongyang No. 2 Magnetic Products and Materials Factory, 134–35
  economic reform and, 126, 132
  Electrical Repair Shop, 135–36
  exportation, 128, 134, 136, 137
  population, 132
  subcontracting, 125, 128, 129, 130, 133, 134, 135
  woodcarving industry, 124–32
Heng Dian Township Industrial Office, 124, 132, 134
Heng Dian Undergarment Factory, 133–34
Heng Dian Woodcarving Arts and Crafts Factory, 124, 125–28
Hong Kong, 11, 12–13, 21
Huailu town, 5
Huang Lisan, 29
Huang Zijin, 48, 58–59

Hu Gong, 196–203
Hu Qi town, 5, 12
Hu Shan village, 113, 115, 117

I

Imitation rosewood furniture, 151–52
Income (Xia Qi Tan), 86–87
Industrial and Commercial Bureau, 26
Italy, 169–70

J

Japanese occupation, 10, 12–13

K

Kui Pavilion, 144–45

L

Land reform
  Li Tang village, 96–97
  Xia Qi Tan village, 76, 79
Lineage
  Guo Zhai town, 109–11, 116
  Li Tang village, 88–90, 93–94, 102–3
  Xia Qi Tan village, 70–72, 74–76
Ling Yin Temple, 42
Li Tang village, 5
  agriculture, 92, 94–99, 108
    cooperativization, 97–98
    land reform, 96–97
    subcontracting, 99
  Ai De Artcraft Products Factory, 105–8
  carpentry shop, 104–5

Li Tang village *(continued)*
  Christianity in, 105–8
  Communist Party and, 93, 96–97, 98–99
  construction contractors, 104
  Cultural Revolution and, 98
  Dongyang Wall Covering Factory, 100–103
  dying materials company, 103
  economic reform and, 96–97, 99, 108
  education in, 99
  exportation, 101, 107, 108
  lineage of, 88–90, 93–94, 102–3
  market days, 90, 92
  metal factory, 100
  mulberry tree cultivation, 92
  population, 92, 94
  religion in, 105–8
  silk production, 5, 92
  woodcarving industry, 92–93, 105–8
  yuan ha production, 94–95
Liu Shi Kou town, 5
Lou Shuiming, 48, 58, 59–60, 65–66, 93, 124
Lou Xi Zhai town, 5
Lu Lianshui, 56–57, 58–59
Lumber production, 5, 8
Lu Zhai village, 9, 42–43

M

Ma Che Bu town, 5
Mao Zedong, 15–16
Market days
  Guo Zhai town, 112
  Li Tang village, 90, 92
  Xia Qi Tan village, 70

Market fairs
  cycle of, 194–96, 206, 207
  modern, 203–8
  traditional, 195–203, 207–8
Mass production, 168–69, 172–73, 174
Master craftsmen, 48–49, 56–60, 62–63, 124, 125, 126–28, 129–32
  Dongyang Woodcarving Factory, 158–60
Ma Youzhang, 48
May 4th Movement (1919), 10
May 30th Movement (1925), 10
Ma Zhai, 12
Metal factory (Li Tang), 100
Migration, 11, 12–13
Mulberry tree cultivation (Li Tang), 92

N

Nan Shang Hu town, 5, 14
Nan Si Ta, 41

O

Operatic themes, 43–46

P

Pan An County, 3, 118
Pan An Electric Lightbulb Factory, 118–19, 123
Photography (Guo Zhai), 121–22
Population
  Dongyang County, 3, 9
  Guo Zhai town, 112
  Heng Dian town, 132

Population *(continued)*
  Li Tang village, 92, 94
  Xia Qi Tan village, 72
Privatization, 25, 26–27, 39–40, 68
  flexible production and, 177, 179–80

R

Religion
  Christianity, 105–8
  Confucianism, 9
  in Li Tang village, 105–8
  woodcarving images, 41–42, 46
    Dongyang Woodcarving Factory, 145, 148–49
Ren Chang Company, 47
Ren Yi Company, 48, 49
Retail shops (Xia Qi Tan), 86
Rural Industrial Bureau, 26

S

Shanghai, 11, 13
  woodcarving industry in, 46–49, 63, 68, 113, 116, 130
Shanghai No. 5 Arts and Crafts Factory, 47
Shanghai No. 1 Woodcarving Factory, 63, 68, 113, 116, 130
Shen De Tang, 44–45
Shen Xiu Tang, 44–45
Shou Ta Tou village, 14
Shuang Hong Tai Company, 47–48
Silk production, 5, 92
Socialism, 15–19, 61–62
  flexible production and, 177–78
Stone Cave Academy, 8, 111–12

Subcontracting, 22–25
  agriculture and, 79–80, 99, 140
  Dongyang Woodcarving Factory, 138–40, 148–49, 152
    wages, 139, 140
  flexible production and, 171–72, 178
  Guo Zhai town, 118–19
  Heng Dian town, 125, 128, 129, 130, 133, 134, 135
  Xia Qi Tan village, 79–80
Su Yong Tang, 9, 42–43

T

Taiping rebels, 9
Technology, 168–69
"Three and Five Anti Campaigns," 13
Three Stars Company (Xia Qi Tan), 84–86
Tripod Abundant Hall, 44

W

Wages, woodcarving industry, 50, 51–53
  Dongyang Woodcarving Factory, 139, 140
Wang Hu Guest House, 143–44
Wang Shen Ji Company, 47
Wang Tiwu, 29–30
Wei Shan town, 3, 5
Women, woodcarving industry and, 53–54, 63
  Dongyang Woodcarving Factory, 140
Woodcarving industry, 5, 21, 26
  apprenticeship in, 50–51, 53

Woodcarving industry *(continued)*
　Dongyang Woodcarving Factory, 155–58
　architecture, 9, 41–46
　　decorative construction, 141–48
　　design specialization, 60–62, 64–65
　　operatic themes, 43–46
　bridal dowries, 46, 53
　Communist Party and, 53, 54
　cooperativization in, 54–56, 61–63
　Cultural Revolution and, 18, 43, 46, 64–66, 142
　economic reform and, 66–68
　　Dongyang Woodcarving Factory, 138, 153–54, 166–67
　exportation, 48, 64, 66–68
　　Dongyang Woodcarving Factory, 147–48, 149, 154, 166
　furniture, 43, 46–49
　　imitation rosewood, 151–52
　Great Leap Forward and, 58, 63–64
　Guo Zhai town, 113–14, 116, 122–23
　Heng Dian town, 124–32
　Li Tang village, 92–93, 105–8
　master craftsmen, 48–49, 56–60, 62–63, 124, 125, 126–28, 129–32
　　Dongyang Woodcarving Factory, 158–60
　origins of, 41–42
　privatization in, 68
　production decline in, 53, 63–64
　religious images, 41–42, 46
　　Dongyang Woodcarving Factory, 145, 148–49
　rural-urban transformation of, 46–53

Woodcarving industry *(continued)*
　subcontracting in, 68–69
　　Dongyang Woodcarving Factory, 138–40, 148–49, 152
　traditionally, 41–46
　wages in, 50, 51–53
　　Dongyang Woodcarving Factory, 139, 140
　women in, 53–54, 63
　　Dongyang Woodcarving Factory, 140
　Xia Qi Tan village, 84–86
　See also Dongyang Woodcarving Factory
Wu Ben Tang, 43
Wu Mantang, 5, 13. *See also* Xia Qi Tan village
Wu Ning town, 3, 5, 12
　development in, 30–36
　entertainment in, 36–39
　lineage in, 36

X

Xiang Shan Paper Products Factory, 119–20
Xia Qi Tan Cement Construction Materials Factory, 81–82
Xia Qi Tan Clothing Factory, 82–84
Xia Qi Tan Steel Reinforcing Wire Drawing Factory, 82
Xia Qi Tan village, 5
　agriculture in, 72, 74
　　cooperativization, 76–77, 80–81
　　land reform, 76, 79
　　subcontracting, 79–80
　bottle cap factory, 86
　Communist Party and, 75–78

Xia Qi Tan village *(continued)*
  Cultural Revolution and, 77–78
  economic reform and, 76, 79–80, 86–87
  education in, 86
  income, 86–87
  lineage of, 70–72, 74–76
  market days, 70
  occupations in, 72, 74
  population, 72
  pork shop, 86
  retail shops, 86
  Three Stars Company, 84–86
Xi Wu Orchards, 120–21
Xu Hai Ji Company, 47–48, 113
Xun Zhi Tang, 43

Y

Yi Hai Hotel and Pleasure Garden, 160–61
Yi Hua Sheng Company, 48
Yi Jing Tang, 43
Yi Wu County, 5, 12
Yuan ha production (Li Tang), 94–95

Z

Zeng Feng village, 113
Zhang Cun town, 5
Zhang Mingyao, 5, 13, 59. *See also* Li Tang village
Zhang Zhengxi, 62–63
Zhi He Tang, 43
Zhou Fangchun, 57–58

Eugene Cooper is Associate Professor of Anthropology and Chinese Studies at the University of Southern California. He has lived and worked in Hong Kong for more than five years, and conducted ethnographic fieldwork in the artisan and industrial communities of Hong Kong and the People's Republic of China. He has published extensively in the areas of Chinese family and kinship, rural political economy, and Chinese folk habit and custom.